CROCODILE ATTACK

CROCODILE ATTACK

HUGH EDWARDS

1817

HARPER & ROW, PUBLISHERS, New York
Grand Rapids, Philadelphia, St. Louis, San Francisco
London, Singapore, Sydney, Tokyo

Credits for insert photos are as follows: Patrick Bollen; Hugh Edwards; West Australian Newspapers Limited; Hugh Edwards; Malcolm Douglas; Malcolm Douglas; Hugh Edwards; Brisbane Courier-Mail, Hugh Edwards; Queensland Police Department; Hugh Edwards; Stan Lamond; Hugh Edwards; Stan Lamond, based on a map in Australian Geographic, January/March 1988, page 96; Ballarat Wildlife Reptile Park; Col Stringer; Hugh Edwards; Bill Green; Malcolm Douglas.

This book was originally published in 1988 in Australia by Swan Publishing.

FIRST U.S. EDITION

Designed by Cassandra J. Pappas

Library of Congress Cataloging-in-Publication Data

Edwards, Hugh.
  Crocodile attack/Hugh Edwards.—1st U.S. ed.
    p. cm.
  ISBN 0-06-016121-3
  1. Crocodile attacks. I. Title.
QL666.C925E34 1989
597.98—dc19   88-45894

89 90 91 92 93 DT/RRD 10 9 8 7 6 5 4 3 2 1

THE CROCODILE

"Consider the chief of the beasts, the crocodile
Who devours cattle as if they were grass.
What strength is in his loins.
What power in the muscles of his belly.
His tail is rigid as a cedar,
The sinews of his flanks are closely knit.
His bones are like tubes of bronze.
And his limbs like bars of iron.
He is the chief of God's works,
Made to be a tyrant over his peers,
For he takes the animals of the hills for his prey
And in his jaws he crushes all wild beasts.
There under the lotus plants he lies
Hidden in the reeds and the marsh
The lotus flower conceals him in its shadow . . ."

THE BOOK OF JOB, OLD TESTAMENT

CONTENTS

The fatal attack on attractive American tourist Ginger Faye Meadows at the King's Cascades on the Prince Regent River in March 1987.

The effect of the tragedy. The search for the body. Crocodile attack on the corpse bag. A husband's ordeal. "Why did no one tell her?" a mother asks. A single red rose.

A comparison of the growing up and formative years of a young crocodile with those of a human child, leading up to that fateful meeting 25 years on.

"I HOPED IT WOULD FINISH ME QUICKLY" *56*

Val Plumwood's amazing escape after being caught twice and
taken underwater by a crocodile in a series of death-rolls in the
East Alligator River. Her struggle to survive her bleeding
wounds and floods in a Northern Territory swamp.

DARK WATERS OF THE DAINTREE *76*

After Beryl Wruck was taken by a crocodile in Barratt's Creek
by the Daintree River, at Christmas 1985, there were
extraordinary Queensland rumours of a drug murder, and a
dismembered body fed to the crocodiles. A shoot-out by
vigilantes destroyed the Daintree's crocodile population before
the 5-metre (16-foot) culprit was caught and human remains
were found in its stomach.

'SWEETHEART' FROM THE FINNISS LAGOON *99*

'Sweetheart' was a huge crocodile who declared war on boats
and outboard motors. He mounted more than 15 attacks without
harming a human being and achieved world fame, defending his
territory against the buzzing mechanical invaders.

FATAL ENCOUNTERS *119*

Fatal crocodile attacks in Australia in recent years. Crocodile-
caused deaths in Queensland, the Northern Territory and
Western Australia. The links between the killings.

ATTACK—EXPECT THE UNEXPECTED *142*

An analysis of what makes a crocodile attack. How to cope with
an attack if it occurs. Means of avoiding attacks. How to live in
crocodile country.

SEE YOU LATER ALLIGATOR—IN A WHILE CROCODILE *162*

The crocodilian family worldwide. The difference between
crocodiles and alligators. A scientific look at the characteristics
of the various species. Monsters, or just misunderstood?

BITING THE HAND THAT FEEDS *187*

Alf Casey, who lost an arm to his pet crocodile. Stories of owners and crocodiles. Bushmen's tales. True and remarkable crocodile stories. The crocodile which up-ended a Toyota truck at the East Alligator River crossing.

MANAGEMENT OF CROCODILES *209*

The change in status from vermin to a conserved creature. Scientific differences of opinion over numbers. Interesting scientific discoveries. Crocodile lovers, and courtship. Harvesting eggs. Economic possibilities. The situation in differing Australian States.

WHAT OF THE FUTURE? *233*

What does the future hold for *Crocodylus porosus,* and the crocodilians in general? Can they continue to exist in the modern world? Or are the surviving relatives of the dinosaurs doomed to join them in extinction?

ACKNOWLEDGMENTS *238*

Illustrations follow page 144

FOREWORD BY PAUL HOGAN

▲▲▲▲▲▲▲▲▲▲▲

Before *Crocodile Dundee* reached the drawing-board stage, I suppose I knew as much as any other average Australian about the croc. In fact, very little.

To me, he was a big, ugly brute who haunted the waters of northern Australia and occasionally made sensational headlines by becoming a man-eater. I couldn't really understand why conservationists made such a big deal out of him.

The research that went into the movie taught me a great deal. The crocodile was no ordinary reptile, no run-of-the-mill predator. He was something else.

I like to think that *Crocodile Dundee* promoted a lot of thought, a lot of discussion about the croc and his place in natural history's scheme of things. He is, after all, a survivor of the dinosaur days and if we kill him off, we destroy one of our last links with prehistoric times.

If you knew little about the beast before, you'll be an authority on him by the time you have read *Crocodile Attack*.

I can also guarantee you one thing: once you've read it, you'll think twice before you go swimming in croc country.

PAUL HOGAN

INTRODUCTION

▲▲▲▲▲▲▲▲▲▲▲

The 200-Million-Year Survivor

*M*illions of years before man invented the death-dealing submarine, crocodiles perfected the art of capturing large prey from concealment beneath the waters.

A large crocodile can make himself invisible in knee-deep muddy water. He can remain below an hour, without a bubble or a ripple to indicate his presence. His heart slowed to an incredible single beat every three minutes.

No movement will betray him, for crocodiles are masters of stillness. He will remain as immobile as a stone until the right moment. Meantime his acute senses register each footfall on the bank, every splash in the water.

When the time comes to attack, the crocodile explodes from below the surface in a whirl of teeth and spray, yellow eyes ablaze, moving faster than the human eye can follow. If need be he can jump and stretch to take prey two metres above the surface. He is rapid enough to catch a bird on the wing, striking quick and deadly as those other reptilian hunters, the snakes.

The crocodile is related to the dinosaurs and once shared the

world with them. A royal remnant from a bygone age, he is one
of nature's most effective amphibious designs for land and water.
A 200-million-year survivor.

Crocodiles are the world's largest non-oceanic hunters. The
biggest terrestrial carnivores. Growing as large as six metres in
length and perhaps 1000 kilograms in weight, they may live 100
years. Some species—notably *Crocodylus niloticus* the African
crocodile, and *Crocodylus porosus* the Australian saltwater crocodile—take human prey and have won the entire species an evil
reputation as man-eaters.

Fear of crocodiles, the terror of attack, has distorted our
human view of all the species. We see them with prejudice, and
few of us know that there is more to crocodiles than a set of
fearsome jaws and a scythe-like tail. In fact they can be ardent
lovers, caring parents, and actually play with 'toys'.

Their nocturnal habits, their trait of concealment, and their
remote habitats, have made them difficult to study. Before 1960
not a great deal was known about them—other than the obvious
facts that they occasionally ate people, and that they were disappearing fast.

For in this century, through destruction of habitat and ruthless
hunting for skins, man has pushed the crocodile to the brink of
extinction in many parts of the world. It was a sad but familiar
story, paralleled in our dealings with whales, seals, bears, rhinoc-
eros, tigers, and other great and wonderful animals whose future
is in jeopardy.

In Australia timely intervention and protection in the 1960s and
'70s averted potential crocodilian disaster with our own two species, the saltwater *Crocodylus porosus*—the largest native creature and man-eater—and the smaller freshwater *Crocodylus
johnstoni*, harmless to humans but still hunted for its skin.

Today, though recovery is far from complete, in northern Australia big crocodiles are more plentiful than anywhere else in the
world. Their future now seems assured provided, of course, that
we can learn to live with each other.

This is not something we should necessarily take for granted.
Crocodiles are so different from ourselves that humans have misunderstood (even sometimes loathed and hated) them as long as

man, the newcomer, and the saurians have uneasily shared the earth.

In the 1970s and '80s research by scientists such as Professor Harry Messel, of the University of Sydney, and Dr. Grahame Webb, a consultant to the Northern Territory Conservation Commission, has given us a new and more sympathetic picture of crocodiles, and done something to soften public attitudes.

But there are still problems. Not everyone in the north—especially in Queensland—wants a half-tonne toothsome predator as a neighbour.

Is there a way to achieve an equable and satisfactory relationship between people and crocodiles in Australia? Can they—or should they—make a major contribution to the economy through tourist dollars?

The chapters ahead look hard at all aspects of crocodile-human relationships. First there is the dark history of attacks and the human fatalities. Then the other side of the coin. The thousands of skins stripped from slaughtered crocodiles and shipped out to become shoes and handbags to feed the needs of human fashions.

The uneasy attitudes of the 1980s, following the much-publicised death of American Ginger Meadows and fatal attacks in the Northern Territory and the Daintree River in Queensland, are examined. An analysis is made of the factors which lead to a crocodile attack and things which can be done to prevent it.

There are glimpses into the world of the scientists, the researchers, the field-workers, and the fascinating facts they have turned up on Australia's most dangerous and controversial wild animal.

The final chapter deals with Wyndham, in Western Australia, a town on Cambridge Gulf which has lived with crocodiles on its doorstep for the best part of a century.

Can crocodiles and humans co-exist? Is there a place for these descendants of the dinosaurs in our modern world?

Is there . . . ?

HUGH EDWARDS, 1988

THE UNSEEN PRESENCE

▲▲▲▲▲▲▲▲▲▲▲

*T*he hornet-buzz of the outboard motor travelled up the river ahead of the speeding boat with its five occupants.

The big crocodile, who ruled the pool below the waterfall of the Cascades, heard the sound before it would have been audible to any human ear.

In a vee of foam-flecked bubbles he slid his olive-green bulk silently below the surface. The two knobs shielding the golden eyes were the last to disappear. He became invisible below the surface of the coffee-coloured tidal water. But he was still there, listening and alert.

The continuing sound of the engine echoed back from the battlements of the ochre-red cliffs lining the river. It penetrated down through the canopy of dripping ferns in the rainforests of the canyons, reverberated among the olive leaves, the pale trunks, and stilt roots, of the mangroves along the banks.

The dark-haired young man with a moustache and miniature vandyke beard—just a tuft below the lower lip—steered with confident, experienced hands on the wheel of the skimming Haines Hunter. He watched ahead for the ripples marking snags. The three girls with their hair blowing in the wind—one sitting

on the bow, legs dangling as the boat bounced along—had eyes
only for the beauty of the scenery around them. They were unaware that shy or hidden animals all along the river were reacting
to the alien engine noise in their own individual ways.

As the boat passed, parrots flew in bright flashes from the
trees. Rock wallabies bounded from ledge to rock to ledge, paus-
ing on the heights to look down with ears erect. On the mud flats
the fiddler crabs stopped and raised red and yellow pincers in
protest against the slap of the waves from the boat's wake.

Below the speeding keel barramundi and stingarees flickered
away unseen to the left and right in the milky waters.

The big crocodile, sensing their coming, was neither shy nor
was he afraid of man. He had submerged from obvious sight for
his own reasons. Acting on 200 million years of accumulated
instinct, he naturally chose the advantage of becoming a secret
presence. He could stay below, invisible, for an hour if he wished.
The silent hunter.

The boat's destination was the King's Cascades, a wide-
rimmed waterfall some 20 kilometres up the Prince Regent River.
The craft was riding the rising tide. That part of the river dried
out to mud and rocks at low water. But at the maximum flood
there could be as much as eight metres of navigable depth in the
main channel.

There was always water in the pool below the Cascades because of the waterfall. That was one of the reasons why the
crocodile had chosen to live there. The fresh water brought wallabies and wild pigs down to the bank, and this suited him too.

When the boat arrived, the staccato motor noise cut suddenly
to be replaced by the softer sound of human voices. There was
no sign of the crocodile. Not even a bubble on the shining green
surface of the pool. But even if there had been any tell-tale indi-
cators the visitors would have missed them. They were intent on
looking up, their attention caught by the rainbow-misted beauty
of the Cascades. The white plumes of water, tumbling down rock
terraces between the fronds of verdant greenery, take the breath
away from any visitor seeing them for the first time.

The falls were first discovered up the spear-straight gorge of
the Prince Regent River by the navigator Philip Parker King in

the 1820s. He charted a good portion of the Western Australian coast, and he would have been pleased to have the Cascades named after him. The falls are one of the most beautiful spots anywhere on the Australian coast. A natural scenic jewel in an often austere land.

His original description still carries something of the wonder of the discovery.

"At the distance of about 17 miles from the basin," he wrote, "we were surprised by hearing the noise of a fall of water. But distrusting our ears we were not convinced of the fact until an opening in the mangroves exposed to our view a cascade of water of 160 feet in breadth, falling from a considerable height."

Aside from their aesthetic appeal, the falls had a practical purpose for sailing ship seamen. In those thirsty latitudes explorers, whalers and pearlers could water there. Send their ship's boats up-river to put the bows under the falls and fill their freshwater barrels straight from the source.

Modern boats like the *Lady G* sometimes take on water there too, and in the steamy climate of the tropics few visitors can resist the temptation to strip off and stand under the cataracts for a cooling, natural shower. Tourist brochures show them swimming there.

By the 1980s a visit to the Cascades had become something of a tradition among yachtsmen travelling around the north of Australia.

The speedboat which came up the river that morning was one of the two tenders of the *Lady G*. She was a white-hulled luxury motor cruiser at that moment lying to anchor in the St George Basin. A sleek, 33-metre aluminum craft, registered in Brisbane in the name of the Gandel Group, a business cartel owned by Melbourne millionaire John Gandel.

The *Lady G* had been in Fremantle, Western Australia, on charter for the summer of The America's Cup, the international 12-metre yacht races. Now the months of hard salt-spray sailing in the boisterous southerly winds of Rottnest Island were completed. The prize was won and lost. The euphoria over. The *Lady G* was making her way back to Australia's east coast by way of Broome, Darwin and the Gulf of Carpentaria. On the way it was planned that she would cruise the Sepik River in New Guinea, picking up her owner at Port Moresby.

While she was sailing to a schedule, there was time on the way to touch at some beauty spots. They had called at Broome and had seen Cable Beach and the pearl-shell shops. They stopped at Cockatoo Island. While they were there they visited Crocodile Creek, leaving their names in the bough shelter where visiting sailors sometimes carved names of their vessels and those of their crews on drift timber. In the tradition they carved 'Lady G' on a board and left their own names. Bruce Fitzpatrick captain, Steve Hilton engineer, Madeleine Janes stewardess, Jane Burchett chef, Ginger Meadows . . . They also swam in the creek with the locals and laughed about the name.

The *Lady G* had every modern device for safety and comfort built into her design. But even the best-planned systems can develop a flaw. There was trouble with the boat's desalination plant which provided fresh water. Those aboard were restricted to one shower every two days, and there was a probability that they would run out entirely before they reached Darwin.

When they reached the vicinity of the St George Basin the skipper, Bruce Fitzpatrick, suggested a run up the Prince Regent River. The girls could have a natural freshwater shower and they could fill freshwater containers to help them through to Darwin. Tourist brochures on board promised that it was one of the wildest and prettiest spots to be found on the entire Kimberley coast. A chance to reach out and touch Adventure Land. They accepted eagerly. The water was a necessity and who could tell when any of them would pass that way again . . . ? Ginger Meadows in particular was keen to experience all she could of Australia's rugged north. It was what she had come all the way from the USA to see at first-hand. She was thrilled at the idea, and took an extra roll of film for her Olympus camera.

So the Haines Hunter tender was winched down from the *Lady G*'s top deck by an electrically controlled davit to lie against fenders alongside. Fitzpatrick, as captain, naturally took the wheel. Madeleine Janes and Jane Burchett—regular members of the crew—tumbled in. They were joined by Ginger Faye Meadows, a 24-year-old red-haired former model who had 'hitched a ride' around the top of Australia with the *Lady G*, and Steve Hilton, the engineer.

They were all in high spirits. Ginger in a beige suede bikini wore pearl and gold earrings. She also had a big gold-and-diamond engagement ring catching the light on her left hand.

It was a beautiful, sun-smiling morning. The river scenery was everything they could have asked for. It was hot and humid, as it always is in March on the tropical Prince Regent. But the boat made its own cool breeze as it skimmed along. There was that exhilarating smell of mud, and mangroves, and sweet tropic blossoms. An excitement in the air. The girls' faces were glowing by the time they reached the most beautiful vista of all, at the Cascades. It was a fitting finale to the journey up the river. They felt almost as though it had all been arranged for them. They were in that kind of mood.

But the prettiness of the scene, viewed from the comfort of the boat's upholstered seats, was deceiving. It was a harsh and primitive land. The lush, green plant life, which had sprouted in such profusion after the monsoon rains of the Kimberley Wet, disguised underlying ridges of iron rocks and knife-edged stones. The green on the slopes was largely a sharp spinifex which speared through trousers and drew blood. The hills were so rough that they had killed the ponies and even the dogs of the first explorers. In 150 years no European settlement had succeeded. There remained only ruins and lonely graves. It was a country that was lovely to look at. But all too often it hurt if you touched it.

The Prince Regent above all was pristine, as savagely primeval as it had been for the past 100,000 years. Unchanged, perhaps unchangeable. The animals who lived there survived by tooth and claw. They lived by strength, cunning or fleetness of foot. The weak, the unwary and the unlucky, perished. In time the hunters themselves were killed by the country or predators, or others of their kind. Then they were eaten too. If they were too old and rank for the flesh-eaters, there were armies of crabs, ants and voracious beetles to act as undertakers. It was the Law of the Jungle. A merciless and unending struggle to survive at the expense of other forms of life. The 'survival of the fittest' as Charles Darwin had accurately described it a century before.

At the King's Cascades the beauty of the scene sometimes masked the reality. The beauty was certainly a truth. But it was dangerous to confuse a pleasant appearance with an imagined degree of softness.

In the depths of the tide-filling pool at the Cascades the crocodile heard the boat stop and the motor cut. He felt the vibrations of movement in the boat and heard the sound of human voices. Then came new sounds which sent tremors down his rows of armoured dorsal spikes. People were walking, splashing, on the edge of the water. He began to move his tail slowly from side to side. It was a long time since he had eaten and he felt the hunger pains inside his green-and-yellow belly.

There were shrieks of laughter as Madeleine Janes fell in while getting out of the boat. The girls disembarked on the rock ledge at the foot of the falls while Fitzpatrick took the boat to find a suitable spot to tie up.

The girls surveyed the climb to the top of the Cascades, to the left of the tumbling water. It had looked easy from the boat. But now they found it was very steep and slippery. Even though they tried to help each other up, the ledges were higher than expected, the rock edges painfully sharp on bare feet. They were beginning to discover some of the hardness of the land.

It was about 11 A.M., with the sun now hot and high in the sky. The date was 29 March 1987.

For Ginger Meadows, about to try the climb up the waterfall, as the unseen crocodile below stirred restlessly, March was a significant month. She was an Aries, an appropriate star sign for a redhead. The next day—30 March—would be her 25th birthday. Maybe her mother and father, Charles and Clara Meadows, would be missing her in the little three-bedroom house in Charlottesville, Virginia? Remembering her by her fond childhood nickname 'Caboose' and thinking perhaps of their girl all that way away in Australia. She would have some stories to tell them!

Perhaps Duanne would be remembering too. Her estranged husband Duanne McCauley, in Snow Mass Village, Aspen, Colorado. Duanne . . . She had better thoughts about him now.

Ginger had spent a lot of time thinking as the *Lady G* forged her way north through the blue swells of the Indian Ocean. There is a lot of time for reflection on a travelling boat. Now that the summer was over, she was beginning to think that she had had her fill of escapism. It might be the right time for soul-searching. For a reassessment. She certainly felt less confused and more certain of herself.

Ginger's story, albeit, was no novelty. It was one shared by thousands of other young women the world around. They had what are called marital difficulties. An antiseptic euphemism for troubles as old as the human race. But to each one of the sufferers the issues were intensely personal, individual and painful. For Ginger, like the others, it was no comfort at all to know that other people had similar woes. The pain felt by someone else means little until we step on a rusty nail, or break a marriage in pieces ourselves.

Ginger was born on 30 March 1962, the youngest of three Meadows daughters. At that time Joyce was already 18 and Charlotte 13. The nickname 'Caboose' was the name for the last car on a railroad train. She was positively and absolutely the last, her father Charles Meadows joked.

After leaving the US Army, Meadows had become a motor mechanic in the picture-book Southern town of Charlottesville, Virginia. The Meadows family had a little stone-fronted, three-bedroomed house in a tree-lined street. There was never a great deal of money. But enough came in, and they were a close-knit and loving family which was something dollars couldn't buy. For Charles and Clara the education of the girls was always a priority. They wanted them to have the best start in life that they could give them, though they were content themselves with their modest style of living.

"Ginger was a truly beautiful little girl," Charles Meadows said. "She was so lively, so full of vitality."

Ginger, as her name implies, was indeed red-headed. She had the Aries fire-sign characteristics of being fun-loving and sociable. She was an excellent swimmer from an early age. As she grew up she graduated from school, worked for a year, and then went to college in Florida. When she came back to Charlottesville she began seeing Duanne McCauley, a friend since childhood. The friendship became serious and no one was surprised when they married and settled in Aspen, Colorado.

Perhaps they were too young after all. Duanne's business was successful. But Ginger had a series of dead-end jobs which dispirited her. She was ambitious. If you had asked she probably would have said she would like to be someone whose name was well known. But she could find nothing that was challenging enough to suit her. Problems developed within the marriage, and when the pressures seemed too great she felt she couldn't go on. "They were young and had a few problems to sort out," Clara Meadows said, with a mother's forgiveness and understanding. "She needed breathing space, time to herself to get some new perspectives on life." Ginger decided to take time off, to travel, to sort out her priorities in the detachment of distance.

It was America's Cup time in Fremantle, Western Australia, and she had become fascinated by Australia after seeing the film *Crocodile Dundee*. "It was about as far from Aspen as I could go . . ." She arrived in Sydney in September 1986, stayed briefly and went on to Fremantle where America's Cup fever had taken over the port.

With her bright personality and gift for making friends, Ginger gravitated naturally into the glamour-filled world of the 12-metre yachts. It was a world in which worries were blown away out on the water on the fresh southerly busters which piped hard every day out of Fremantle. Talk was all of races lost and won, of broken gear and men overboard, of faster sails and winged keels.

After the sun had set on the victors and the vanquished for the day there was a whirlwind of social life at night. The atmosphere was international and exciting, with racing crews and teams from the United States, France, Britain, Italy and New Zealand adding colour and unfamiliar accents to the port.

There were regular dinners, dances and functions associated with the Cup, as well as hospitality from the home yacht clubs like Royal Perth or Royal Freshwater Bay. Or it was fun just to move around the waterfront bars at night with a group of happy friends. The time passed almost too quickly. Ginger met an *Eagle* crewman called Charlie Dwyer. Through his introductions she became part of the team of workers and supporters associated with the *Eagle* syndicate. She worked part-time in the New Orleans Beefsteak and Bourbon Bar, filled in as a hostess aboard the charter boats out on the Cup course on the ocean, and generally became a happy part of the Cup scene. It was a good time. She laughed and smiled with a lot of new people, and in her natural way made many friends. When *Eagle* was eliminated, and bundled out of Challenge contention, she hurt too. Then she experienced the heights of joy shared by all Americans, when Dennis Conner finally won the Cup back for the United States. History records that he triumphed in straight races with his strong-wind flier, *Stars & Stripes*, in February of 1987.

Suddenly, the Cup was over and with it all the camaraderie of those weeks of a halcyon summer. The visitors went home, the crews began to pack up. The yachts were lifted out on hoists and stripped of their masts and gear.

As the first signs of the Australian autumn began to appear Ginger had had time to think. The therapy had been just what she had needed. Life wasn't so serious after all. Her problems no longer seemed insurmountable. There was nothing that couldn't be fixed with a smile and a little common sense. And she was beginning to feel just a little homesick. Perhaps she and Duanne could make it work after all? "I still love Duanne very much," she confided to a friend in Fremantle. "I'm really looking forward to getting back with him."

But she still hadn't seen a lot of Australia, apart from the urban sprawls of Sydney, Perth and Fremantle. Having come so far she wanted to see more of the 'real' Australia. The country outside the cities and suburbia. Most of all she wanted to experience at first-hand that wild frontier land of the north. The bush she had glimpsed tantalisingly in the movie *Crocodile Dundee*.

Most of the boats from eastern Australian ports which had come to Fremantle for the Cup were going back 'around the top' of Australia. Ginger had no shyness when it came to asking around. She tried a number of boats asking whether they had a spare berth. At the *Lady G* (she told her friends) she 'struck it lucky.' The ship was going around northern Australia to Port Moresby with a minimum crew of five. There was room on board and they would be glad of company. Ginger was welcome, Captain Bruce Fitzpatrick assured her.

Ginger was overjoyed. "Over the moon!" The voyage seemed

to offer the kind of adventure she had always dreamed about. Even the name of the boat—*Lady G*—seemed appropriate. She told her friends so with a laugh.

"Watch out for crocodiles," they told her jokingly in the New Orleans Beefsteak and Bourbon Bar. A man had recently been killed in the Northern Territory in the East Alligator River, by a crocodile in gruesome circumstances. Decapitated in front of a horrified crowd watching from the river bank. The watchers had included his son.

"I've been all over the world," Ginger replied, with a grin and a toss of her red hair. "I can take care of myself."

Now, on 29 March, at the Cascade falls on the Prince Regent River the minute hands on the wrist-watches on the slim, brown arms of the girls were already sweeping toward 11.30 A.M.

The girls began to climb the falls, laughing and helping each other up the steep ledges. Bruce Fitzpatrick smilingly snapped a picture from the boat with his camera of Jane Burchett helping Ginger up the slippery rocks, while Madeleine Janes stood higher up the slope in the fall of water. Ginger was conspicuous most of all by her red hair. Jane only went a little way. She had broken her neck in an accident three years before, and was nervous about the risk of falling.

Then Fitzpatrick climbed up, finding it easier than the girls but still puffing with the exertion as he neared the summit. Reaching the top he looked back and saw that two of the girls had descended to water level again. Jane Burchett went back to the boat and then decided to swim around to the left of the falls to see whether there might be an easier way to climb up.

It was such a beautiful morning. The sunlight sparkled in twinkling points like diamonds on the water, and dragonflies danced above their own reflections on the surface.

Bruce Fitzpatrick, breath still coming short with the effort of the climb, went on to explore the rock pools above. Steven and Madeleine also climbed the falls, but Ginger had climbed down again. She had to watch her footing carefully on the slippery natural ledges of rock, and discovered that it was a lot harder going down than up.

Jane swam unhurriedly back from her exploration to the left of the falls, and found Ginger sitting on a rock, enjoying the sunshine.

"Hi," Ginger greeted her with a wave. "Take my picture?" She smiled. "The camera's in the boat!"

Jane climbed into the tender, dried herself and took a photograph of Steve Hilton and Madeleine Janes with her own camera. Then she focused carefully with Ginger's unfamiliar Olympus. Ginger posed laughingly for the picture, but Jane frowned and made a face. The film was finished and she wasn't sure how to reload the Olympus.

"I'll do it," said Ginger.

She swam out with easy strokes to the tender, now drifting at the end of the line tethering it to the rocks and climbed, dripping, over the stern.

The crocodile, submerged on the muddy bottom a little distance away, heard the splash of a swimmer and stirred uneasily again, hunger rumbling in his stomach.

But even as he swung his snaggle-toothed snout to an angle to pick up the vibrations, Ginger heaved herself out of the water and into the boat. The yellow eyes glinted fiercely in the depths and the crocodile became motionless again. Listening.

Unaware in the boat, the girls loaded the camera and looked up to see what the others were doing. Bruce was still out of sight on the level plateau above the falls.

"What shall we do?" Ginger asked Jane brightly. It was pleasant being lazy in the sunshine in the boat. But she felt the urge to do something. To see more of this exciting new countryside while she had the chance. After all she might never have the opportunity again. She should make an effort, and now she rather regretted not having persevered and made more effort to reach the top of the falls with Bruce.

"Isn't there an easier way to climb on the other side?" she asked Jane, screwing up her face as she looked up into the sun.

Jane shook her head. "It gets steeper," she replied. "I just swam around that way." She shrugged her shoulders. She was covered with sun cream now and had her book. She was happy enough to stay in the boat.

"How about that track—or is it a clearing—over there?" Ginger persisted, pointing toward the left of the rock ledges of the main falls where a tributary creek came in. "We could take our shoes and maybe swim over and do a bit of exploring?"

"Okay." Jane, always amenable, made the fateful decision.

Later she wondered why. It was 11.20 A.M.

It was especially important for them to leave by 11.30 so that the *Lady G* could catch the tide out of the St George Basin.

It would have been physically impossible for the girls to swim to the 'track', climb up to the top of the falls and be down again in 10 minutes. For the rest of her life Jane will wonder what strange last-minute compulsion made them set off.

They pulled their track shoes on, wriggling their toes to get them onto damp feet, and did up the laces. Ginger's shoes were white IW Sports.

The big crocodile, hidden and stationary below the surface, heard bodies splash into the pool, and now there came again through the water the fluttering vibrations of humans swimming. His tail stirred the mud and he began to move forward slowly, rising imperceptibly.

The two girls had swum only a little distance when Jane began to feel uneasy. She explained it later by saying that she 'lost her nerve'. Whatever the feeling was—premonition, or sixth sense—she suddenly felt deeply afraid. It was strange because previously she had been quite unconcerned and confident on her own in the water below the Cascades. "Suddenly the water seemed dark and dangerous. I just had this awful feeling . . ."

Her immediate instinct was to get out of the water. All her senses seemed to be urging her to go back, GO BACK!

"Come on," Ginger pleaded. "We've gone this far, we might as well go the rest of the distance. Look—I'll go in front."

Jane glanced around her. There was nothing there. She laughed nervously. Perhaps Ginger was right . . . but the feeling came again as she swam on with Ginger now in the lead.

Ginger was a strong swimmer, totally confident in the water. Jane began to feel a little ashamed of her nervousness. Silly really . . .

But there it was again. Unmistakable. She felt a tinge of panic. GO BACK! This time the premonition of danger was so strong that she stopped to tell Ginger she couldn't go any farther. She had to go back to the boat.

At that moment Bruce Fitzpatrick's shout split the morning above them.

"Crocodile!" he shouted down from the top of the falls. "CROCODILE! GET OUT OF THE WATER!"

"GET OUT OF THE WATER!"

Bruce Fitzpatrick had taken his photographs of the picturesque pools and paperbark trees in the rock formations on the top of the falls. He had stayed a little longer than he intended, seduced by the sunshine and the tranquillity of the morning.

Now he glanced at his watch and frowned self-reprovingly. It was nearly 11.30 A.M. Time to be thinking about getting back. Time and tide wait for no man . . .

He picked his way through the uneven rocks to the edge of the falls, guarding his camera carefully in case of a slip. On the edge he paused, thinking about another picture. He noticed Steve and Madeleine on a ledge below the crest, perhaps two to three metres beneath him. Ginger and Jane were swimming at the edge of the cliff on the left-hand side where a massive growth of tree-fern cast a shadow on the water.

Then his eye was caught by something else. Movement in the pool behind the tender. A long, olive-green shape, sinister in outline and bulky, had risen in the coffee-coloured water. It began to move with purposeful sweeps of a massive tail toward the side of the falls.

A crocodile! For a moment Fitzpatrick stood stunned by what he saw. The ugliness, the threat, seemed unreal, somehow inappropriate in that beautiful place . . . He blinked in disbelief. But it was real and now it was moving with unmistakable menace in the direction of the two girls.

"CROCODILE!" Bruce Fitzpatrick yelled so loudly he almost overbalanced. Ginger and Jane looked up inquiringly.

"Get out of the water!" Fitzpatrick shouted again, and the two girls understood him and began to scramble in alarm toward the overhanging cliff.

"Quick Steve!" Fitzpatrick ordered. "Get the boat over to them!"

Steven and Madeleine had already started on their way down the cliff when their descent was arrested by Bruce's shout. "I don't think I believed it was happening at first," Steve said. For those few seconds when, for all of them, everything seemed to be happening in slow motion, Madeleine did not seem to understand what was happening. Or perhaps she understood too well. She remained frozen with horror on the spot.

Steve looked at the crocodile, looked again at the girls to see whether they would have time to get out of the water. Then he began jumping down the slippery ledges of the cliff, risking life and limb, to get to the boat and the girls before the crocodile.

On the way he added his voice. It seemed as though everyone —Bruce, Steve, Madeleine—were all shouting to the girls to get out of the water.

But the girls had nowhere to go. They stopped, trapped, waist-deep on a ledge, their back against a solid wall of rock with no footholds, water falling in front of them. The crocodile, they could plainly see, was very close now, and barring the way between them and the tender. In fact it was little more than five metres away. Horror paralysed them.

The crocodile was now so near that Jane Burchett could see every detail of the dragon face. With the horned eyebrows, the noduled reptilian skin, and the flaring single nostril, the awful yellow eyes, and the teeth—those dreadful exposed wolf-like dagger teeth—it looked like the Devil himself. Terror!

The humped and threatening movement of its body showed unmistakably that it was going to attack. "Ginger was holding onto my arm," Jane said. "I screamed as loud as I could to scare the crocodile and took off my shoe and threw it . . . I think it hit the crocodile. It stopped and looked disconcerted, as though it had lost its bearings. Ginger looked at me and said 'What shall we do?' . . ."

They were the last words she would ever speak.

Jane was about to answer her, to say, "I don't know, but let's stay here." But before she could speak Ginger had let go of her arm, dived away to the right and struck out for a piece of dry bank 25 metres away.

The others above saw the crocodile stop momentarily nonplussed when it was hit by the shoe, and then watched in horror as Ginger swam. What followed was a tragedy in slow motion.

While Jane remained frozen the crocodile surged forward, foaming the surface.

"The crocodile seemed to go around the back of her, then it got her," Madeleine Janes recalled in her statement later. She watched, powerless to help, as though in a nightmare.

"She only got a few feet," Jane said. "I was thinking 'why, oh why did she do that?' Then it happened."

The crocodile seized its victim in a lightning grab by the upper legs and hips, the jaws extending past her bikini-clad body on either side.

Bruce saw Ginger dragged under the water. "Then she came back up clear to about her waist with her hands in the air and a really startled look on her face . . . She was looking right at me . . . but she didn't say a word."

That look of anguish would haunt Bruce Fitzpatrick and the others in the aftermath.

Jane Burchett was the closest, still standing, rigid with disbelief on the ledge. She saw her friend's arms outstretched in mute appeal. "She looked at me as though to say 'what's happening?' " Then the crocodile dragged her down again, jerking her beneath the surface.

"Swim!" the others shouted to Jane. Terrified, she struck out in the opposite direction, to the place where she had tried to climb the waterfall before. She dragged herself out and sat shaking on the rock ledge only a foot above the water. "Why didn't it take me?" she kept asking herself.

Steve Hilton saw Ginger seized even as he reached the boat. "I saw Ginger away from the cliff, and her arms waving up and down. She made no sound at all." He jumped into the boat, started the motor, revved it with a roar and a cloud of blue exhaust smoke to try to frighten the crocodile into giving up its victim. Then he jammed the handle hard into gear and drove as quickly as he could to the spot where he had last seen Ginger. "All I saw was a lot of bubbles come up . . ."

He revved the motor again and again, the din reverberating back off the cliff-face and sending birds shrieking in alarm. He

must have been within a couple of metres of the crocodile and
the girl. But despite the shallow water he could see nothing because of the murk and tidal discolouration.

"Bruce was yelling for me to get Jane," so he went and picked
her up, shivering in fear, from the ledge, and told her to stay on
the bottom of the boat and not to look.

"Once she was on board I turned back to where Ginger was
taken and I saw the crocodile reappear on the surface with Ginger
in its mouth. It appeared to have her by the upper part of the
legs and her torso was in the water. There was no sign of movement from her." She was limp and almost certainly drowned at
that point. But there was always hope. Steve gunned the motor
again . . .

"I went over to where she was and once again the crocodile
submerged . . ."

For Bruce Fitzpatrick the horror had a kind of cotton-wool
unreality. Even though he was terribly aware of what was happening it all seemed inconceivable. The events had the quality of
a bad dream.

He jumped down the cliff, ledge by ledge. He was about half-
way down when he reached Madeleine. "She was yelling, and
sobbing, and stamping, up and down." He was worried that she
might fall off the rocks and into the pool.

He grabbed hold of her and shook her, and told her that he
didn't want anyone else hurt. He suggested she make her way
down the cliff slowly while he hurried on. Steve was below in the
boat where the attack had taken place. Bruce watched a moment
or two then he went back up the cliff to Madeleine and helped
her down to a point where the boat came in to pick them up.
They put Madeleine on board and sat her on the floor with Jane.
Both girls were now in shock.

The crocodile appeared and submerged once more as though
playing a macabre game of hide-and-seek.

After that there was no trace of anything in the water. Not even
blood, Bruce Fitzpatrick said. They tried everything they could
think of, revving the engine, trying to scare the crocodile into
letting go of its victim. Nothing happened. Then, at the very left-
hand side of the falls they saw the eyes of the crocodile and what

looked like flesh in its mouth. Steve picked up an oar and they steered toward it. But as they got near to the crocodile it disappeared for the last time.

They never saw it again. Or Ginger.

Once more the pool below the falls was a shining stretch of placid water. It was as though the crocodile had never been. As though it was all just an evil dream. Except that where there had been five of them, now there was four.

Ginger's Olympus camera was still on the boat seat, and her bag, a blouse. That was all. But now the terror, the realisation of what had happened and what it meant came crowding in on them.

They were all appalled, white-faced, especially Bruce Fitzpatrick, who realised what he had to do.

He had to go back to the *Lady G*, calm his voice and call the Darwin Overseas Telecommunications Centre on the radio. To tell the world that Ginger Meadows was dead. Killed by a crocodile.

The time was 11.30 A.M., the date 29 March 1987. That date—along with the fact that it would have been Ginger's birthday the next day—would be etched in their minds forever.

The nightmares began at once. The horror of the recollection that—try as they would—they could not drive from their minds. The vision of the beautiful pool. And the crocodile.

And Ginger reaching out soundlessly to them in those last moments . . .

BAD TIDINGS

▲▲▲▲▲▲▲▲▲▲▲

When the news reached the outside world in the Monday newspapers and the television bulletins, there was general shock at the way in which Ginger Meadows had died.

The story broke on the morning of the day which would have been her birthday. By the end of 30 March 1987 her name was known to millions of people around the world because of her bizarre wilderness demise. Ginger Faye Meadows became a posthumous celebrity. The newspapers—particularly those in the United States—naturally made the most of a sad story.

Some of the facts were muddled from the start.

One cause may have been poor radio transmission from the isolated area. Perhaps also Bruce Fitzpatrick was not as crisply coherent as usual when he sent the message with the *Lady G*'s call-sign VK4131.

Whatever the reasons, at 1600 hours 29/3/87 Broome police had received a telex message from 'Norlaw' their counterparts in Darwin. It read:

"FEMALE [AMERICAN CITIZEN] SWIMMING FROM A RUBBER RAFT
TO THE YACHT WAS ATTACKED BY CROCODILE. CROCODILE IM-

MEDIATELY DISAPPEARED BELOW SURFACE WITH THE FEMALE
AND NEITHER HAVE BEEN SEEN SINCE."

The location was given as 'ST GEORGE SOUND.' This temporarily mystified newspaper editors and some others who tried to
find it in an atlas because it is not listed and does not exist. There
is a King George Sound, in southern Western Australia, and the
name 'George' (after the English monarch of the early Australian
exploration era) appears frequently on rivers and prominent landmarks of northern Australia, including Port George IV not far
from where the *Lady G* was lying in the St George Basin.

Even with the uncertain facts and a general lack of detail,
Ginger Meadows was guaranteed front-page news.

Her untimely death was the latest in a series of crocodile attacks in northern Australia. The most recent fatality, a father of
three decapitated at the East Alligator River, had occurred only
three weeks before. There had been eight humans killed over two
years by crocodiles which had been protected wildlife in Western
Australia, the Northern Territory and Queensland since the
1970s.

Once the first news bulletin went out there was an immediate
call for more news. Telexes flooded into Australian newspaper
and television offices from other media syndication groups
around the world. They all wanted to know more details about
the attack. But Australian news sources themselves knew little.
Even the police had only the first garbled radio message.

It was no use trying to contact the boat. After sending that
message which electrified the world the *Lady G* had gone off the
air. She became a white cocoon of private grief.

Anticipating the probings of the press, those aboard had
switched off the outside world. They retreated into their own
state of shock. It was a miserable night.

They could not hide with their pain indefinitely. Next morning,
about the same time that the attack had taken place on the previous day, there came the distant snarl of an aero engine. A float
plane settled down on the St George Basin in a cloud of spray,
and then motored up to the *Lady G* with its propeller turning over
slowly. The world had arrived on their doorstep.

It was a Beaver float plane chartered from Kununurra, with the company name 'Alligator Airways' down the side and a crocodile painted on the tail.

Aboard were Senior Constable John Litherland, from Broome regional police office, and Fisheries and Fauna Department Inspector Peter Johnson.

Litherland was to begin inquiries at once and set in train the official investigation. Johnson was there on behalf of the Department of Conservation and Land Management to represent the crocodile. If it had to be shot, to recover remains, he would do it. Otherwise his duty was to protect the animal and prevent anyone else taking the law into their own hands and shooting it out of grief or anger, as had happened on the Daintree River in Queensland.

Also with the aircraft were a television news reporter and photographer, who had joined the plane in the hope of being first in for a news scoop.

Bruce Fitzpatrick did not allow them on board. He and the others were desolated and angry inside themselves at the fundamental 'unfairness' of what had happened to Ginger. They saw the press as intruding into their private grief. People often do in such circumstances. What newspapers see as a 'good' story too often means blood and tears for those directly involved. Naturally they resent the press's eagerness for the kind of harrowing detail which causes them pain.

No press interviews were granted. But there was no escaping the official statements necessary for a Coroner's investigation into the cause of death. Until the aircraft, the first contact from outside, had arrived it had all seemed so unreal. It is often like that after a fatality. Those close to the dead person keep anticipating the familiar. Looking up and half expecting to see Ginger walking through the cabin door with her usual cheerful grin and greeting. Then that jolt of pain deep in the stomach and the knowledge that it could never happen again. Ginger would never ever again walk through that door . . . Or anywhere . . .

Patiently Constable Litherland began to piece together the story of what had happened. Extra police were coming, he told Fitzpatrick. Two small vessels with search parties were already on their way from the island mining town at Koolan. Their mission would be to look for the body. Or what the crocodile might have left.

But meantime they had to inspect the scene. Fitzpatrick had expected it and steeled himself to go. The trip up the river in the Haines Hunter was very different from the happy expedition of the previous day with the girls smiling and their hair blowing in the wind of the boat.

The Cascades were the same—exactly the same as when they had first seen them on the Sunday morning. The lush greenery, the sun reflecting on the water in just the same way. But now the men saw the beautiful falls differently. They seemed to have a sinister air. Particularly that patch of shadow beneath the ferns growing on the cliff at the left-hand side, where the two girls had stood waist-deep, with their backs against the wall of rock . . . The place where it happened. They did not want to look at it, yet their eyes kept turning there.

They kept half expecting to see the crocodile appear from the milky water. The two knobs rising up to reveal the blazing yellow-green eyes. Then the triangular head, the dragon serrations along the back coming up like a submarine surfacing with the water running off the armoured spine. Last of all the long, powerful, frilled sweep of tail, as it surged forward, primeval and prehistoric. A creature with death in its eyes from the age of the dinosaurs.

But there was no crocodile to be seen.

No sign of Ginger. Was it real? Had it really and truly happened?

The sound of the motor mercifully removed the need to talk, or to answer questions as they returned glumly to the *Lady G.*

Bruce Fitzpatrick now wished to continue the voyage. Apart from the bad memories he was behind the schedule required by the owner. The open sea probably also appealed as its own kind of refuge. As captain he would have his own tensions, though the Coroner's finding, months later, on 21 August 1987, cleared him of any responsibility for the tragedy.

He asked Constable Litherland whether he could take the *Lady G* out of the St George Basin on the high tide at 4 P.M. He did not relish attempting the tricky rock-strewn passage at the mouth, he said, with a falling tide in gathering darkness.

The Constable agreed. There was no reason not to. And so it came about that the official declarations, sworn under oath, were taken at Cape Wellington after 5 P.M. They took the usual form.

"I Bruce Duncan Fitzpatrick, Captain, of Coronation Avenue, Mosman 2088, Sydney, New South Wales, IN THE STATE OF WESTERN AUSTRALIA MAKE OATH AND SAY . . ."

Now it was really true. The statements made it an accepted fact. Was it only yesterday? It seemed so long ago. Already some things were hazy . . .

The Constable was experienced and patient, helping them through. He was handed tourist brochures, showing coloured photographs of people swimming and splashing and having a good time at the Cascades in the area where the attack took place. The other visitors had been luckier, it seemed. He also noted that there were no warning signs in the area. It was symptomatic that Bruce Fitzpatrick made an error he would probably never have committed in ordinary circumstances.

He described the attack as having taken place at the 'western' side of the Cascades. In fact it was on the east side.

Stephen Hilton, Madeleine Janes and Jane Burchett each gave their oath and accounts of what had happened, and signed their names to the official forms.

At the end of their statements each of them spontaneously paid tribute to Ginger. "She was good to have on board. Very friendly, a good personality," Bruce Fitzpatrick said. He added miserably what the whole world would soon know. "It would have been her birthday today."

"She was very friendly and happy," Jane said. "I found her very easy to get on with."

"Ginger was great," said Steve. "Very outgoing."

They had dreaded having to make the statements. They seemed so formal and final. But now that it was completed there was a feeling of relief. A duty finished and done. The recollections might take longer to disperse.

Now they were all anxious to be away from that place of dreadful memory. None of them wanted to be there if the official search party found Ginger's body, or—what seemed more likely—a mutilated part of it. That would be altogether too much to bear.

But they had to wait until next morning, Tuesday, 31 March 1987, before the two boats, *Voyager* at 8.28 A.M. and *Penguin* at 9.24 A.M., arrived from Koolan Island. The *Voyager* was a 23-foot half-cabin fibreglass cruiser, skippered by Sean Rowles. *Penguin* was a 23-foot aluminum half-cabin boat of similar design, skippered by her owner Peter Tyler. She was particularly suitable for working shallow water.

With the party were Senior Constable Michael Scanlon, from Koolan Island, and Vic Cox, a crocodile expert from Cockatoo Island. Scanlon was to lead the search up the river. He had particularly requested Vic Cox's inclusion in the party.

Cox knew more about crocodiles than anyone else in the area. He had a pet crocodile himself, a fierce-eyed creature called Henry, which had grown to 14 feet (4.27 metres) in the 27 years it had lived in a pen by Cox's house. It was a pet in name only. Despite the fact that Vic fed him and was a familiar figure, he knew that Henry could never be trusted. Given any chance he would have snapped up the rest of Vic, along with the hand that fed him. It had been years since Vic had been able to get in the pen with him to clean out the concrete swimming pool that once belonged to Vic's kids. Aside from this day-by-day knowledge of crocodiles at first hand, Vic Cox had also been a professional crocodile hunter, and he knew the Prince Regent River and its tributary creeks well.

With their arrival the *Lady G* was at last free to go. Her captain and crew would have to face the ordeal of fire, the press questioning and explanations at Darwin where there could be no escape. But for the moment there was the welcome anonymity of the open sea.

The press meantime chafed 300 kilometres to the south at the Search Control Centre in Broome. They were restless at the lack of information coming from the Prince Regent, and frustrated by the fact that they had no means of reaching the remote area. "What are you *doing?*" editors inquired in frequent telephone calls.

The reporters seized on snippets. Despite the lack of 'hard' news they found a good deal to fill their front page columns. The Perth *Daily News*, of 30 March, led its main story with a local crocodile scare in Broome, 'CROC FEARS HIT N-W RESORT', ignoring the fact that it was the tourist off-season and teasing the government's Department of Conservation and Land Management with residents' suggestions about culling 'killer' crocodiles.

Reporters scoured Fremantle to find former friends of Ginger Meadows and seek out their comments and thoughts on the events at the Prince Regent, for the late editions of that day.

The *Daily News* quoted Adelaide sporting commentator Ray Fewings, who had met Ms Meadows during The America's Cup.

He described her as "a typical American—confident about the world.

"I could just imagine her diving off the boat without fear," he said.

A friend of Ms Meadows, Sydney sports commentator Patrick Bollen, said she was a vivacious woman with the world at her feet.

"She had split up from her husband and decided now was the time to get out and see the world," he said.

For readers with a taste for the macabre the newspaper added an extra unsubtle touch:

> "Officer in Charge of the Broome Police, Sergeant Alan Hall, said that Ms Meadows would have been 'ripped to pieces' once the smell of blood was in the water.
>   Searching for the body was 'just an exercise,' he said.
>   Broome Regional Officer, Chief Inspector Arnold Davies, said that Mr Meadows accepted that his daughter's body may never be found."

Meantime, 2500 kilometres farther north from Perth and Fremantle, at the St George Basin, the search for what might remain of Ginger Meadows was under way. *Penguin*, the aluminum boat, was heading purposefully up river. The craft, with Constable Mick Scanlon, Inspector Johnson, Vic Cox and Peter Tyler, arrived at the falls on the rising tide at noon.

Vic Cox, the professional, quietly disagreed with the reports of the pessimistic but widely held view that a body would not be found.

"It will be there," he said. "Though it may not be a pretty sight. Crocodiles' teeth are not adapted for chewing. When they capture big prey—human or a cow—they have to let it go soft for a few days until they can tear it in pieces. He'll store the remains somewhere. There are two creeks at the Cascades. That big crocodile dominates the pool there, and my guess is that he'll have taken her up one or the other of them. We'll probably find her in the mangroves by the high-tide mark."

Cox added a caution to the others in the search party. "There's a fair chance that the croc will be close by, keeping a watch over his property. We'll need to exercise a bit of discretion."

At the Cascades Peter Johnson, the fisheries inspector, climbed the falls, reaching the top at 12.18 P.M.

"The rocks were steep and slippery," he recalled later. "Some of the steps were quite high, four feet or more. I found it quite difficult, and it was certaintly not a place you could go up or down in a hurry."

Looking down he immediately saw two crocodiles in the entrance. But they both appeared to be only about eight feet long. Though crocodile sizes are notoriously hard to judge from the bank, Vic Cox considered that neither was big enough to have been the one described as the aggressor in the attack on Ginger Meadows.

The party split up to search the two creeks, each man with mixed feelings. The object was to locate a body, but they were individually apprehensive about what mangled horror they might find. Each hoped that one of the others would find the remains— if there was anything to be found.

They were also naturally wary about the crocodile. If it had killed once would it attack again? Would it be aggressive defending its prey? There was only one rifle (Broome police high-calibre firearm 223) between them. For efficient search they had naturally split up in different directions, so that most of them were unarmed and unprotected.

For lack of immediate news, the media accent now swung from the personal tragedy of Ginger Meadows to the contentious subject of crocodiles in general. The question was naturally asked: how far protection and tolerance should be extended when crocodiles killed humans?

Crocodiles had been protected in Western Australia, the Northern Territory and Queensland since the early 1970s. In the early days of exploration and settlement they had been relatively common in tropical mangrove areas. But shooting saltwater crocodiles, of the species *Crocodylus porosus*, in northern Australia for commercial skins in the 1950s and '60s had reduced numbers to such a low point that shooters themselves called for controls.

With the years of protection the reptiles had recovered and bred back to an extent which surprised even optimistic conservationists.

In 1987 rival Australian scientists in the field disagreed with some heat about their current counts and counting methods. But there was no questioning the fact that the numbers had significantly increased, particularly in the Northern Territory. It was also agreed that there was now a larger percentage of big crocodiles over three metres, the size at which they become dangerous to humans.

Some northern residents, particularly in Queensland, had resented an influx of dangerous animals into their rivers and favourite swimming holes. They pointed out that the government approved the culling of other wild creatures when there was sufficient reason. This approval included the annual shooting of one and a half million kangaroos, a species which had never physically hurt anyone. What was so sacrosanct, they asked, about a crocodile, an unpleasant animal which ate people? What was the difference between a forbidden bullet for a reptile and a million and more approved ones for the marsupials of the national emblem?

In the heat of the controversy some interesting things were said. They included a statement by the then Federal Minister for the Environment, Barry Cohen.

"We will be investigating the possibility of fines for people who place themselves at risk," he told reporters. "If they were not there they would not be eaten."

For someone being torn to pieces by a crocodile, the prospect of being fined posthumously by Mr Cohen's department may not have been the matter of most immediate concern.

Cohen went on: "We have been desperately worried for some time. That is why we put up signs for people's protection. They still want to ignore them and we don't think that can go on."

But the signs he referred to, funded by the Federal Government, were in the Northern Territory some hundreds of kilometres from the Prince Regent River where the attack took place. There were no signs at the time on the river at the King's Cascades. None on the unpopulated areas of the Kimberley Coast. However it was a long, long way to either the Northern Territory or the Kimberleys from Canberra where the most dangerous wild creatures were nesting magpies.

The West Australian Minister for Conservation, Barry Hodge, was almost as far distant. Warning people not to shoot at crocodiles he said, "Crocodiles are a rare and endangered species, and the penalty for killing them is a fine of up to $10,000."

In fact, in March 1987, crocodiles were neither rare nor endangered. There were probably about 400 in the St George Basin and Prince Regent River, according to scientific estimates, and from 60,000 to 100,000 throughout northern Australia, increasing (if you accept the Northern Territory Conservation Commission figures) at a rate of 6 per cent to 9 per cent each year.

Some conservationists also pointed out the self-evident fact that had Ms Meadows been an unattractive, middle-aged spinster who drowned while swimming, or slipped on the Cascades rock and fractured her skull—died in an 'ordinary' accident, in short —the matter would hardly have raised a flicker of press interest. interest.

It was the manner of her death, they said—a pretty girl in a bikini being seized by a crocodile in front of her friends—which grabbed the headlines, and attracted 'undue' publicity of a sensational and unbalanced kind.

Quite so. But freakish affair or not, the world's interest could

not be denied. Every headline and newspaper confirmed it. In
the light of the attack the ongong question of crocodiles and
people and their respective rights was not one which was going
to fade quietly away.

A story syndicated to the Perth *Daily News* told of other aspects of a family's grief under the heading PLEA BY VICTIM'S
FATHER and subtitled "Please Find Her Body." The article
read:

> "SYDNEY: The father of crocodile victim Ginger Mead-
> ows today made a plea for rescue squads to find the body
> of his daughter.
>
> Mr Charles Meadows said he hoped if the body was
> found it could be flown back to the US for burial.
>
> And the victim's husband arrived in Australia today to
> join in the search for her body.
>
> Dwayne McCaulley (27) was too distressed to talk to
> the media 'after arriving at Sydney Airport shortly before
> midday.
>
> Holding back tears he said: 'Leave me alone, for
> Christ's sake.'
>
> Mr McCaulley is scheduled to fly to Perth later today
> to catch a connecting flight to Derby.
>
> Mr Meadows, speaking from Charlottesville, Virginia,
> said the tragedy had devastated his family.
>
> 'We are all in shock,' he said.
>
> 'I just wish somebody had warned her, because I'm
> sure she was unaware of the dangers.'
>
> Miss Meadows was taken by a crocodile on Sunday
> as she swam near a chartered yacht, the *Lady G*, as it
> moored near the mouth of the isolated Prince Regent
> River in the northwest of WA.
>
> Mr Meadows said his daughter had gone to Australia
> to escape the trauma of a broken marriage.
>
> Information about how the incident occurred is still
> sketchy."

The newspaper also reported, as a side-issue, some supposed
local resentment:

"There isn't a shred of sympathy in the Kimberley for Miss Meadows," it claimed.

"Residents of the towns of Derby and Broome, which rely heavily on tourism during the winter months, were outraged that she was silly enough to put her life at risk."

In fact—while there may have been an initial reaction—the people of the north were not so hard-hearted as the article implied.

In Broome and Derby there was as much genuine sorrow for the way Ginger Meadows died, and as much sympathy for her stricken family as there was anywhere else in the world.

At the steamy Prince Regent River, meanwhile, the searchers —unaware that they were the subject of world press attention— spread out along the slippery, muddy banks of the mangrove creeks. They watched warily in the midday heat for abrupt or sudden movement that might indicate the presence of the crocodile.

Vic Cox moved slowly and studied the ground carefully. He looked for crocodile tracks along the banks and for unusual bird or fish activity. Peter Johnson carried the weight of responsibility for shooting the crocodile if it became necessary. Though, because he had to climb the waterfall, the firearm had been left in the boat for the time being. He took the most likely bank, running to the east of the place where the crocodile had last been seen. He pushed his way through dense undergrowth 600 metres before increasing thickets blocked his way and he began to feel uneasy. He had a feeling that the crocodile was close, though he could not see it.

"I didn't feel like wading along in the water without the rifle," he explained later. "So I turned back to find another way around."

Meantime Cox on the opposite bank continued on and clambering over the rocks around the head of the creek saw something pale and catching the light among the mangroves, about 100 metres past the spot where the Fisheries Inspector had been forced to turn back.

It was Ginger, face down in the water, and approximately where Vic Cox said she might be found. He looked at once for the crocodile. There was no sign, though like the inspector he had a strong feeling it was in the locality and aware of him.

The body had no arms. But as yet it had not been dismembered. The crocodile had 'stored' its prey, apparently intending to eat the remainder at a later time.

Cox returned to the boat at 1.45 P.M. with the grim news. The rest of the party were alerted, and body bags and a camera were brought from the boat for official photographs. These would be the brutally detailed kind, for the Coroner's files. Pictures which no one in their right mind and not officially involved would ever want to see. But they were necessary, of course, for identification, for the forensic medical reports, and for a Broome Coroner's finding as to the cause of death.

It was hard for the men to stay detached as they carried out the official duties of photography and measurement. Peter Johnson stood guard with the police rifle, watching with Vic Cox in case the crocodile appeared to dispute possession of his prey.

They dreaded the moment when the body—a poor armless broken doll, with back, buttocks, and legs scarred and torn by myriad toothmarks—was turned over. Would the face show the horror of the death? After two days in the heat of tropical mangrove mud would there be a face at all? But they were surprised. The face at this time was neither injured nor damaged, and the expression showed no sign of trauma. It was pale and almost peaceful, with the eyes closed like a little child asleep.

Perhaps, in her own way, Ginger Meadows was indeed at rest.

A little distance from her body they found a single white IW Sports shoe. There was no other clothing.

They discussed, as a matter of course, the question of the crocodile. Should it be shot? Vic Cox was confident that it would return to feed and that someone concealed with the high-powered rifle would not have to wait long. One reason for shooting it might be that Ginger's very valuable gold-and-diamond ring was presumably inside it. It was believed to be worth thousands of dollars.

Peter Johnson was against shooting the crocodile. The police also felt that getting the body back as quickly as possible should now be the main priority. Johnson's view was that he would have shot the crocodile if that were the only way to recover the remains (like Beryl Wruck on the Daintree, or Lee McLeod at Borroloola, whose body was found inside the crocodile). "But shooting it just for revenge seemed senseless," he said. "It wouldn't bring the poor girl back."

Carefully, gently, they placed her on a plastic sheet, then into two body bags, wrapped in a tarpaulin. Then, slung below a sapling, with the men panting with exertion, blinded by sweat, and struggling over the steep rocky ground of the creek bank, Ginger Faye Meadows began the long journey home to Charlottesville, Virginia, where she began it all.

Meantime, travelling in the opposite direction from Colorado in the USA to Western Australia, came Duanne McCauley. He had booked his flight in the outside hope that perhaps Ginger might not be dead after all. He thought, in some far-out flight of fancy, that maybe she might have managed to escape from the jaws of the crocodile. There were instances in history and in popular fiction where crocodiles had carried people off and let them go. Or where victims had escaped from their underwater lairs. Perhaps, somewhere, Ginger was waiting to be rescued by a search party . . .

It is a long journey across the Pacific at any time. For McCauley, reliving old memories, it must have seemed interminable. Then there was the change of aircraft in Sydney where he found the reporters were waiting for him. It was an unhappy confrontation, with McCauley begging them to leave him alone, and the press persisting with hard questioning.

At Perth Airport before the last leg of the flight to Broome, press representatives were waiting again.

This time they had news for *him*, they said as he tried vainly to escape. Perhaps they were not aware of how he had built his hopes up, as they brought them crashing down.

The body had been found at the Prince Regent. What did he think about *that*? They shoved the police telex message in front of him so that he could not ignore it. But still his eyes did not want to see it.

The younger and more naïve of the reporters found it hard to comprehend why Duanne McCauley reeled away without saying anything, his right hand clutching the side of his head. But some of those who had been in the business longer understood. So did many of the readers, who were repelled by the pictures. For they photographed him regardless of his wishes and printed portraits of a man in grief. It was not one of the greater moments of Australian journalism.

At Broome they were waiting again. In desperation he telephoned the police from the airport coin phone booth, and Inspector Arnold Davies came to the airport at once and whisked him away in a Toyota four-wheel-drive vehicle. McCauley was "distraught at the loss of his wife," Davies told the press firmly. He asked that there should be no further harassment.

The reporters were disappointed. But they did not have to wait long for the next story. The next news bulletin from the Prince Regent would be satisfactorily sensational, and there were more crocodile headlines to come.

It took the men carrying the burden sagging from the pole an interminable time to struggle over the rough ground at the head of the creek and back to the *Penguin*. They arrived back at 4.35. Meantime a radio message sent to their consort vessel *Voyager* (which had gone to Kuri Bay to pick up more fuel for the search) was intercepted and misunderstood by a coast watch radio listener in Sandy Straits. With the best of intentions details of what was supposed was a new crocodile attack were passed on to the national Sea Safety organisation in Canberra which in turn alerted Darwin and Broome police.

The Press were naturally agog. ANOTHER CROCODILE ATTACK? . . . WHERE? . . . WHEN? . . . WHOM?

The message which caused the furore read:

"At about 1536 hrs this date Sea Safety Canberra advised HQDO (Headquarters, Darwin Office) that a Sandy Straits volunteer coast guard operator received a message on marine emergency CB 27.88.

Details were unclear as the message was received on skip, but basically a boat called *Penguin* calling *Voyager*, reporting a crocodile attack.

Radio communication appeared as though call was made in a desperate manner or extreme urgency.

Further details unable to be supplied, as communication only on the skip. Please keep HQDO posted!"

There was a sigh of disappointment among the media when the mystery was unravelled. It was only, it turned out, *Penguin* reporting the finding of the body to *Voyager*, so that the information could be relayed to Koolan Island and Broome. *Penguin*'s radio, despite the freak interception, had limited range and a rendezvous was being arranged. The urgency was, of course, the feared complete deterioration of a body which had already been decomposing two days in tropical heat.

Penguin, with her sad burden, went down to the mouth of the Prince Regent River, and there the anchor was dropped in a sheltered creek. The five men aboard prepared to settle down in the cramped space for a less than comfortable night. The body, enclosed in its bags and wrapped in a tarpaulin, was lashed securely on the foredeck. They were quite unprepared for what was to happen.

"CROC LEAPS AT BODY ON BOAT," was the sensational report in the next edition of the *West Australian* newspaper. "Dramatic End to Grim Search at River Mouth." The report said:

"BROOME: A big crocodile jumped 1.5 metres from the water and tried to drag a woman's body from a four-metre boat as it left the Prince Regent River area . . .

Searchers recovered the body, believed to be that of American model Ginger Faye Meadows (24) of Virginia, from the river on Tuesday.

A positive identification is expected to be made today by the dead woman's estranged husband, Mr Duane McCauley, who arrived in Broome yesterday.

Search co-ordinator Chief-Inspector Arnold Davies said transport problems had prevented the body being flown from Koolan Island to Broome yesterday afternoon.

Former crocodile shooter Vic Cox, from Cockatoo Island, led a search boat to the body about a kilometre from the King's Cascades about 2.30 P.M. on Tuesday but searchers could not retrieve it till about 4 P.M. that day.

Mr Davies said Mr Cox's long experience was instrumental in finding the body on tidal flats behind some mangroves about a kilometre from the attack scene.

It had decomposed in the hot estuary, he said."

The body, it should perhaps be explained out of fairness to the searchers, was on the bow of the boat for two reasons. One was that, with five men and equipment, the little boat was crowded beyond its normal capacity. There was no lack of respect for the bag or its contents. On the contrary they did not want to be falling over it or accidentally disturbing it. Also, quite naturally, after two and a half days of tropical sun, there was a considerable aroma and some seepage of fluid. This was what brought on the crocodile attacks.

The men of the search party had had a gruelling day, physically and emotionally. Peter Johnson received a shock when he was sitting on *Penguin*'s gunwale after dark. "Something made me look over the side, and I was startled to see an eight-foot crocodile lying right alongside the boat. A little later there was a thump and a bang on the side of the hull, and a similar-sized crocodile —perhaps the same one—jumped out of the water, grabbed the body bag and its contents and tried to drag it overboard."

A shotgun was fired to frighten it off.

They shone a torch on the surrounding water and were startled to see the reflected eyes of crocodiles all around them in the creek.

"About 9.30 P.M. there was another disturbance and another crocodile jumped and seized the bag." This one jumped twice and succeeded in tearing the end out of the bag. It had to jump a metre out of the water to get hold of it with its teeth.

That was too much. It was obvious that the crocodiles would keep harassing them through the night. If a big one came along it might wreck the bag and its contents. Perhaps drag the poor remains away altogether.

They decided to up-anchor and pass the night out on the rougher open water of the St George Basin, rather than fight for the body with the crocodiles in the creek.

"It was unlikely that the original crocodile had trailed us down river," Johnson said later. "That was the obvious inference a lot of people made. But it was more than 15 kilometres from the Cascades. Altogether too far, I think, for it to have followed us. The crocodiles which attacked the body bag were probably considerably smaller than the one which killed her." Was it a dangerous situation? "Not so far as it had gone," he said. "But it was decidedly uncomfortable and unpleasant. If the scent attracted the small and medium-sized crocodiles there was also the distinct possibility that a really large one might come along later in the night. If it tried to climb in or on the boat to get to the body it would have been a very different story. Certainly it wasn't a nice thought to try to go to sleep on."

The eerie incident spooked all the men. They spent a wretched and largely sleepless night rolling at anchor out in the open reaches of the St George Basin.

Early next morning—5.15 A.M., 1 April 1987—*Voyager* came alongside and at 6.30 they met at Customs boat *Jackana* where the body was transferred to the *Jackana*'s dinghy for towing. At Koolan Island at 2.10 P.M. Dr Andrew Barclay examined the remains and performed his official duty of pronouncing life extinct. In fact by now the condition of the body had deteriorated to such a degree that he said it could not possibly be placed in the waiting aircraft. He recommended that they chill the bag and contents for a period in a low-temperature refrigerator unit for 24 hours before it was flown on. This was done and a flight was arranged for next day. At 9.30 A.M. on 2 April, the body was flown to Broome and taken to the town mortuary.

A favourite story in Broome afterwards was that the police there gently dissuaded McCauley—who wished to view the now-disintegrated body—from doing anything of the sort. They did this out of kindness, it was said, and in technical contradiction of their formal duty. The proposition was supposed to have been put that Ginger would undoubtedly have preferred that Duanne McCauley should simply remember her as she was in life. Bright, vibrant, cheerful and pretty. Not as a dead and damaged object.

It was a nice story, but incorrect.

It was true that the police tried to persuade him not to view the body bag's contents. It was not necessary for him to see something in a morgue that bore no resemblance to what he had known because there were other scientific means of achieving positive identification. It was eventually achieved in Perth through dental records. McCauley had already suffered enough, it was felt, and there was a fear that his sanity might not have stood looking in the body bag.

But McCauley himself insisted. He needed to know, he said, that there really would be no tomorrow. That Ginger was actually dead.

He could not identify what he saw. He 'knew' that it was her, but there were no physical identifying features he could point to for official records. He staggered when he came out of the identification, and broke down finally in the police vehicle.

Later police took from him the single red rose he had brought for her, and gently placed it with Ginger. They attached a note to the bag which ensured that it remained with her 'at all times' until she was returned to America and her parents. That flight left Perth Airport at 4 P.M. on 13 April 1987.

Sometimes the police in northern Australia are accused of being heavy-handed. Keeping the law in frontier land is not always easy. But in the Ginger Meadows case they showed an understanding and a human decency that won them the warmth and commendation of their fellow citizens.

In any complete study of crocodile attacks, and in particular the sad story of Ginger Meadows, it is necessary to follow through to the end. This is not because of any unhealthy interest in the macabre. But because events before and after the attack take in all aspects of the often-uneasy relationship between human beings and crocodiles.

Any death is a reason for sadness, particularly when there is no point to it. There are lessons to be learned from the incident at the King's Cascades on 29 March 1987, which may very well save someone else's life, somewhere else, some time in the future.

It would be wanton not to try to learn from what occurred, and to put the knowledge to positive future use. To waste it would be a waste indeed. Ginger Meadows would probably agree.

All of the people killed by crocodiles in northern Australia over the preceding two years had their own individual poignant human stories too.

Kerry McLoughlin, a 40-year-old storeman working at Jabiru, who was taken at Cahill's Crossing on the East Alligator River only 12 days before Ginger died, had three children. One of his sons actually saw him seized by the crocodile which decapitated him.

Similarly people killed in motor accidents throughout the country in the same weekend left behind some who loved them— wives, children, fiancées, parents, as may be—even though they did not receive the same degree of publicity. It is a rare person who does not have someone to cry for him or her or say "If only . . ."

The strong bond between humans, whether they are related or not, is an important part of our development as an intensely gregarious species. Whatever our shortcomings, love for our fellows is surely one of the most redeeming features of the human race. Ginger was loved and mourned by thousands of people she had never known or met.

In contrast, it has been said, crocodiles are a murderous, joyless lot, dividing their lives between fear of each other, fratricidal aggression and the brutal assassination of other animals. And people.

They appear to have no traits which would redeem them in our human eyes. None of the devotion (to humans) of a dog, nor the playfulness of a kitten, the friendliness of a dolphin or sea lion . . . None of the ability of a horse or an elephant to accept training—A dangerous beast, in short, with no practical purpose in our scheme of things.

Some people would rather see them eliminated altogether. Exterminated. But how comfortably could we live with the knowledge that we had terminated a life-form which evolved with the dinosaurs, and has survived on earth nearly 200 million years . . . ?

The proposition arouses some interesting questions about the way we perceive things. For instance is a crocodile crueller than the cat toying with a mouse? Or the dog running down a rabbit? Or a dolphin throwing a herring up in the air to catch it?

Yet we love all those creatures.

In terms of actual cruelty—the infliction of physical pain and suffering which most of us reasonably find objectionable—how does man himself rate with his guns, fishing rods, hooks, nets, gin-traps, and poisons?

Or take the higher question: Is man the only animal form with a right to life?

In the past not many people considered questions of this kind seriously. Those who did were thought to be cranks, or—at best —'soft.' But it is a changing world. The human conscience, with more knowledge about other creatures of this planet, has developed new dimensions. The status and survival of wild animals everywhere has become one of the important issues of our time. Caring about nature—one of the more significant changes of attitude of the late 20th century.

Finding answers to the problems, including the various dilemmas on crocodiles, will require a measure of honesty not especially evident in our past. It may be a useful experience for us all. Lessons learned with animals may perhaps help with the ultimate problem of our time. The one we will not be able to turn our faces away from indefinitely. That is the problem of living with the rest of the human race in the mushrooming population explosion, as the year 2000 approaches.

A DIFFERENCE IN LIFESTYLES

▲▲▲▲▲▲▲▲▲▲

*T*he crocodile that killed Ginger Meadows may have been born about the same time. His size in 1987 indicated a creature of a similar life span.

There could be no greater contrast than the lives of the two young creatures. The little girl growing up through her ages of hair-ribbons and skipping ropes, and the small reptile struggling for its very existence in the muddy reaches of a tropical river.

The girl with the red hair and the wide smile was surrounded by love and care each day of her life. The tiny crocodile, in contrast, found enemies waiting at the bend of each creek. Creatures which saw him only as a part of the food chain.

For the small reptile death could come from the air on the rush of wings and the outstretched talons of a fish-hawk. On the land there were the stiletto-sharp beaks of wading birds, the crushing coils of water pythons. Most dangerous place of all was the water where big barramundi and cod with cavernous mouths waited, and where sharks came up on the tide.

But the greatest threat for our little crocodile came not from the finned creatures—though they took their toll—but from his own peers. Crocodiles themselves are cannibals. For a tiny crocodile trying to escape there seemed to be almost nowhere he could flee where another crocodile could not follow.

Luck played a considerable part in his survival. Several times it was a matter of a simple choice, and a despairing brother or sister was snapped up beside him. Disappearing forever in a flash of cruel teeth. A gulp and a swirl of muddy water and a small life extinguished. The tinge of blood on the tide the only sign that moments before there had been a living creature there.

Each escape hardened the little crocodile. The brushes with death made him cautious and cunning, and desperation gave him the strength and meanness to catch his own prey in turn. Nonetheless his chances of survival were not high.

Nature had played a cruel joke on his mother. She had laid her 50 eggs in the mound she had so carefully built in the swamp. As the summer advanced and the sun's heat on the compost increased the life-giving warmth, she lay beside the nest in a wallow she had especially dug there.

Week after week, mother-love belying the warty ferocity of her natural expression, she watched over the eggs as inside the buried shells dots in the yolks grew to form tiny crocodiles in her own image.

As the time for hatching drew near she became increasingly anxious. A big monitor lizard which dug incautiously in the side of the nest saw his danger too late. He vanished down the mother's gullet in a couple of bloody gulps. A welcome morsel in a time of compulsory fasting. There were wild pigs to be driven away before they could snout at the mound. Once a dozen buffalo, led by a grizzled, battle-scarred old bull, came grunting and stomping through the swamp, their hairy backs gleaming with wet mud.

Buffalo give way to no other creature. But the mother crocodile came out of her wallow with her mouth open, growling and hissing, and barred the way to the nest.

When the bull lowered his head she humped her back and snapped her jaws in bluff, defiant of the scimitar horns and trampling hooves that could have ended her own life.

For moments they remained locked in confrontation. The yellow blazing eyes of the crocodile, the anger-red eyes of the bull, each glaring at the other. The bull snorting, head lowered, paw-ing the ground, with the herd pressing behind him, impatient to get to the river. The mother crocodile, jaws open, ready to give her life for the unborn young in the nest behind her.

Then the bull blew hard through his nostrils and threw his head up. Stamping his cloven hooves he backed off, pushing his rump into the group of cow buffalo, before leading them away again in a different direction. The little lizard-like creatures in the buried eggs—50 separate beating hearts—unaware of the drama that had taken place on their behalf.

There came the day when a faint frog-like croaking came from the nest side. The mother heaved herself up from the wallow, muddy water rivuleting from her scaly sides. Then she waddled up to the high ground where she had built the nest safe from flooding.

She cocked her head delicately to one side, listening. The croaking chorus came louder. She extended a clawed reptilian paw and began to dig slowly at first, then more quickly. The first of the babies were already breaking through the shells of the eggs, aided by a little horn on their snouts—nature's can-opener —which would drop off soon after birth. Some of the babies were having difficulty. The mother rolled the eggs in her mouth, between that horrendous palisade of teeth, and gently crushed them just enough to crack the shells. The bite that meant death to so many creatures, now bringing life to her own young.

The little crocodile was one of those who had found it hard to break out of the imprisoning shell. It was not the most promising beginning, but it was the first time that his life was accidentally saved by outside circumstances.

The first of the babies to break out of his shell and head instinctively for the river—the strongest and fittest, and logically the one with the best hope for survival—lost his roll of the dice before he even reached the water. A whistling kite swooped down and scooped him up, carrying him off, writhing and broken-backed, to its own young in a distant nest high up in the gorges.

The mother shepherded the others to the shallow water, carrying some in her mouth. For the first weeks, perhaps even a month or two, she stayed with them while they snapped dragonflies out of the air, and crunched beetles and riverside spiders.

Then one day she was gone, thin and wasted, to make up for

all that long period of vigilance. Nature's joke on her was that despite all her love and labour, all the time of watching, the vast majority of her babies would perish before reaching full adulthood.

Crocodile mortality—if they were to consider it themselves as a species—is appalling, especially in the early years. Due to flooding, interference by other species and predators, only a small percentage of the total number of eggs laid in a summer survived to hatching. Thereafter the hatchlings who had crossed that uncertain bridge found themselves constantly embattled. There was so much against our little crocodile surviving. Luck played a major part in those early days, as brothers and sisters fell one by one along the way. But each escape was an experience. A piece of knowledge to add to inherited instinct. He grew at the rate of 12 inches or 30 centimetres a year, and began to add cunning to his natural strength and agility.

The most dangerous ages (after the first weeks as a hatchling) came when he was between two and four years old, and vulnerable to smaller predators. Later when he was two metres or about six and a half feet in length he had grown enough to be free from threat from birds (he was already stalking and eating them instead) and safe from fish and most sharks. But the main threat now came from his own kind, *Crocodylus porosus*.

As the summer began and the thunder-clouds mounted in the build-up for the wet season, the big male crocodiles with angry, raised tails and gobbling grunts, began staking out their breeding territories along the river. Sun temperatures mounted and the heat-waves quivered along the mud banks.

The advent of summer brought on a mating madness. It began with the gladiatorial contests for the favours of the females.

The protagonists rolling, jaws crashing, sending vast sheets of spray flying with flailing tails, as they fought for holds on throats and feet.

A five-metre monster held the balance of terror in the river where our young crocodile reached his first two metres. This ogre to a small *porosus* was 900 kilograms in weight. A mouthful of embedded catfish spikes and a stingaree barb beside his eye kept him in a state of permanent bad temper. Added to this was the remembered pain from the battles of the years. He trusted no other creature and gave no mercy.

When November came and the duels between the older crocodiles began, the younger crocodiles had to flee the river. It was not safe to remain. Defeated rivals took their spite out on anything that moved a tail. Lords of the river brooked no other male —even those too immature to breed—on their domain. The big crocodile ate two-metre adolescents when he could catch them and crunched their bones with personal relish.

Our crocodile had felt himself safe in a mangrove tributary. But one sunny afternoon in a rare moment of carelessness he dozed on the surface and woke—too late—in a maelstrom of frothing water. As he was rolled around and disoriented he felt the dreadful grip crushing his chest and he knew that he was about to die.

A row of ribs and a foreleg cracked with the pressure. The air was gone from his lungs. A roaring blackness descended on him as the four-metre crocodile that crushed and shook him in its jaws prepared to change grips to finish him off.

Then suddenly the crocodile was free. He flailed blindly to the surface, jaws open, feeling the stabbing, choking pain of his broken ribs. At the same time, instinctively, desperately, he swam for the mangroves, tail lashing the water. If he could only reach the line of green foliage at the river edge he could dive to safety among the stilted mangrove roots like a rat down a hole. Every moment he anticipated the sound of pursuit, a renewal of the crack of jaws around his body. Another roll and the waves of blinding crushing pain. But they did not come.

He reached the mangroves, pushed and wriggled through roots and crevices until finally he came to rest, terrified, exhausted, swooning with fright and pain. There he lay in a cave of roots, buried to his eyeballs in the mud.

Only then the sounds of outside conflict reached him and he realised why he had been saved. The five-metre ogre, taking advantage of the aggressor's preoccupation with his prey, had seized the chance. Surfing across the coffee-coloured water of the creek he clamped his great, grim jaws on the other big saurian's foreleg and threw himself into the crocodile's deadliest manoeuvre, the death roll. The small crocodile owed his release to this providential intervention. Now it was the four-metre beast's turn to know fear. Try as he would there was nothing he could do to break that fatal grip. Over and over the adversaries rolled until there was a sudden wrench and a sunburst of red and the foreleg tore away at the shoulder.

The dying crocodile tried to flee, but everywhere he forced his mutilated body there was a huge shadow behind him. No need to come to close grips now. The end was inevitable. Simply a matter of waiting and following the thickening trail of blood. Death on the river.

With hundreds of others of his size the small crocodile was forced down the river, alternatively hiding from the savagery of the larger male crocodiles, or running the gauntlet of their territories. He travelled slowly, moving from cover to cover, nursing his wounds. In a backwater he found a long-necked turtle under a log and cut off its escape. He cracked its shell with a savage crunch of jaws. The protein rebuilt his strength. But it would be a long time before his confidence returned.

In time he reached the sea and the saltwater swamps. This was a no-man's-land where he was safe from harassment by the big crocodiles. But it was no land of milk and honey. It was poor in food (else the big crocodiles would have been there) but it was rich in danger. Whaler and hammerhead sharks foraged regularly on the rising tides.

Only about 30 per cent of the harried juveniles who sought refuge would survive the sharks, the hunger and the harshness of the habitat, to venture hopefully again up river after the breeding season.

But the little crocodile kept beating the odds. It may have appeared that he had a charmed existence. But the fact was that even at his tender age he had a stronger urge for survival, a shrewder estimation of risks, than his fellows. It was nature's cruel way of ensuring that only the best and fittest survived.

He learned to shepherd fish against a bank and surprise them with a whirling turn that trapped them. He ambushed an occasional wading bird in the reeds, and was not too proud to wolf at the carcass of some poor drowned creature floating down the river.

Like the big crocodiles he learned the importance of artificial temperature control to a reptile. Spending nights in the water, letting the morning sun raise his blood warmth on the mud banks and hiding in some cool spot in the heat of the day.

The price of his survival was eternal vigilance. His yellow eyes were always watchful, his senses alert.

Ginger Meadows, the human child, grew up with bedtime stories and cuddles from her parents. She went to school fetes and sports days and rode her bicycle in a world of warmth and safety and approval. But every living thing in the crocodile's life seemed to be against him.

In the next year, up the river after the breeding season, death introduced a new element. There came the alien noise of engines and human voices. Two ex-pearling luggers, which had been turned to another use following a calamitous drop in the price of mother-of-pearl shell, arrived behind the sound. When night fell they swung little boats overboard on davits and sent them up the river. They carried spotlights which shone brighter than day and sent beams dancing across the water to dazzle any crocodiles in their path.

The men seemed pleased with what they saw when they reached the main stream.

"Holy Christ!" exclaimed a bearded man in the leading boat. "Will you look at all them eyes!" There was a metallic rattle of .303 rifle bolts.

Like fire-flies on the water the eyes of crocodiles reflected along the broad expanse of the virgin stream. There came a strange crashing sound which echoed and echoed. It was like no noise the little crocodile had ever heard before.

"Got 'im!" cried a voice and a big crocodile stood up on its tail and fell back thrashing, belly up.

The rifles cracked all night, and next day the men spent all the daylight hours flensing the corpses, cursing the tormenting sand-flies, and salting the skins. They rolled the sad remains, white and naked without their pelts, back into the water. At night the shooting began again. BANG! . . . BANG! . . . BANG! . . . went the rifles. SPLASH! went the tails slapping the water convulsively, as crocodile after crocodile rolled in its death throes. The dark-skinned Aboriginal boys brought along by the white

shooters harpooned the dead or wounded crocodiles and drew
them with lines attached to barbed darts to the dinghies. Sometimes they dived over with a line in their teeth. Plunging down to
tie it around the scaly leg of a shot crocodile which had sunk to
the bottom. They loved the work, returning to the surface with a
white gleam of teeth.

"You-ai, boss, I gottim orright!"

A wide grin for a risk taken, another quarry secured.

For a few days all was confusion and panic. Crocodiles fled
into every tributary of the river. But once darkness fell the lights
sought them out remorselessly.

Those who survived learned what to do. When they saw the
flash of the lights and heard the sound of the motors, they submerged among the mangrove roots, or under floating mats of
vegetation until the sound of vibrations passed. The shooters
tried sitting it out, but though they notched a few more skins to
strip off, roll up and salt away, the crocodiles had learned well.
Those few that had survived.

It was another lesson in the life of the little crocodile. The big
five-metre monster, who had terrorised the river—and inadver-
tently saved the life of the little one—had been too old to learn
new tricks. His was one of the first skins secured by the shooters
as he cruised arrogantly out to see who was trespassing in his
domain.

All his mighty strength and the pent-up anger of the continual
battle to secure his section of the river were of no avail. He could
have crushed the dinghies with his bulk. Bitten any of the hunters
in half with a snap of his giant jaws if he had closed with them.
But he was defeated by a small piece of lead weighing less than
an ounce. A .303 bullet—designed for killing men, not crocodiles, but effective for both—lifted the top off his skull. The
mighty one was no more. Humiliatingly stripped of its armoured
hide, pathetically naked, the great corpse was left to strand on a
sand bar and feed the mud crabs and carrion birds. His skin went
off to make suitcases for people who required a distinguished
look to their luggage. The smaller hides became shoes and handbags.

The largest of the remaining crocodiles would battle to fill his territory, and to sire the lady crocodiles he had acquired by strength and serviced so many years. The small crocodile did not know it, but the dead monster had been his father.

A new crocodile took his place. The King is dead; long live the King. But because the elevation to the peerage took place in unnatural circumstances the new lord was nowhere as big, as strong, as ruthless, or as arrogant as the old master. He had been 17 feet 10 inches long, and had been many years in domination of the river. The little crocodile watched and learned.

Nothing would ever be quite the same again in the river. The shooters came back again and again with their lights and barking rifles. When the crocodiles became too wary, they tempted them with snares and baited hooks and even poison. As a last resort they set heavy nets across creek entrances.

But by that time, the end of the 1960s, there were so few crocodiles of any size that the hunters ceased their expeditions. "The game's not worth the candle," they complained in the pubs in Darwin and Derby. "There's not a bloody croc bigger 'n a gecko (small tropical lizard) between Cape Londonderry and the bloody Buccaneer Archipelago."

Despite their gruff tone—making it sound as though it was somehow the crocodiles' fault—the hunters were troubled.

Men who live close to animals, even when they have to kill them for a living, feel themselves a part of the natural world. The hunter loves the hunted. They felt bad in themselves about the decline in crocodile numbers and there was no longer the same joy or challenge in the hunt.

The small crocodile—not so small now, as he filled out—saw it all. Watching from his careful series of chosen refuges, he was aware that things had altered along the river. With the removal of the large crocodiles from the river systems he was safer than he ever would have been in natural circumstances.

But the hunting had destroyed a delicate balance. Few crocodiles had actually been breeders. The bulk of the female crocodiles had been serviced by a few old and powerful males. Nature selected the biggest and fiercest animals to father future generations. They held their positions by continual trial by battle.

Because of their size they were the first to be shot. A few

survived the slaughter to become legendary 'Old Man' crocs, so wary now that no human ever saw them. Occasionally their tracks would be seen, or a bullock carcass scarred and crushed would bloat in the shallows. A reminder that not all the big crocodiles (the old hunters called them 'alligators' or 'gators') were gone.

By the time Ginger Faye Meadows reached high school and went to her first school dance, the crocodile was taking his place in the world. He had beaten most of the odds nature had stacked against him and become a survivor where scores of his contemporaries had perished. He had his healed scars, including the beaked nodules on his broken ribs and the broken foreleg. But he was healthy and strong and now only a bigger crocodile—or a human—could kill him.

The birds which once had tormented him, he snapped off the bank with a wicked 'clop' of white teeth and a flurry of feathers.

His diet was changing. He trapped an old and feeble wild pig and found that the mammal blood answered an age-old instinct after the years of fish, turtles and stingarees.

There was also something else. Strange new urges were stirring in him. He was reaching sexual maturity and a restlessness, a hungry desire he had never known before, seized him.

When a female crocodile arched her back and raised her nose in the submissive pose one November evening, he felt a beating pulse in his loins and drove towards her in a flurry of foam. For days they touched or rolled and rubbed together in the titillation of courtship. When she was finally ready and he captured her, it was exactly as nature had intended. He had passed his trials of pain and humiliation. He had starved and suffered and proved himself in the hardest school his world could provide.

He took the female crocodile with all the hunger of new discovery. Interlocking with her, twining, rolling, in the ecstasy of lovers of whatever species, world around. He had her for the better part of a fortnight before the big crocodile who now controlled that part of the river came angrily on the scene and drove him away with threatening displays.

If it had been the old crocodile of previous years there might have been no display. Just a terrible crash of jaws. But the new master was uncertain—and the crocodile's increased bulk was beginning to earn him respect.

Next time a female crocodile sought him out he did not retire so easily. Instead he humped his tail and opened his jaws and growled to show he was ready to fight to retain his pleasures. The contest was brief, a series of snaps and lunges, before the big crocodile—who had won the responsibility of that part of the river before he was really ready for it—fled in cowardly fashion. The crocodile was left with his lady love. They retired to a tributary creek and, because there were so few crocodiles of any size remaining in the Prince Regent, spent a happy summer honeymooning undisturbed.

Sometimes the drone of a beetle reminded the crocodile of the boats and he would tense waiting for the sound to grow louder. But in the world of men, legislation had been passed protecting crocodiles of his species, *Crocodylus porosus*, in Western Australia, as well as the other Australian crocodile species *Crocodylus johnstoni*—the little freshwater Johnstone River crocodile.

The men with the guns would never come again. At least not in the old way. The year was 1972. The crocodile was 16 years old, nearly three metres in length, green, shiny, with yellow and black interlocking markings and in good health. He was handsome in the eyes of his ladies. Already he weighed about 150 kilograms. He was young to be living with breeding females and he would have been severely punished for his temerity in previous years by one of the old bulls. But then things had changed on the river.

Ginger Meadows was growing up. "She was a truly beautiful child," her father said. "She was so lively. So full of vitality."

She loved the water and became an accomplished swimmer. A skill which, in the final analysis, may have eventually been a disadvantage.

Little girls growing up in America are much like little girls growing up in Australia. In their early teens they suddenly turn from children to young women. They have their first dates with boys (usually carefully supervised), wear lipstick and high heels for the first time and go to their first school dance in a tremble of excitement and anticipation.

The high school years end in graduation. Ginger felt she had studied enough and chose to work for a year before she changed her mind again and went to college in Florida. By that time the crocodile was growing towards four metres in length. He was now a magnificent specimen of his species.

He no longer feared any other saltwater crocodiles and the memories of the men with the guns and lights had faded. He had taken over a prime territory at the junction of the two mangrove creeks at the King's Cascades waterfall, driving the previous male occupant out and down river with a ferocity which impressed his growing retinue of lady crocodiles. The breeding instincts of the females were triggered and excited by such male conflicts.

Stretched on a mud bank in the mornings sunning himself, with the typical mirthless grin of the saurians which sends shivers down the spine of any human observer, he was the lord of all he surveyed. A magnificent, primitive sight. With his shining scales and frilled back and tail he was a creation from another age. He was now a prince by conquest and of royal blood by birth—a lineal descendant of the great dinosaurs which once ruled the earth in the age of the reptiles. Crocodiles and dinosaurs together came from ancient stock—the Archosaurs. They had shared common ancestors in the Cotylosaurs, during the Palaeozoic era evolving through the Mesozoic. Why the dominant dinosaurs, the great lizards, died away and crocodiles survived is one of the earth's great mysteries. But survive they did.

For 200 million years the Crocodilians did well, changing little in a changing world. They were well adapted to their amphibious life and it carried some important advantages for them.

Crocodilians could retreat to either land or water to escape from enemies. At the same time prey from both land and sea was available to them, with odd offerings from the air in the form of water birds and flying foxes. For reptiles the control of body temperatures is vital. There may be as much as 17°C variation between night and day temperatures ashore. But water temperatures remain constant, seldom altering as much as 3°C.

The crocodile, by shrewd movement between land and water, sun and shade, kept his temperature constantly within a few degrees of 30–32°C. Temperature was as important to him as sex or eating—in fact neither of these two activities could take place satisfactorily if his temperature was not exactly right for the occasion.

Being amphibious allowed the female crocodiles which the crocodile fertilised to lay their eggs ashore in a nest where they could be guarded, unlike the spawn of marine creatures which often floated away on the tide.

Water supports a much greater body size, allowing our saltwater crocodile to reach one day a maximum length of perhaps somewhere between five and six metres and maybe a tonne in weight—the largest natural Australian creature.

Because of their size, big crocodiles, in the days before man, had had nothing to fear from any other living creature. Except other large crocodile rivals.

Observing the crocodile on his mud bank, mouth slightly agape as a fine tuning of his temperature balance, there would be many interesting evolutionary features to see.

His teeth, for example. That ferocious, perpetual grin. The jaws—immensely powerful—form a formidable spiked clamp like a bear trap. A careful scrutiny shows that they do not open and close with a normal scissor motion. In fact the top and lower jaws are offset, like multigrip pliers, for a more even and powerful grip. Once the jaws lock, with crushing power, nothing seized escapes until the crocodile himself voluntarily opens his mouth. As with sharks—whose teeth are also at risk in the hurly-burly of catching prey—crocodiles grow new teeth to replace any fangs that are knocked out or broken.

The skull of the animal on the sandbank is solid bone, to protect against the kicks and struggles of desperate prey. His nostrils and gullet have flaps which act as valves to keep water out while the crocodile is engaged in violent threshing and rolling to kill its victim.

The nostril is easy to see, set high on the tip of the nose. The eyes are on top of the skull. Immersed, the crocodile need only show the merest fraction of his huge bulk while he breathes and observes. The ability of a crocodile to drift downstream stalking prey, while appearing to be a small and totally innocent piece of

floating branch, is legendary. Our crocodile has developed it to
an art, a part of the reason for his survival where so many others
of his hatching never reached the rewards of adulthood.

And the eyes—those yellow blazing eyes, which inspire
so much human fear when seen in confrontation at close
quarters . . . Crocodiles see well above and below water. Movement on the bank is their trigger for action or concealment. The
eye has three membranes, or eyelids. One works as a goggle, for
underwater vision. Another—a clear membrane—is a wiper for
cleaning away mud or grit while ashore. The major one is a heavy,
crinkled, true eyelid which protects the whole optic like a human
eyelid.

Though the crocodile is now big enough to take large prey,
including wallabies and wild pigs, he still does not need to eat
often. His species converts an amazing 30 per cent of food they
eat into biomass, or more body growth. Birds and humans only
convert 3 per cent. Consequently people have to eat a lot more
often to maintain activity.

But perhaps the most remarkable physical attribute of the
crocodile is his ability to conceal himself. Two hundred million
years before man invented the submarine, crocodiles learned
how to submerge and become invisible. Even on the surface, with
only the 'walnuts' of the eyes and the tips of the nostril showing,
he is extremely difficult to see in his tropical river system, when
drifting logs, branches and yellow mangrove leaves are a normal
part of the surface scene on the running tides.

Young crocodiles can bury completely in mud to escape the
persecution of their peers. 'Old Man' crocodiles can remain submerged up to an hour. They become adroit at using natural cover,
like lily pads, floating or overhanging vegetation, as disguise
when they do take a breath.

It is our crocodile's natural preference, inherent, age-old instinct, to see and not be seen. The secret presence.

Our crocodile on the mud bank, growing towards his prime at
around 25 years, has perfected these techniques of submerging.
He is able to wait under water up to an hour because, like all of
his species, he can unconsciously control the rate of his four-
chambered heart to a remarkable degree.

In bursts of activity his heart may pulse at a rate of up to 46 beats a minute. In repose where we see him on his morning sandbar, or drifting idly on the surface current, it may drop to 16 or 20 beats. But when he dives to 'lie doggo' for a deliberately long period, his heartbeat will reduce to an incredible one beat every three minutes. Almost suspended animation.

With his ability to submerge as his most useful weapon, the crocodile has also perfected his ambush technique. The attack from concealment. With animals and birds he commonly observes their movements for some time. Most animals and people, as we have already observed, are creatures of habit.

At their regular time of approach to the water he had learned to position himself in advance. Waiting and listening, below. Feeling the vibrations of footfalls. Able to see the shadows of movement on the bank, waiting for precisely the right moment. Then, like an uncoiled spring exploding out of the water, he was able to strike with flashing teeth in the lightning sideways movement that seldom failed.

To the crocodile, animals had always had to be considered either as predator or prey. As he reached maturity, fewer and fewer animals posed a threat. But he became more involved with the rivalry with other large males for territory and breeding females.

The Prince Regent River is so remote that apart from that first traumatic experience with the shooters years ago, the growing crocodile had seldom needed to consider whether humans were a likely threat, or were possible prey.

But by the late 1980s more and more human visitors began to pass by. They came from yachts sailing around Australia, or charter craft from Kimberley centres like Broome and Derby, which turned in to the St George Basin and went up river to see the Prince Regent and the beauty of the King's Cascades. Boat parties sometimes came too from the big BHP mining operations at Koolan and Cockatoo Islands.

People had fun at the waterfalls. They climbed the Cascades, stood under the falls and had shower baths. The picnic parties saw a lot of beer drunk and some of the more daring went swimming in the pool with whoops and laughter.

At first no one saw the crocodile and so of course—in human logic—they thought he wasn't there. But he watched, from his cover in the mangrove shadows, and waited, invisible. With every group of visitors he learned a little more about these strange two-legged animals who made so much noise and who seemed so unaware. With every visit he became more confident and bolder. Soon he ventured out and sometimes cruised quite close to the boats. People sometimes threw him fish carcasses and took his photograph. He studied them and felt less and less fear. Each visitor who fed him contributed to that future day.

Meantime Ginger Meadows had grown up in her own civilised world of people. She had completed her schooling, spent a year at college, entered into marriage—run the normal gambit of training and activity for a young human female adult of her age.

Statistically, the chances of her being killed or injured in a motor accident before she reached 60 years of age were something to consider seriously. There was a significant chance. On the same basis of figure analysis, the possibility that a young lady from Charlottesville, Virginia, could be eaten by a saltwater crocodile were so infinitesimal—billions to one against—as to be not even worth considering.

Yet by 29 March 1987, she had travelled to the Prince Regent River and now the odds had altered dramatically. There was so much of fate involved. Ill-luck for poor Ginger Meadows. All the things she had believed were bringing her good fortune—the trip to Australia, the passage on the *Lady G*—were in fact bringing her closer to the King's Cascades.

On that day the element of random chance still played its part. While the crocodile, the silent and invisible hunter at the bottom of the pool, waited for his opportunity, any number of factors could have thwarted his intention. The human actors in the drama were, of course, completely unaware that he was there. But if Bruce Fitzpatrick had returned five minutes earlier . . . if Jane Burchett had had her forebodings earlier and declined the swim to shore . . . If Madeleine had already returned to the boat instead of being half-way down the cliff . . . All questions they asked themselves in the aftermath. But, of course, how could they know?

Speculation as to what might or might not have happened is probably unfair. Certainly it cannot now change the events of that day. The girl who had spent 25 years becoming a woman, and the crocodile which had spent perhaps a similar length of time learning to survive in his own harsh environment, came together.

We know how the story ended for Ginger. For the crocodile— unless it has since fallen victim to some illegal shooter in search of Ginger's gold-and-diamond ring, the hunter, hunted—the story continues. Life, in one form or another, goes on.

Ask Valerie Plumwood.

"I HOPED IT WOULD FINISH ME QUICKLY"

▲▲▲▲▲▲▲▲▲▲▲

*P*utting one foot in front of the other was something Val Plumwood did well.

Bushwalking was an enjoyment for her and it fitted in naturally with her occupation as a lecturer in environmental philosophy at Sydney's Macquarie University.

She found that while she walked, her mind worked better than it did when she was sitting at a desk. Walking and thinking, thinking and walking, allowed her to observe environmental problems at first hand in the most pleasant and effective way.

From the time she was a young woman she took comfortable strides through the escarpment country of southern New South Wales. She loved the smell of eucalyptus and the sound of bird songs. She built her own house of stone there in the bush, five kilometres from the nearest neighbour.

"That's not to say I'm a hermit who doesn't like people's company. I do, and often seek it out. But sometimes I do like to be on my own. I'm very comfortable with myself and I enjoy my own company." She called the house Plumwood Mountain, after the Plumwood, a beautiful rainforest tree which grows there.

Val Plumwood did most things in a wholehearted fashion. Her

bushwalks were no casual strolls to the bottom of the garden. In a motorised age when most city dwellers consider a kilometre walk from a concrete park an epic of endurance, she backpacked for days at a time. Some of her 'walks' were as long as six days with groups of other walkers. She would spend up to four days on her own, walking and camping out overnight, enjoying the bushland solitude, the smell of earth and trees, and the sweet and secret sounds that town folk seldom hear.

With this background it was hardly surprising that she took a keen interest in environmental politics. She was involved in campaigns for saving native forests and particularly uranium and energy issues. She tended to have strong opinions. "But what's the point of believing in something if you don't stand up for it?"

She rejected the austerity of old-school philosophy which concerned itself only with abstract argument and held aloof from living issues. "There's nothing wrong with having a strong emotional opinion and supporting it with rational argument. If you like it and believe in it, go for it."

If you had asked her the reasons for walking she could have given you a list of positives. Bushland appreciation. An uncluttered mind. Getting a feeling for the power of the earth and its forces.

"There isn't anything Amazonian in it," she says. "I didn't need to prove anything physical and I certainly don't relish pain for the sake of it. My attitude to walking is still one of enjoyment. Of being in a nice place and being able to appreciate the things around me. I've never been one for marching along in military fashion. Rather I tend to set the pace that suits my mood and the moment."

There was also the personal reward of getting there . . . Reaching goals. Achievement. It felt good. And if you did it often enough, there was the fine, taut feeling of being really physically fit.

Without realising it Val Plumwood was actually in training for a day when she would need all those reserves of physical strength. All her accumulated determination, simply to stay alive.

When she went to Kakadu National Park in the Northern Territory in February 1985, she had no particularly strong thoughts about crocodiles.

"They were animals. They were a part of the environment and they were protected—that was good.

"But they weren't in my specific field of interests. I was far more concerned with birds and I didn't even expect to have anything to do with crocodiles. So far as a wild animal risk went, I'd given much more thought to buffalo, creatures I expected I might bump into on a bushwalk and which can sometimes be dangerous."

Crocodiles were a part of the water and not a part of her expectations.

Val Plumwood stayed in a privately owned caravan at the park ranger base at the East Alligator River. "It wasn't official accommodation, but was arranged by a friend. I appreciated it."

About 10 February, she completed a three-day bushwalk in the Mt Brockman area. A stimulating experience. "It was really hot —quite different from what I was used to. But the Kakadu escarpment country is so beautiful. It surprises and delights you at every corner."

When she finished the walk Val Plumwood was probably as fit as she had ever been in her life.

Birds had always fascinated her. She spent a good deal of time in previous summers working on forest bird-breeding studies in New South Wales. She wanted naturally to see some of the Kakadu bird life and asked the advice of one of the rangers on the best places to study the water birds. Kakadu is a feathered paradise and a joy for those who like to watch birds. On the floodplains and billabongs there are magpie geese in thousands, flocks of pelicans and armies of ibis. As well as herons, egrets, brolgas and magnificent solitary jabiru storks, more than a third of Australia's bird species are found in Kakadu.

Her friend, who worked in the area, suggested she take a fibreglass Canadian canoe moored close to the ranger station. It was a good way to get close to the birds and allowed access to swampy areas difficult to reach on foot or by conventional boat.

"It seemed a good idea at the time," Val Plumwood recalls. "Canoes weren't a strong part of my experience. But it was easy to handle. It was about 14 feet long and there was no problem about balance. As canoes went it was a substantial sort of craft.

"The thinking at the time was that crocodiles didn't attack people in boats and though the thought did vaguely cross my mind it wasn't a serious worry. After all, a lot of local people had been using it."

In fact Canadian-style fibreglass canoes had been used a good deal in the Northern Territory. Wildlife officers had often employed them in fieldwork, for bird studies, for locating crocodile nests and for crocodile counts. They were considered as safe as any other small craft. A perception which Val Plumwood was about to change.

On the first day she went out with the canoe she experienced no problems. She felt happy in the craft and confident in handling it. The rangers had told her not to go out in the mainstream of the river because the current ran strongly. They recommended she stay in the backwaters and this suited her. The birds were exciting. She took her binoculars, ate lunch on the bank, had a brief walk and returned later in the afternoon. It was a good day.

The second day, 19 February 1985, was quite different. The Northern Territory Wet was running late and the countryside was very dry. Thunder-clouds had been building up in the usual way. But the annual monsoon deluge was well behind schedule.

The day was overcast and fine rain was falling. She had not intended to go out on the river again—her plan had been to go walking. "But I was feeling unwell, so I thought that, after all, I'd use the canoe once more to get to where the birds were. Then I'd have a short walk."

She went down to the landing and launched the canoe about 11 A.M. Almost at once she felt that the atmosphere was quite different to the previous day.

"I was immediately uneasy. I felt that there was something there, that hadn't been around the day before. It's hard to describe—a feeling of unseen menace, I suppose. Whatever it was I felt vulnerable. The canoe seemed very close to the water."

She paddled down river in the backwater, the blade dipping in regular strokes. Trying to talk herself out of the unease.

It was a sort of anabranch joining the main river at both ends.

A quiet backwater and normally very pretty. But not that day. "The rain began early and soon became so heavy that I had to keep stopping to empty the canoe. Because of the unease I was very careful not to get out in the water. I always stepped onto land." She stopped again for lunch and went for a short walk in the escarpment country with her binoculars, observing the birds.

"The rain became heavier and heavier until it became an incredible deluge. It was actually the start of the Wet, though I didn't realise it at the time."

The feeling of vulnerability, that she shouldn't be there, persisted.

It was particularly strong at one spot on the river. "I could see a particular rock formation some distance away across the East Alligator River—one rock balanced on another. Every time I looked at it I got scared. The other circumstances of the day troubled me. It was a sort of non-specific feeling that something just wasn't right. I shouldn't be there.

"I had no idea why that balancing rock should frighten me and it was irritating. Rational thinkers aren't supposed to be like children afraid of the dark."

However, rationalise as much as she could, she couldn't rid herself of the feeling. An instinct that somewhere there was trouble about.

For that reason she turned the canoe around and set off for home in the rain much earlier than intended. It was about 3.30 P.M. and the rain and squalls of wind were still increasing.

She reached the place in the waterway, a bend, where she had experienced particular uneasiness earlier.

Later an old crocodile shooter told her that the crocodile would have been watching her and that she was probably subconsciously aware of the presence.

The crocodile would have awaited her return.

As she paddled back that way something caught her eye. "I noticed a piece of driftwood and thought to myself 'That wasn't there earlier' . . ."

In a short time she realised that the 'driftwood' was a crocodile ("I saw its yellow eyes") and that she was going to pass quite close to it.

"At that point I hadn't connected my uneasiness with crocodiles. The popular notion was that you wouldn't be attacked in boats. So when I saw it I thought, 'That's all right. A crocodile. How interesting' . . ."

Nonetheless she paddled intending to go wide of the crocodile, not wishing to pass too close to it. It was a discourtesy to intrude on wild animals. Besides—now she saw those eyes—there was the start of a shiver up her spine.

But whatever she did with the paddle she seemed to be on a collision course. At the time she thought that the current—now running faster because of the rising water—was carrying her towards it. It did not occur to her that the crocodile was deliberately intercepting her. Events began to occur quickly.

Canoe and crocodile converged. "There was a tremendous bang on the side of the canoe. I didn't know whether the crocodile was lashing out with its tail or banging with its head. I was too petrified to look.

"For a moment I froze. I thought, 'No. This isn't happening. Not to me. They don't attack boats!' "

But the crocodile was real, it was there and it was unquestionably hostile. "It kept bashing at the canoe. One part of my mind kept asking, 'Why?—Why me?' The other part was trying to be practical, trying to decide what to do.

"The problem was that it was all so unexpected. Obviously I had to make a split-second decision. Over to the right was a shallow, wide sandbank which I would have had to wade across. On the other side was a steep muddy bank, two to three meters high, and growing out of the water a couple of big paperbarks with low, spreading branches. It seemed a great idea to go over there and climb up into the tree. The rain didn't help. It was still pouring down."

BANG! BANG!

The crocodile kept hitting the canoe. Plainly something had to be done and at once. She paddled for the bank, mind in a whirl, the rain still came down hard.

"They said later that the crocodile might have been being territorial and had mistaken the canoe for another crocodile which had to be driven out of its area. But crocodiles see well, I understand, and the canoe looks nothing at all like another crocodile. Also the canoe was bigger, so if that was the reason it was a pretty brave crocodile. But looking back, I recall that it was looking at me and I think that was the crux of it."

Val Plumwood paddled hard, trying not to panic. When she reached the paperbarks the crocodile was still alongside. Those yellow eyes blazing up at her.

She stood up in the canoe. The crocodile looked even more interested. "Go away!" she yelled, waving her arms as though it were a naughty child, or a disobedient dog. Trying to bluff and hide her fear.

The yellow eyes continued to blaze back, unblinking.

"We had a minute or so of staring into each other's eyes. I was trembling with fear, absolutely terrified. Yet there was still a part of me that couldn't believe it was real. This couldn't be happening to me . . ."

The crocodile seemed to be tensing, humping its back. "I had the feeling it was getting ready to do something. So I jumped for the tree. There were three or four branches like steps and I pictured myself climbing up them to safety."

She jumped and reached the first branch, seeking to pull herself up higher into the tree. But in the same moment the crocodile also leaped. Faster by far than her. It was a lightning upwards thrust out of the water that was quicker than the human eye. The typical Crocodilian strike which anticipates the movement of the prey.

There was an instant of shock and horror as it surged up and grabbed her with a crash of jaws between the legs. "It was unbelievably fast. I had sort of stepped up with one leg and it came up in a blur from below like a giant pair of spiked pincers. Before I could move or react it had grabbed me at the top of its jump. As it fell back it just tore me out of the tree by throwing its body into a roll.

"Once it got hold of me I had no chance at all. I couldn't believe the strength. The sheer power was enormous."

The crocodile took her down underwater into a series of death rolls, seeking to disorient her, to exhaust her and then hold her down and drown her.

"Gee, that roll! I'd never experienced anything remotely like it. I was helpless against that kind of strength. The river was a kind of black, watery pit and I was being thrashed around like some rag doll in a berserk washing machine. At that time there wasn't a lot of pain. But because of where it had grabbed me, up between the legs, I thought I was going to lose my sexual organs. One tooth, in fact, had gone in beside the vagina and back as deep as the coccyx—about four inches. That kind of worry may have seemed irrational—after all I knew I was going to die. But I didn't want to be mutilated. Just terror, terror, terror . . ."

The washing machine motion stopped. The jerking, tearing, threshing rolls. The crocodile was holding her down now, to drown her.

With astonishment Val Plumwood realised that her head was just high enough for her to catch a breath at the surface. She had water in her lungs. She was choking, breathing half water, but now she could at least get air. Sweet, pure, wonderful air. It tasted so good.

If the water had been deeper, if the rolling had lasted another minute, she would probably have drowned. "But the crocodile had a bad grip on the lower part of my body and the water was too shallow, only up to my chest. With an effort I was able to get my head up and breathe.

"There were two sets of rolls, then a distinct gap between, as though the crocodile was getting its own breath back. When it rolled me it seemed like eternity.

"I expected it to roll me again. To keep on doing it and force my head underwater. I thought every breath would be my last so I sucked in as deep and hard as I could. I was just astonished that with that strength it didn't do exactly what it wanted with me. There seemed nothing I could do to stop it."

But there was. As she choked and gasped and struggled for breath she saw within reach one of the overhanging branches of a freshwater mangrove. "It was just so lucky!" She grabbed it as hard and strong as only a drowning person can.

Disconcerted, the crocodile let go. It had used a good deal of its own strength in the attack and in the rolling, and the prey was still vigorously alive.

It would try for a better grip.

As it opened its jaws Val Plumwood dragged herself towards the mangrove by her grip on the root. "And sort of dodged around behind the tree . . ."

But where next? In her confusion Val repeated her earlier mistakes. Awkwardly, fumbling, blood running down her legs below her torn shorts, she dragged herself up into the tree again.

It seemed like one of those nightmares where things keep repeating themselves. Once more the crocodile leaped from the water. The blur of movement, the flash of spiked teeth, the physical impact and the crash of jaws across her body—this time the upper left thigh.

As it dragged her out of the tree again back down into the river she felt pure despair, her breath choked off by the splash as they struck the water together. Predator and prey.

Again the rolls, disorientation. "I thought I'd rather go through anything than one more of those rolls. There wasn't a lot of pain. But there was a hot feeling in my thigh. I knew the teeth had gone in deep. It all seemed so wasteful. I thought, 'I'm going to die and no one will ever know what happened. How I've suffered. They'll think I've just drowned!' The crocodile was growling in its throat—it seemed terribly angry. I was just so terrified. An agony of terror—I thought, 'Please no—don't let it roll me again!' But it did. A third time.

"By this time I was weaker. It would have been impossible to feel any more fear. But I was despairing. It seemed so futile, so stupid to die like that, without a reason. I tried to feel back along its head—thinking of jabbing my fingers in the crocodile's eyes. I found two sort of leathery sockets. I had a sort of debate with myself as to whether I would make it angrier or not if I attacked it. Then I decided to try a jab. But there was no response and I realised I had my fingers in its nostrils.

"By the end of the third roll I thought I'd really had it. I was thinking 'I wish to God it would finish me off quickly. I don't want to die so slowly and unpleasantly.' Then my waving arms touched the tree branch again—almost as though I was reliving the first effort—and I grabbed it with whatever strength I had left. I knew I couldn't last through any more rolls.

"Then, astonishingly, when it seemed to be all over—The End —it released me again. I guess it was to change grip, maybe to try to get me higher up the body so it could hold me under. But once again I managed to dodge around the tree. This time I didn't make the mistake of trying to climb up into the branches.

"I flung myself up the bank. But it was steep slippery mud. Twice I just slithered back. That was the real nightmare—picturing the crocodile waiting for me at the bottom to grab me again.

"The third time I found that if I stuck my fingers into the mud I could claw myself up inches at a time. I had no idea where the crocodile was—whether it was a few inches behind me, or still back in the water. I didn't dare look around. I was concentrating all my efforts on dragging myself up that slippery bank.

"But I reached the top—to my utter, utter amazement, because I never expected to get away—and I stood up and set off on a sort of hysterical flopping half-crawl, half-run, trying to put distance between me and the river. I knew immediately I was hurt but I didn't dare pause or look back.

"So I flopped along not being able to run fast because my left leg wouldn't work properly and I actually thought it (the crocodile) had done something to my knee. I kept thinking 'the bastard's done my knee.'

"But nothing mattered in the face of the wild elation—an absolute euphoria. I was alive! Against all expectations I was alive! I had got away! It sounds silly now. A crazy, light-headed feeling."

The euphoria did not last long. She was in a serious predicament. Somehow she had to get back to the East Alligator ranger base. It was out of the question to go back and look for the canoe. But without it she had to cross the swamp and some tributary streams. For her now, any water held terror beyond her physical capacity. But water was everywhere.

She was aware that her injuries were serious—she hadn't the courage to take off her shredded shorts to see exactly how bad— but she knew that she could not go long without medical attention. She took off her singlet, then her bra and used them as bandages and a tourniquet. "A big piece of my left thigh was sort of hanging off and flopping about. It was a miracle the bite missed the femoral artery. But it ripped the muscles and tendons. At one time I had wanted to die. But now I wanted to live. The desire, the determination was very strong."

Gritting her teeth she set off. Every step was pain and her left leg simply would not do what she wanted. But the training of those years of walking stood her in good stead. Putting one foot in front of the other. Making distance, even when it hurt. "Concentrate, Val, concentrate! . . ."

Meantime the rain poured down, huge drops, splashing on the leaves. Bouncing in the puddles, washing the blood off her legs. Rivulets spreading across the earth to join up into a continuous shining sheet of water as the monsoon broke. The ground seemed to be moving water. The flood was coming. Squalls of wind tossed the treetops. There was an eerie grey-green light over everything. The end of the world could have come on just such a day.

In her shocked state, stumbling along, Val Plumwood began to be afraid of losing consciousness. She still had on her raincoat and shorts with her familiar compass swinging around her neck. The temperature was a hothouse 35°C with steam rising up from the rain. But she felt cold and was shivering from shock and fright, and sick and nauseous. The numbed and dizzy disorientation of clinical shock after a serious injury.

Minutes seemed hours, as though time was part suspended.

The attack had occurred about 4 P.M. The struggle felt as though it had lasted an eternity. Now it seemed ages ago.

The events and the abnormal darkness of the day, the rain sluicing down, all created an atmosphere of impending doom and her spirits sank correspondingly lower.

"The worst thing was that I knew that I was in a swamp that was likely to become flooded with such heavy rain. I was terrified that if I passed out and became unconscious I would drown and be washed away. No one would ever know what had happened to me. Strange how important that was. It seemed so cruel to have survived something as dreadful as the crocodile and then die out there in the mud."

As daylight faded she began to feel increasingly light-headed and apprehensive. Twice she had to cross deeper streams. With great effort, concentrating on each step, she walked up them until she found overhanging branches she could hold onto to cross.

She knew she could not get back to the ranger station across the water on her own and that she would have to rely on being found. The closer she could get to the swamp the better chance she had of being found. But she could not expect a search party until the next day and by then she might be dead. How could she maximise her chances of being found? How would she survive the coming night?

She was getting very weak and dizzy now and knew she could not go much farther. Her left leg was a weak, useless, floppy thing, foreign to her body, except that it burned with pain. Several times she blacked out momentarily. But she was dreadfully afraid that if she lay down where she was, no one would find her. So she staggered and crawled on, to try to find a better place to lie down for the night, a place where her body could be seen.

"Concentrate, Val! You can do it! You know you can!"

Forcing one foot after the other. Making distance. She tried all the old bushwalking tricks to goad herself along. Each tree passed was a progress. Each bend in the creek an event.

At one stage her paddle passed her floating down the creek. She looked around hopefully for the canoe. But no such luck. She had had too much luck already. Just to get away from those jaws! She looked behind her apprehensively, the horror still upon her.

Now as she walked she began calling out, tears running down her cheeks, imploring the crocodile to forgive her for intruding in its territory. Apologising to it, over and over. "I'm sorry. I'm sorry. I shouldn't have come to your place. Just let me go!"

Meantime, as darkness fell at the ranger base, each family was isolated in its own house by the rain pouring down. Rain hammering on the roofs, splashing on the patios, a deluge. It was no night to be outside. Everyone was indoors.

Val Plumwood could have died in the swamp that night. She was quite right in her fear that no one would have known what happened. By morning the whole area was under water. The paddle washed far, far down the river.

But one man noticed that there was no light in her caravan. Rangers are more conscious about these things than other peo-

ple. The darkened van troubled Greg Miles. He knew that she
had been out in the canoe on the previous day and the canoe was
normally kept down at the mooring. He supposed that he could
at least go down and check that it was there. The darkened
caravan nagged at him. When he knocked there was no response.
There was nobody there. Where could she be on a night like
this? She should have been back hours before . . . Miles started
the three-wheeler bike and steered out into the slush. The road
was a running muddy river, though the rain had temporarily
eased.

At the mooring the rain had stopped. But now his eyes nar-
rowed in concern. The canoe was definitely missing. If Val Plumwood had gone out in it she should have been back in the
afternoon. It was now well after dark. He consulted his watch. It
was after 8 o'clock. He peered out into the darkness. The night
was now still.

Val Plumwood had reached the edge of the swamp. For the
last part of the distance she crawled. "Concentrate, Val, concentrate. Don't give up!"

Dragging herself through the mud and sticks. "Concentrate . . . " But still a sheet of water divided her from the ranger
base. She could go no farther. She settled on a spot and lay down
to await the coming night. Her chances of survival seemed remote.

As darkness fell, she hoped for unconsciousness but it did not
come and the line between recognisable reality and tortured fan-
tasy became blurred. It was not surprising. After what had happened, and as a normal reaction of shock to the injury, she had
become part delirious.

She became convinced that the crocodile was somewhere
around. She hoped for unconsciousness but it did not come.
Worse still, as she lay there in her pain she heard splashings.
It was no imagination. There were crocodiles about in her area.
She also heard dingoes howling close by. "They had different,
distinctive voices. I thought there were about six of them. I knew
they wouldn't hurt a healthy person. But what about someone
wounded, weak and bleeding? Someone unconscious on the
ground . . . ?"

Then she saw a light and heard a distant sound of a motor. It came bobbing through the darkness and stopped. She was vaguely aware that the rain had stopped and the wind quietened into what seemed an unnatural hush. She raised herself on her elbow and called with all her strength across the dark swamp, "Help!" again and again. "Help! . . ."

Greg Miles thought he heard a sound. A cry? . . . A despairing human cry? He cocked his head and listened. Yes, there it was again. A long way away. But unmistakably a human voice. "Stay there. We're coming back to get you!" he called across the black water.

Confronted with an emergency the Australian National Parks and Wildlife Service rangers are a well-trained body of men. Greg Miles could have no knowledge of what had happened to Val Plumwood, of course. But he recognised an emergency. For anyone to be out in the darkness, crying out, something serious must have happened. At any rate she needed help and quickly, by the sound of it.

He started the bike, spun it around and roared off to raise the alarm. To put into practice the accustomed emergency routine of organising the ranger boat and the other people to help in an immediate search.

Van Plumwood could not understand why the light went away. It seemed so cruel to see that faint flicker of hope disappear. But then nothing seemed to make much sense any more.

Had the voice—whoever it was—heard her call? Would they come to find her?

Despair. As she lay in the rain, hordes of mosquitoes—happy for the Wet—buzzed around tormenting her. "The whining was dreadful and they bit and bit. There was nothing I could do."

At last, at last the boat. The sound of lights and voices. She was too weak even to sit up. Thank God there was still a lull.

"Help!

"Help!

"Help! Oh, God help me!"

"I shouted for all I was worth. Just lying on the ground, too weak to sit up or do anything else . . ."

But they heard her. An hour earlier in the downpour, with the wind roaring in the trees, she would have had no chance.

Even so it took them some time to locate the injured, terrified woman, lying among the trees. But eventually the spotlight, filtering between trunks, lighted on her. It paused, then returned and held her in its beam.

Rescue!

"I was never so pleased to see anyone. I greeted them with an enormous smile, despite my injuries. I was go glad, so glad to see human faces. They were so capable, so comforting."

The rangers in their turn were shocked when they saw her injuries and heard her story, garbled and incoherent.

Val Plumwood recalls little of that time. She had used all her determination and reserves of strength to reach the perimeters of safety. Now she let go—pain and consciousness together came and went in waves. But she does recall hearing two of the four rangers in the boat talking matter-of-factly about shooting the crocodile. She was horrified. "I really asked them in the strongest possible terms, in fact begged them, not to do it. It seemed so unfair." It wasn't the crocodile's fault, she said. She had been the intruder . . . It was the crocodile's territory.

Greg Miles and the other Australian National Parks and Wildlife rangers found her five hours after the attack. The following day Darwin newspapers carried an account of her ordeal and the 13-hour, all-night drama involved in getting her to hospital in Darwin after the boat rescue in the swamp.

"DARWIN: Val Plumwood, from Braidwood in the NSW southern tableland, was admitted to Royal Darwin Hospital about 8 A.M. yesterday after an all-night rescue operation to get her out of the floodbound Kakadu National Park to an ambulance for the 200-kilometre journey to Darwin after being attacked by a 4.5-metre saltwater crocodile.

In teeming rain she was transported in three separate cars and three boats across potholed bush roads and through swamps before reaching the ambulance (at the South Alligator River crossing).

She is understood to be in a serious but stable condition after undergoing surgery for deep gashes in her buttocks and legs."

Greg Miles was quoted:

"She was not a pretty picture. She was very desperate and there was a lot of blood. She had the horrific experience of having to assess her own wounds but she was still able to smile.

"She is an extremely courageous woman to have survived the terror of the attack in the first instance, and then to tourniquet those horrible wounds and then try to get help."

Val Plumwood remained seriously ill in the hospital for some time. As a complication to her major injuries she contracted a pseudomonas infection, either from the swamp mud or from the crocodile's teeth, which caused her doctors grave concern and which also could have killed her. It was the third time her life had been at risk. She survived the infection as she had the other ordeals. After a long month in Darwin she was transferred to Sydney's Royal North Shore Hospital for skin grafts and further surgery over another month.

For a time she feared she might never walk normally again. But skilful surgery and her own determination saw a remarkable recovery. Nonetheless there were some permanent effects from the injuries.

The incident with the crocodile, naturally enough, changed important aspects of her life. People wanted to know how she now felt about crocodiles. Did she want them shot? Or was she some kind of crazy eco-nut who had a masochistic affection for the beast that had almost killed her?

Three years after the event Val Plumwood still mused over the new perspectives which the experience has given her.

"When it first happened," she recalled. "I didn't want to talk to the press. I thought they'd use it as evidence to make a case for shooting crocodiles—like the later shoot-out at the Daintree River in Queensland.

"But, while I didn't know much about crocodiles beforehand, I learned very quickly and found I was able to make environmental points on behalf of crocodiles and Kakadu which were worth-while. So I have made statements to the press.

"It was a bit ironic that being attacked seemed to make me an authority people would listen to. Whereas if I'd ventured an opinion before—for whatever reason—it would have carried no weight.

"But my efforts to exercise some control of the use made of my story were not always successful. Some of the press stories, while they sometimes contained part of the message I wanted to put across, were very wide of the mark. They were too often sensational, exaggerating for example the size of the crocodile, and seeming to misunderstand what I actually said. In the main they made me out to be a ridiculous animal lover, an absurd extremist who would never lift a finger against a creature in any circumstances.

"That isn't so. I would have gladly shot the crocodile if that were possible, during the attack, to escape from that awful situation.

"Even now I don't *like* crocodiles—how could you? They're a pretty hard, tough, distinctly unlovable kind of animal.

"But I do believe that crocodiles are entitled to their life and their piece of habitat. We humans think that the world is ours to do with as we like, regardless of the needs of all the other creatures which may be affected.

"I think non-human rights are one of the most important issues of our time.

"In the crocodile debate which arose, particularly after the Daintree River incident, a lot of people wanted to use me for their own purposes in the arguments of culling, relocating or getting rid of the crocodiles.

"The problem on the Daintree and other places in the north was that after the shooting years of the 1950s and '60s, people got used to unnaturally low crocodile numbers and hence a low risk. Now that we have a resurgence in numbers, the risk factor is higher, though still not nearly as high as driving your motor car down the street.

"As humans we seem to think that whenever there's a conflict with an animal like a crocodile, the crocodile has to go to suit the humans. I think that's unfair. The world is not just a place for human beings. It's a crocodile world too. That goes for other less-than-popular (with humans) creatures like snakes.

"In the case of crocodiles the risk should not be removed by removing the crocodiles. Humans think they should be inviolate —but we don't think that should apply to other creatures.

"I can't see why people can't live with crocodiles in Queensland. They do in the Territory. It's mainly a matter of modifying expectations. Obviously you don't swim in a river where there are large crocodiles, any more than you go swimming at Cairns or in Darwin Harbour when the sea wasp season is on. If you ignore the notices and get fatally stung, or are bitten by a crocodile in a non-swimming area, who is to blame?

"But it's not always a question of *blame*. There is always a certain amount of risk in being in crocodile country. It has to be accepted I think as part of the price of being there."

Was there blame then in her own case?

"That's something I've obviously thought about a great deal. I think the answer is simply that it was an accident, something which everyone (especially me) has learned from. I think it could have happened anywhere to anyone in a canoe. I was just unlucky and the word 'blame' doesn't really apply. I did receive a certain amount of criticism from other people for the incident, unfairly I think, because usually they didn't know the facts.

"People said I was foolhardy for going out in a canoe on a crocodile river. I had to bite my tongue. I couldn't say who owned it or they might have been held responsible. Nor could I say that all the locals used it. That they considered it to be all right. That would have appeared to have been shifting the blame on to them and would have been very ungrateful. The canoe was loaned out of kindness and willingness to help. Maybe it was my behaviour in the canoe which caused the problem. But it's pretty hard to know what to do in extreme circumstances where you have no time to think. And I think what I did was probably the best in the circumstances, although it's hard to be sure. But in any case the rangers certainly saved my life and I'll be forever grateful for the way they got me to a hospital against enormous difficulties and at great inconvenience and risk to themselves. That was why I kept quiet. I believe that the incident caused trouble for some of the people there. I really regret that. It seemed so unfair to me. I was sorry to have been a cause of any difficulty. And I can't see why anyone should be blamed!

"Anyway I was stuck with the 'foolhardy' tag and this is the first time I've given a total account of all that happened. But to learn from incidents of this kind it's important to examine all the aspects. Canoes have been withdrawn despite the fact that they were used by the wildlife people, and Aborigines have used dug-out canoes for more than a century. After all there were a lot of attacks on boats in the Finniss River in the 1970s. Despite this small boats still go out on all the crocodile rivers. I think there is always a certain amount of risk in any small craft in crocodile country. It has to be accepted.

"However, to get back to crocodiles. I think that the decision to cull or relocate the crocodile population of North Queensland is dismal. It would be far more constructive if people learned to live with crocodiles. This means more public education.

"Crocodile farming is being promoted as an alternative to preserving crocodiles in the wild. This would be a disaster. Crocodiles should be able to live where they always have.

"Habitat is essential to all creatures and especially to crocodiles. It has been terribly important for the birds, crocodiles and all the wildlife of the area to conserve and protect habitat, especially Kakadu. The major priority of the present is to stop mining in Kakadu National Park. This is because of the danger, especially, of the release of heavy metals in the headwaters of the rivers, particularly the South Alligator. But also habitat destruction from mining, settlements, roads and human encroachment pose other problems.

"My major environmental interest now is stopping mining in Kakadu National Park through the group I am associated with called 'Friends of Kakadu'."

So much for Val Plumwood, the environmental philosopher. What about Val Plumwood the person? How did the crocodile attack affect her?

"There are continuing personal side-effects. I don't recommend a crocodile attack to anyone. I have coped with the injuries but they have slowed me down. There are scars. They're not pretty. I'm still having major problems with the medial muscles of my left leg, which may require further surgery. I had a long period taken out of my life and I'm getting it together again. The worst aspect was that I was very fit. Now, because I can't walk as long or as hard, I've lost some physical tone. But I learned a lot about my friends and how supportive people can be. And of course it could have been much worse. Apart from my left leg all the other injuries healed and I'm quite normal."

What about post-accident traumas? People involved in life-threatening situations—wars, train wrecks, rape, motor accidents—sometimes have permanent psychological scars. Does she have crocodile nightmares, loss of confidence, poor concentration?

Val Plumwood shakes her head. "I did a lot of reliving—experiencing the attack over and over in my mind. I still do it occasionally. But I think I have it under control. I think a good deal of the secret of handling bad memories is not to be afraid to face them. If you live the situation out you can bring it back from being a bogy to right proportions. And talking it through with loving friends is great therapy. Perhaps becoming involved in crocodile politics was a helpful therapy too."

And the crocodile?

Somewhere in the East Alligator River and billabong system, in Kakadu National Park, it almost certainly swims to this day.

"I wish him luck," says Val Plumwood.

DARK WATERS OF THE DAINTREE

▲▲▲▲▲▲▲▲▲▲▲

*T*he Daintree River, on the Cape York Peninsula, winds lazily in from the sea between banks lined by a curtain of green mangroves and rainforest. A broad and noble stream.

It is one of the most beautiful waterways on the scenically spectacular far North Queensland coast.

Upstream at the little township of Daintree—so small that it does not even boast a pub—the banks have been cleared in areas by previous generations of cane and cattle farmers. Rank grass grows chest high where once forest stood.

But a good deal of the Daintree remains pristine in the blue shadow of 4200 ft Mt Thornton.

For the best part of 100 years the Daintree was also poor. It was almost the last outpost of the civilisation which came creeping up from the south along the edge of the Cape York Peninsula. A hot and humid place deluged by the monsoons in summer, prone to flood and cyclone damage. So far from markets that the handful of primary producers in the area struggled to make ends meet.

Even today the Daintree is close to the end of the track. The only town farther north on the east coast and accessible by an inland road (of such doubtful reptuation that in the past most travellers went by sea) is the port of Cooktown. At Daintree the pavement ends. People wishing to push farther north along the actual coast have to take a ferry across the river with their vehicles. From the far bank they enter wilderness, to bump over rugged dirt mountain roads, unbridged creeks and boulder-studded washaways.

But in the 1980s the tag of poverty was becoming a part of the historical past. Wealth was beginning to come into the town. It rolled in on the wheels of hundreds of cars and buses filled with people coming to see the beauty of the area. Tourism arrived somewhat later in the Daintree than in the south. But when it did come it was with a rush.

By 1985 all Queensland, from Surfers Paradise and Noosa Heads north to the Whitsunday Passage, Cairns and the Great Barrier Reef, was riding on a tourist wave of prosperity. Even little Daintree, at the end of the line, took its share of the visitors. Perhaps a little more than its share. After all it had some unique features.

Daintree had crocodiles.

It was the only large river system accessible in Queensland where wild *Crocodylus porosus*, saltwater crocodiles up to five metres in length, were present in numbers, and where they could be readily seen by visitors in their natural environment.

"The Crocodile Express" river cruises, begun by Michael Turner, were an instant success, and were soon followed by other boat operators.

The cruise boats took in all the Daintree wildlife. Herons, egrets, ibis and other wading birds, as well as Torres Strait pigeons, sea eagles, brilliantly coloured kingfishers and the occasional wild boar snouting on the river bank.

But it was the big crocodiles which people really came to see. From daily familiarity they became unafraid of people. They could be seen sunning on the banks in typical crocodile pose. Mouths agape, eyes part-closed with a deceptive air of grand prehistoric indifference. The boatloads of tourists edged ever closer with clicks of cameras and gasps of awe and horror—the normal human reactions to dangerous animals they don't understand.

At Christmas 1985, the mood of the handful of local business

people on the Daintree was jovial. The tourist trade had boomed
that year and the prospects for 1986 looked even better.

Michael Turner, who—with his attractive wife Jacqueline—
had moved into a new and flourishing business enterprise, the
Daintree Butterfly Farm, decided to give a Christmas party for
their friends and business associates. There were about 10
guests.

Invitations were sent out for 7 P.M. on 21 December 1985. A
date they would all remember long after. Among the guests were
David Martin and Beryl Wruck, who ran the Daintree general
store and liquor outlet; John Robb, a tour operator; Maurice
Mealing, a local grazier and his wife Rosario, and Kathleen
Booth, a Daintree housewife.

The party itself was a barbecue in the usual informal North
Queensland style. Drinks flowed freely. Beside the popular
Queensland beer XXXX in its conspicuous yellow cans, there
was chilled champagne, wine and spirits. Michael and Jacqui
were good hosts, and the party was similar to hundreds of other
such gatherings in Queensland and around Australia that night.
Good friends meeting to celebrate a good year and a happy start
to the festive season.

The difference on the tropical Daintree was that it was probably a good deal hotter than elsewhere. The thunderstorms were
building up for the coming Wet, which was expected in January.
December on Cape York sees hot, humid days, when human
perspiration runs freely. A month when only mad dogs and southern visitors who don't know better go out in the midday sun.

By evening it was particularly hot and humid, even for the
Daintree. Apart from enjoying the good food and drinks, some of
the guests had been dancing on the Turners' verandah and they
were gasping and dripping with perspiration by 11 P.M.

John Robb, one of the dancers, suggested a dip to cool off in
Barratt Creek which formed one boundary of the Butterfly Farm
and joined the nearby Daintree River.

"You're bloody mad to go swimming down there," David
Martin said flatly, and Kathy Booth and some others agreed
with him.

But the others laughed and went pattering off barefooted down
the 50-yard boardwalk which led to the three-stage landing at the

creek. So there were crocodiles in the Daintree? Well, everyone knew that. But in all the long years people had lived in the area no one had ever been attacked. Most people who had lived in the Daintree a long time, and especially those who had worked boats professionally, had spent a lot of time in the water without harm or even a fright.

It was OK, they said, to take a dip on the edge. A splash only. Provided you were careful, of course. And after all it was low tide. And Christmas.

Michael Turner had been in the water himself often, when it was necessary to heave a boat off a sandbar or remove a snag. He and Jacqui and friends had sometimes splashed briefly in the creek at the foot of their garden. But that was in daylight. And though Barratt Creek—a beautiful little waterway overgrown with rainforest—was off the mainstream, he and his wife had seen crocodiles by the landing. One about 2.5 metres was there quite regularly. It wasn't big enough to hurt a human but it showed that crocodiles could use the creek on occasion.

It was David Martin who had the darkest feeling. He had lived there all his life and knew crocodiles and the Daintree well. A hot December night, with fresh water in the creek, offered optimum crocodile conditions. "You're bloody mad!" he said again, this time with emphasis.

But the perspiring dancers were all adults, free, and over 21 years old. It was Christmas. The drinks had inspired a mood of reckless *bonhomie*. There was nothing anyone could do to stop them going down to the creek if they had made up their minds. But Martin couldn't hide his concern. After all he and Beryl Wruck, one of the intending swimmers, lived together as man and wife.

But she was a spirited lady who knew her own mind. A dynamic and forceful presence in their business, despite her slight build. Beryl was popular in the area. At 43 she had the authority of years. But she retained the physical fitness and appeal of youth.

"David was so fortunate to have a woman like her with so much business drive," said Bill Kromhout, owner of the arts and crafts shop next door to the Martin and Wruck store. "She was a good companion to him too."

If David Martin thought of going after Beryl he changed his mind. You didn't tell Beryl what to do, and after all it was Christmas.

He tried to put it from his mind, drink in hand. But try as he would the forebodings would not go away. When he heard the shout from the landing a few minutes later he spun around almost as though he had expected it.

Down at the creek the merry group had stripped off down to their underwear. The tide was low and the water was only knee-deep—45 centimetres was the actual measurement.

They were laughing and splashing. John Robb was standing next to Beryl who was wearing her bra and panties, and had crouched down to get herself wet.

What took place was so quick that they were all bewildered, and for a long time afterwards none of them were quite sure exactly what had happened.

"There was a gigantic swirl," John Robb recalls. "I was pushed aside. At first I thought I had been hit too. But later I found it was just water pressure.

"Beryl went up in the air and over and then she was gone. There was no sound, no scream. It was so quick that if you'd blinked an eye you'd have missed the whole thing.

"She didn't even cry out. I'm still convinced that at first she may have thought it was one of us skylarking. Grabbing her and throwing her over into the deep water.

"But there was no question about what happened. Even though it was dark I could see this huge, frightful head as it swung toward her." Two years later he said he could still see it in his mind and hear Maurice Mealing shouting out, "A croc's got Beryl!"

Maurice Mealing at the later Coroner's inquiry said that he had just happened to look around. "I saw the head of a crocodile. It struck Beryl and her hands flew in the air. It rolled her to the right," he said.

"There was no cry for help. There wasn't a sound. It happened so quickly."

Rosario Mealing said at the inquiry that she too saw "a long dark object with a scaly back rise to the surface of the water" on

Beryl's right and take her. "She made no sound. There was no blood," she said.

The water was about two metres deep right next to the 45-centimetre shallows at the foot of the landing where the party were splashing. It was the classic situation for a crocodile ambush. When Beryl Wruck, a slightly built lady, crouched down to get wet and cool she unknowingly reduced her size as a target so that she became the automatic choice for the crocodile.

The alarm was raised at once.

Michael Turner found torches and an immediate but fruitless search was made of the creek in his aluminum dinghy. David Martin and some of the others set a net across the mouth of Barratt Creek to try to cut off the crocodile's escape.

The police at Mossman, where Sergeant Kevin Turner was in charge, were notified.

When morning light came, with no sign of the crocodile or the body, they were all still numbed by the disaster.

It had been so quick. So unexpected. There was no trace. Sometimes it was hard to believe that the tragedy had taken place at all. Everything else was just as it had been before. Only Beryl was not there. But as the day wore on reporters, photographers, policemen and curious onlookers came swarming around the landing at Barratt Creek, and the activity was confirmation itself of the grim reality.

At first there was only grief and sorrow.

But during the day, as people had time to think, other emotions began to surface. There was a natural anger in some quarters at the crocodile. An understandable desire for revenge, not only on the animal concerned but on the whole crocodile species.

"What if it happens again?" some residents were asking. Forgetting that in all the previous century on the Daintree, it had never happened before.

There were some people who wanted all the crocodiles in the river shot. A life-threatening danger removed, they said. Most of these were graziers who had lost stock, farmers and locals who saw the crocodiles as ugly and dangerous nuisances.

The tourist operators naturally perceived a different aspect. Without the crocodile attraction the interest of their river cruises would be considerably reduced. Beryl's death was a tragedy—that was agreed by everyone. But how could it help the situation to kill a lot of crocodiles which were an economic asset to the area, and which had nothing to do with the incident?

David Martin, who had had such strong forebodings, had his own ideas. He wanted the crocodile which had killed Beryl at all costs. He wanted it dead. The views of conservationists and tour operators—whom he regarded as having a financial reason for preserving the crocodiles—were of no interest to him.

He stated unequivocally that he did not intend to rest until he had that crocodile dead on the bank. Dead, with proof positive that it was the beast which had killed Beryl Wruck.

For now rumours, ugly as the black midnight death itself, and totally false, were beginning to fly about the district. Rumours which caused Martin and Beryl's family anger and keen distress.

Some people were questioning whether Beryl really had been taken by a crocodile at all. They suggested that the story was a cover for murder.

There was a darker side to the Daintree than the buoyant tourist trade, and the traditional cane farming and cattle holdings.

The Daintree was a reputed drug area. Some people claimed that it was a gateway to the Cape York wilderness where a good deal of marijuana was said to be grown in remote, mysterious rainforest clearings. Some of the well-organised drug operations in Australia were supposedly out there under cover in ideal climatic conditions.

The long and deserted coastline, dotted with uninhabited islands, also offered hundreds of potential spots for drops of heroin and cocaine.

There were many little fishing boats on the coast which worked the area. Strange boats could mingle and work in and out of the reef without fear of detection. Once ashore drugs could be run south by road.

Police could never search every camper's vehicle, tourist's four-wheel-drive, or prospector's truck.

Not long before Beryl Wruck's death a man named Frederick Ivan Cox had been found dead on the Upper Daintree Road. Some packets of heroin were in his pockets. His grey Toyota

Landcruiser stood empty nearby. Blood-spattered banknotes blew around like leaves on the ground.

Cox, who had previous drug convictions, had, it appeared, been executed in gangland style for supposed breaches of the drug-runners' code. He had seven shotgun blasts in his body in a ritual pattern. The shots were to his head, his hands and the front and the back of his body. A warning to others engaged in the nefarious trade.

The rumours said that Beryl Wruck had been a witness to the murder. They claimed that she had been killed to prevent her testifying in court. Some of the rumours even specified that her body had been cut up with a chain-saw and fed to the crocodiles.

The stories were so persistent, even for a country area where gossip is an art form, that they aroused attention more than 1500 kilometres to the south in the Queensland capital of Brisbane. There questions were asked in State Parliament.

The *Cairns Post* of February 1986 ran an unusual story datelined from Australian Associated Press in Brisbane:

> "BRISBANE (AAP)—Police yesterday dismissed rumours that Daintree woman Beryl Wruck had been murdered and her body fed to a crocodile.
>
> Cairns regional police superintendent, Supt. Gordon Duncan, said rumours had been circulating in the region since the 43-year-old Daintree storekeeper disappeared on December 21 last year.
>
> Questions were also asked in State Parliament on Thursday as to whether Mrs Wruck was to be called as a Crown witness in a murder case or drug trial before she vanished.
>
> But Opposition national parks spokesman, Mr Bob Gibbs, said yesterday he was far from satisfied with the answers he received from the Attorney-General, Mr Neville Harper, and intended to pursue the matter.
>
> Supt. Duncan said he had been satisfied from the outset that Mrs Wruck was taken by a crocodile while cooling off with three friends at the edge of Barratt Creek—a tributary of the Daintree River.

He said there were no suspicious circumstances surrounding her death, and there was no evidence to indicate that she had been murdered.

Mr Harper told Parliament Mrs Wruck had not been
subpoenaed to appear as a witness, but her son would
give evidence in a court case over the alleged murder of
Frederick Ivan Cox.

Cox's bullet-ridden body was discovered on the Upper
Daintree Road north of Mossman in November last year.
Two packets of heroin were found in his pocket.

Mr Gibbs replied yesterday that he had been con-
tacted from within the Police Department saying there
were concerns about the circumstances of Mrs Wruck's
disappearance.

'The information suggests to me she did not disappear
as a result of a crocodile attack,' he said.

'There was no noise, nobody saw it, she simply disappeared.'

He also said he believed there were inconsistencies in
evidence given to police.

Supt. Duncan said there had been no intention to call
Mrs Wruck as a witness.

Supt. Duncan said he was also satisfied with the statements of three people who were with Mrs Wruck on the
night she disappeared."

The extraordinary allegations could be made in Parliament
only because of the protection of parliamentary privilege which
prevented legal action for defamation.

The people whose reputations and truthfulness were being
questioned had no forum of their own. They had no means of
defending themselves against the rumours or the allegations in
the Queensland Parliament. It seemed unfair and it was a testing
time for those who had been close to Beryl Wruck. The innuen-
does extended to all the people who had been with her when the
crocodile struck—and indeed everyone who had been at the
party.

For by implication, if a murder had been committed, everyone who had been there must have somehow been involved in a giant conspiracy. It was a notion so impractical and so absurd that it would seem to be self-defeating. It was, of course, completely false, and proved to be so by the finding of the Coroner that Beryl was taken by a crocodile, and that no human was in any way at fault for her death.

But rumour, the black art of ugly and slanderous invention, did not let truth spoil a good story.

In the circumstances it is hardly surprising that the little Daintree community—once a happy and harmonious group—was split down the middle by the crocodile debate.

Gunshots echoed down the river late at night for weeks after the attack. Most of the larger crocodiles, and the medium-sized animals, left the river or were killed. Estimates of the toll varied from a minimised half-dozen crocodiles killed to a top (and likely exaggerated) estimate of 60 to 70 crocodile corpses. Probably about 30 were actually shot. But crocodiles learn quickly and once hunting started the larger survivors would have departed quickly.

Crocodiles, of course, were protected in Queensland, and technically this wholesale slaughter was illegal. But that had little effect on the Daintree where there were always people ready to take the law into their own hands.

However, David Martin was not involved in any large-scale killings. He said categorically that he was after one animal only. The crocodile which had killed Beryl.

At first officers from the Queensland National Parks and Wildlife Service had tried to catch or kill the creature.

When they were unsuccessful and the official hunt was called off, Martin was given permission by the Mossman police to continue efforts to catch the crocodile himself.

Some of the methods used, including baited hooks, were indiscriminate. But he denied any wholesale slaughter.

Who, then, did wipe out the bulk of the big crocodiles on the Daintree?

As with the rumours, whose origins remained darkly obscure, it was very difficult or impossible to track down the real identity of the shooters.

While David Martin maintained his hunting operations openly, there were others in the district who had no love for crocodiles. They were people who had resented the build-up of numbers since they had become protected in Queensland after 1972.

Some of the shooters were graziers and farmers who saw crocodiles as a threat to stock and were glad of a chance to be rid of them. Others, nameless, secretly resented the influx of tourists and the river tours which they considered were disrupting their comfortable rural life. They did not want the strangers. They were envious of those who made money from them. Secret shots at crocodiles were a way of getting back at the tourist trade.

Others again were simply trigger-happy yokels delighted with a chance to blaze away at something other than wild pigs. Here was a chance to actually shoot a crocodile!

The official sanction, of course, had only been extended to David Martin. But the others took it as applying to themselves anyway.

The Minister for the Environment, and member for the area, Mr Martin Tenni, said that despite the overall Queensland policy of protection he believed that all large crocodiles should be removed from the Daintree River. "People are more important than crocodiles," he said.

Michael Turner, who was at the time President of the Daintree Tourist Association, vigorously defended the crocodiles.

"Beryl's death was a tragedy," he said. "It was most unfortunate. But there has been an enormous overreaction to it.

"The Daintree is a crocodile area. It will never be 100 per cent safe to swim in the river because it is open to the sea with a lot of other crocodile habitats nearby. You could never be sure that another big crocodile had not come up the river from somewhere else. They move around a lot.

"But it isn't necessary to clean out the crocs. People can live with them quite comfortably providing they observe certain basic commonsense rules. The most important of those is that you simply do not go in the water. Especially not at night. Poor Beryl broke the rules and you can't blame the crocodile.

"But it was the first accident of its kind ever in the district. In

Melbourne you don't put all the trams off the road because someone makes a mistake and gets run over by one."

He said that the killing of the crocodiles on the river was economic madness.

"The Daintree takes $4 million a year in tourist income," he
said. "Seventy per cent of the visitors come to see crocodiles.

"The Australian and Queensland governments are spending
millions of dollars a year overseas trying to attract tourists. The
Daintree was one of the few areas in the world in a stable country
where visitors could see wild crocodiles easily in natural sur-
roundings.

"Martin Tenni and the cabinet are trying on the one hand to
get the next *Crocodile Dundee* film shot on the Daintree, and to
promote the area. On the other hand they're getting rid of all the
big crocodiles. The breeders. It's crazy. But the end result is
simply going to be that there won't be any crocodiles left in the
Daintree."

Ian and Melva Osborne, who run 400 Brahman cattle on their
202-hectare property on the river, represented the opposite point
of view, together with other graziers, farmers and net fishermen.

Melva Osborne was quoted in a Daintree article titled
'Crocodile Fury' in the national magazine *New Idea*, in November 1987.

"There has been a big build-up in crocodiles since they became
protected in the 1970s," she said.

"One big crock took our stud bull in 1979. We believe it was
the same one that killed poor Beryl. It just goes to show the
strength of them that one could kill a massive Brahman bull.

"Beryl's death was a tragedy and it's just torn this town apart.

"But we've got to make the river safe for everyone, locals and
tourists. I'm simply terrified a crocodile is going to kill my husband Ian when he goes to round up our cattle."

Irene Kromhout, who ran the Daintree craft shop with her
husband, disagreed. "We'll be killing the goose that lays the
golden egg if we get rid of the crocodiles."

She said that there had been a developing anti-crocodile lobby
in Daintree even before the Beryl Wruck tragedy. "They used
her death as an excuse to kill the crocodiles. They dynamited

Barratt Creek and killed and killed. When we said they should stop we were made outcasts."

Letters were written to the *Cairns Post*, the newspaper in the nearest major town 140 kilometres south. On 11 January 1986 the *Cairns Post* ran a story under the headline:

"RESIDENT REPORTS CROCS BEING SHOT IN
DAINTREE AREA."

The story, by reporter Vicky Jennings, read:

"Unlawful shooting and baiting of crocodiles has occurred in the Daintree River over the past two weeks according to a resident of the area.

The resident (who did not want to be named) said that since the memorial service for 43-year-old Daintree resident Beryl Wruck, believed to have been taken by a crocodile in a Daintree River tributary last December, there have been several parties seen hunting, and shooting incidents have occurred.

'I don't know who the people are, but on quite a few nights we have seen people in dinghies with lights going up and down the river, and we have heard a number of shots.

'We have also smelled the rotting (crocodile) bodies,' she said."

The *Post* reported that it also had at least three other independent reports of shooting.

Official and public responses were predictable. A Queensland National Parks and Wildlife Service spokesman said that they had also heard of the shoot-out, but were not at liberty to comment further. A police spokesman said that if such shootings were occurring and those responsible were apprehended, they would be prosecuted.

The Minister for the Environment, Martin Tenni, announced that a survey showed increased numbers of crocodiles in North

Queensland rivers. There were in excess of 237 adult crocodiles in major rivers between Port Douglas and Innisfail.

He was attacked by the President of the Cairns branch of the Wildlife Preservation Society, Dr Lesley Clark, on the grounds that the survey had been carried out by a commercial firm which had offered to cull crocodiles from the Daintree. The firm proposed to breed crocodiles for the skin market. She said that the Minister had "a record of known antipathy toward crocodiles" and he had ignored expert research available from the government's own National Parks and Wildlife Service. Instead he had accepted "unknown methodology provided by a commercial enterprise which stands to gain from crocodile culling."

Tenni replied in the same article that he was not going to be drawn into a "silly debate about the actual size of each crocodile in the far north."

"I think that it is about time the conservationists put the lives of people ahead of the welfare of crocodiles," he said.

"It would be much more sensible for the conservationists to ask themselves if they would feel comfortable about having one of these 1.8-metre crocodiles as a neighbour near their families," he continued.

He was in print again on 15 January 1986. On that date, Martin Tenni threw the cat amongst the conservationist pigeons by telling a Brisbane press conference that he hoped his Barron River electorate would eventually be a crocodile-free zone.

"I don't think you could say any area would be completely free of all crocodiles, but they could be free of all known crocodiles," he told the conference, leaving a few of those present scratching their heads trying to understand what he meant by that.

He added: "Lives are more important than crocodiles. We want to be like you in Brisbane. We want to live free of crocodiles."

This hardly correlated with his previous statement in the *Cairns Post* of 4 January.

Mr Tenni said, contrary to the criticism of some conservationists, it had never been his aim to attempt to establish 'crocodile-free zones' in the far north.

"All I am interested in doing is reducing the crocodile numbers in a humane and sensible way, close to our major populated areas between Cairns and Port Douglas and the Daintree township," he said.

However, the Minister did also speak out against the unauthorised hunting parties.

"I fully sympathise with Daintree residents upset over the death of Mrs Beryl Wruck," he said. "But I cannot support illegal shooting expeditions to wipe out crocodiles.

"I appeal to the good people of Daintree and other residents in the far north who are planning to take the law into their own hands with these revenge killings to put their guns away.

"This is a time for cool heads, not trigger-happy hunting parties."

And so it went on, along established battle lines. On 16 January, David Martin himself entered the debate for the first time with a strongly worded letter which was published on the front page of the *Cairns Post* under the heading 'A Few Thoughts From A Citizen Of Daintree.'

The *Post* headed the letter by saying that it was David Martin's first comment since the tragedy, and that he had asked the newspaper to publish his response to previous statements about crocodiles made since Beryl Wruck's death. He began with an oblique thrust at scientists and conservationists who had publicly commented on the Daintree crocodile debate.

"Here are a few thoughts from another 'Citizen of Daintree,' " he wrote. "One of Beryl's loved ones, offered in an effort to clarify some of the hysterical misinformation which has been bandied about lately.

"A few thoughts on crocodiles, world authorities and experts with letters after their names.

"One such 'expert on crocodiles' did his thesis on geckoes (small tropical lizards), crocodiles being very similar, it was believed. Another was arrested in the NT, his boat freezer full of magpie geese. Sydney University paid his fine. (The conviction of Professor Harry Messel was however quashed by the High Court in 1986.)

"You believe them if you wish. I tend to believe people who have hunted crocs for a living—not just a year or two, but those who have been at it for a lifetime; who have been up a thousand lonely creeks on dark nights; walked the banks in daylight and seen sights that one sees once in a lifetime.

"Bullocks pulled into the water by big crocs (what chance a frail human?), birds disappearing in a swirl of feathers, dogs and horses taken, sometimes from the very hands of their owners, hundreds of stomach contents examined after the skin has been removed; friends, relatives or acquaintances taken by crocs.

"They had seen the sad epitaph of a fisherman's shack —below in the soft clay were found the marks of his desperately clawing fingers and the claw marks of a huge croc.

"Poor Peter Weimes (at Weipa) was aware of the danger; he was careful, never took any unnecessary risks. He was just washing his breakfast plates.

"Some time in the near future a touring family will pull up on the bank of the Daintree. Mum and Dad are tired and just sit down above the bank while little Willie runs off down the bank to explore the edge of the water. Perhaps it's late afternoon, it is peaceful and the hot sun has receded, the tide is swirling in, bits of driftwood sail past, little Willie is calf deep in the water on a little sandy beach. He doesn't see the croc's head, so like just another piece of driftwood, only metres from him.

"A rush and a crash of those terrible jaws; a shattering of bone; another life disappears in a swirl of water. Horrified parents screaming and a lifetime of remembering. And who would expect such a thing could happen? After all they were driving through Cairns only two hours ago, even had a milkshake at Mossman. It all happened so quickly.

"And now, here are a few facts which may interest those who have been following this sad story.

"1. Sharks come up rivers and creeks with the tide and then go back out again when the tide turns.

They do not remain behind in a shallow creek. Beryl was taken at low tide. The same goes for large cod and groper.

"2.   When a croc grabs a large, active prey which is larger than his usual diet of fish, bandicoots, birds, etc., the croc, in order to subdue the struggling prey, will spin and roll.

"However we are not looking for a 3–4 metre croc, but rather a 5–6 m animal, and a human to an animal that size is like a bandicoot to a 2 m croc. We are talking about a croc that weighs in at three-quarter of a tonne or more.

"A full bite from a croc this size would shatter a human's spine and pelvis, drive the air from the lungs, and probably kill instantly.

"3.   It is a guiltily concealed fact that certain tourist operators have been feeding crocodiles. They have been cautioned against this several times by wildlife officers as it links food and humans together in the croc's mind, and worse still, helps to take away a croc's natural fear of man. In the U.S. it is an offence to feed wild crocodiles.

"We think a big croc in the 5–6 m range came up with the tide, smelled a piece of rotten meat on the bank, stayed around to investigate, or possibly was hanging around a female croc. He would have left the shallow water of the creek in the early morning on the next tide.

"4.   After Beryl was taken the desperate searching and indiscriminate shooting continued for about four days with full knowledge of wildlife officers who even took part in it, or tried to, totally missing one croc above the bridge on Barratt Creek (about 3 m), and another at the mouth of Barratt Creek.

"They finally managed to hit one near the ferry, not with one shot at point-blank range, but with two shots—

a poor little 2.5 m croc hardly big enough to handle a big dog. Four or five other fruitless shots were fired by wild-life officers on the same night.

"All in all four crocs between 2.5 and 3.5 m, and six very small ones have been shot—all a waste of bullets and time. Since then, no further crocs have been killed, despite hysterical reports by sundry ratbags.

"Unfortunately, Mr Martin Tenni seems to believe anything anyone tells him, though his concern for further victims is not misplaced and he is well regarded in the Daintree area.

"The so-called 'irresponsible shooters' will continue, not to shoot anything that moves, but to look for one very large croc, not so much in a spirit of revenge, but in an effort to stop a repeat of this tragedy, to stop other lives being vandalised as ours have been, and this will surely happen if the croc responsible for Beryl's death is not shot.

"Really, this is the responsibility of the Department of National Parks and Wildlife, however, they do not have the expertise to do it, as they have amply demonstrated.

"And so, to those tourist operators, and to those con-servationists they manipulate, who have fed and pro-tected this crocodile in the past and continue to do so now.

"Who, the night after Beryl was taken, went down the river frightening every croc they saw, making it impossi-ble for the guilty croc to be shot.

"Who have actively hindered Beryl's loved ones in their efforts to hunt that one croc, as is their lawful and moral right to do, not vindictively, but to prevent further grief.

"Can you justify yourselves? How will you live with yourselves when the next person is killed? You have stopped NPWS from removing a couple of large crocs from the Daintree in the past, and you are trying to do so again, all for monetary gain.

"Another little-known fact is that about three years

ago a 5–6 m croc attacked a couple of professional fishermen in a dory in the mouth of the Mowbray River. He
tried to climb into the dory and was kept at bay with a
singlet dipped in fuel and lit on the end of an oar.

"Some time later the same croc was snared and then
let go when it was found that he was protected and
couldn't be sold. He has not been seen in the Mowbray
since. Is he in the Daintree?

"The croc that killed Beryl was no new chum. He took
her from among three other people. He wasn't a small,
or even a medium-sized croc.

"He can and will carry out a bold attack at short notice, and he will attack again.

"In closing, I would like to sincerely thank Mossman
and Cairns police for the prompt and professional handling of the situation."

David Martin and the crocodile were to have the front page of
the *Post* two days in a row. The day his letter was published in
the *Cairns Post*, a huge crocodile had already been found struggling on one of Martin's set-lines in the Barratt Creek tributary
of the Daintree River.

It had taken a bait of wild pig on a shark hook on a line set by
David Martin. A sensational discovery was made when the creature's stomach was opened.

Senior Sergeant Kevin Turner, officer in charge of Mossman
Police, confirmed that human remains had been found in the
crocodile's stomach. These included long bones and fingernails
with nailpolish. "We can't positively identify the body as being
Mrs Wruck," he said. "But who else could it be?"

The bones and other such remains were sent to the Department of Anatomy at the University of Queensland. There Dr
Wood confirmed that the remains were from a mature, slightly
built human female. This was a fair description of Beryl Wruck.

The crocodile was a huge beast measuring 16 feet 3 inches (a
fraction short of five metres). There seemed no doubt that it was
the creature that had killed Beryl Wruck.

The *Post* quoted David Martin as saying that "he felt some
satisfaction at catching what appeared to be the killer crocodile.

"A lot of things have been said about us," he said. "That we wanted to wipe out the whole river of crocodiles. That's not true. All we ever wanted to do was to catch the killer croc," he said.

"The officer in charge of Mossman Police, Sen. Sgt Kevin Turner, said yesterday that when the hunt was scaled down, a number of local residents nominated by police continued to make nightly observations in the Daintree River and Barratt Creek and baited several set-lines."

The *Post* also, curiously, reported a widespread impression which would be directly contradicted at the inquest which followed the find of Beryl Wruck's remains.

"Although none of the people with Mrs Wruck at the time saw her taken," the *Post* reported, "they said she vanished without a sound following a violent disturbance in the water.

"It was assumed she was taken by a crocodile as Barratt Creek and the Daintree River are known habitats of the reptile."

In fact one school of marine thought had insisted for some time that the villain of the piece must have been a shark. It was not a crocodile at all, they claimed.

However the evidence from the crocodile's maw was incontrovertible.

The discovery of the remains prepared the way for a Coroner's inquiry, which was held on 19 February 1987 in the picturesque timber colonial-style Mossman Court House.

The Cairns Coroner, Stipendiary Magistrate Mr Tom Bradshaw, heard evidence from nine people including those who had been in the water with Beryl Wruck on that Christmas party night at the Daintree Butterfly Farm—a night which had begun so happily in the time before Daintree became a divided community. A night which now seemed so long ago.

John Robb (47), tour operator of Daintree, testified that he had been in the water next to Beryl Wruck when she was taken. He had felt the swirl so close he thought he had been actually brushed himself and saw the head of the crocodile. "There was no sound—or any sound of distress," he said.

Maurice Mealing (43), grazier, of Daintree, told the inquest that he had seen Beryl Wruck in 45 cm of water at the end of the catwalk. "I happened to look around and I saw the head of a croc. It struck Beryl and her hands flew in the air. It rolled her to the right. There was no cry for help. There wasn't a sound. It happened so quickly."

His wife Rosario Mealing (39) said she saw a long dark object with a scaly back rise to the surface of the water on Mrs Wruck's right and take her. "She made no sound and there was no blood," Mrs Mealing said in a *Cairns Post* account of the inquest proceedings.

David Martin (47), proprietor of the Daintree General Store, told Coroner Bradshaw that he had continued to search for the crocodile which killed Beryl Wruck after official efforts to locate it had been abandoned. He had been helped by Barney Booth and Richard Ralph, a former crocodile shooter.

They had rigged a set-line, with a shark hook baited with a large piece of pig-meat and suspended it above the water in Barratt Creek, about 300 metres from Daintree township.

The rig eventually caught and killed a five-metre crocodile. The animal's stomach was opened in the presence of police prosecutor Doug Tanzer and his wife, who were visiting the area. Bones and nails were found inside the crocodile and passed on to Sergeant Kevin Turner, the officer in charge of the district police station at Mossman.

Sergeant Turner told the Coroner (the *Post* reported) that the material had been examined by Dr Wood, of the Queensland University Department of Anatomy, and identified as human remains from a slight, mature female. Specifically they were portions of the hip bone, fibula, tibia, twelfth rib, and scapula (shoulder blade). Manicured fingernails were also present. The bones had been "forcibly crushed and broken off."

After giving his technical evidence the Sergeant went on to make a strongly worded defence of the witnesses. He said that he "had no doubt that the witnesses to the incident had initially and afterwards told the truth.

"The media hype about her (Mrs Wruck's) disappearance should be disregarded," he told the Coroner. "She was not at any stage a witness into the death of a man named Cox who was disposed of in a drug murder in the Daintree region.

"Her son was an incidental witness. At the time of Cox's death, she and her *de facto* husband David Martin were fishing on the (Barrier) Reef.

"A lot of vicious rumours," the Sergeant said, "are to be treated with the contempt they deserve.

"She left no last will and testament and nobody could have gained by her death. All the people involved in the incident are people of integrity and honesty."

When Coroner Tom Bradshaw gave his official finding he concurred with the police sergeant.

"I find each of the witnesses truthful and reliable," he said. "And I find that the witnesses obviously gave their best and most truthful evidence.

"I accept that a large crocodile attacked Mrs Wruck and pulled her underwater at approximately 11.45 P.M. on the night in question." (21 December 1985.)

"I find that no person shall be committed for trial and there was no criminal negligence on behalf of any person present at the time of the incident."

The inquest killed the rumours, rumours ugly as the black back of the crocodile breaking the surface of Barratt Creek. Perhaps after the hearing in the little white-painted Mossman Court House, and the Coroner's finding, Beryl Wruck should have been allowed to rest in peace. The relatives, who had endured two miserable Christmases in the 14 months since the tragedy, permitted to go home with dignity.

But it seemed that the crocodile controversy which had arisen was not going to go away from the Daintree River and its surrounding districts.

The issue came to a head with a public meeting of people in the district hall in Mossman in mid-1987, and the Mossman Road Board. Speakers from both sides addressed the crowd. When a vote was finally taken, 134 residents held up their hands in support of the government culling programme in the Daintree, while 95 voted against.

The cullers carried the day.

In November 1987, I took a river cruise with John Robb's Daintree Wildlife Safaris. In many respects the trip was excellent value. The tour guide, David Armbrust, gave an interesting nature commentary. He was obviously a man who knew the area and cared about it with some personal passion. The Daintree rainforest and mangroves were magnificent. We saw overgrown

winding Barratt Creek—a crocodile trap, if ever there was one—
and the fatal landing below the Butterfly Farm. The bird life was
beautiful, including ibis, egrets, reef herons, nesting boobook
owls and kingfishers. There was even a brief glimpse of a rare
Great Billed Heron—the bird whose call is commonly mistaken
by the inexperienced for a crocodile 'bellow'. It was the nearest
we came to anything live connected with crocodiles.

Aside from that, in nearly two hours of cruising, we did not see
a single crocodile.

There were no pairs of 'walnut' eyes in the stream. No slides,
nor tracks on the banks. No trace of the large saurians, once
plentiful in the Daintree River.

Just the memory . . .

By 1988 small crocodiles were returning to the lower reaches
of the river. I saw one in May and it was something of an event.
There was no doubt, of course, that given the chance the bigger
ones would eventually return. The Daintree was prime crocodile
territory, open to the sea, with well-populated crocodile habitat
nearby.

But the vital question was whether or not crocodiles would be
tolerated again in the Daintree system by local people, regardless
of the benefits from tourism. Whether the hostility which still
simmered would result in Ku Klux Klan–style covert killings. The
secret and solitary snipers. Impossible to prevent, difficult to
detect.

Time alone holds the answer.

'SWEETHEART' FROM THE FINNISS LAGOON

▲▲▲▲▲▲▲▲▲▲

Sweetheart' was a giant crocodile who lived in the Finniss River, south of Darwin. He achieved world fame in the 1970s for his private and intensely personal war with outboard motors whose noise annoyed him.

He took his name from the billabong he ruled below Sweet's Lookout. A shiny pool lined with river gums and pandanus palms on one of the most beautiful reaches of the Finniss. His story is one of the sad chronicles in the history of relationships between man and crocodile in northern Australia.

Between 1974 and 1979 there were a series of crocodile attacks on boats and outboard engines in the Sweet's lagoon. Northern Territorians still argue about how many incidents there actually were, whether more than one crocodile was involved, and about the real identity of Sweetheart. However the Sweetheart legend now seems firmly established.

About 15 attacks are on record. But quite a number of other confrontations may have occurred which were not listed—which basically means that they were not reported in the newspapers or to the Conservation authorities.

This was because some of the recipients of Sweetheart's unwelcome attentions did not want the publicity. "Being made to look like a bloody galah," as one of them put it. For this reason more Sweetheart stories may come to light as time goes by and people become less reticent.

Max Curtain, at that time publican of the Mandorah Inn, was one who tried unsuccessfully to avoid newspaper exposure after the huge crocodile sank a dinghy containing himself and his manager in September 1978. "Ian Watson and I decided not to say anything to anybody," he said. "It sounded too much like a cheap publicity stunt to be believed. The Loch Ness monster, and all that sort of thing."

Despite his reluctance he was tracked down and interviewed for a nationwide television show. By 1979 Sweetheart, through press and television coverage in Australia and overseas, had become the most famous Australian wild crocodile in history.

On one occasion a television crew presented what may have been the most extraordinary spectacle ever witnessed on the remote Finniss River. A boat overloaded with journalists clutching notebooks and pens, cameramen aiming big lenses, and sound recordists holding out microphones on long booms, trailed a 'decoy' craft ready for the crocodile to attack on cue for the national *Mike Willesee Show*.

The secret wish of the few observers was that Sweetheart would go for the press boat.

He missed a rare opportunity.

He became the darling of the press, which usually referred to him inaccurately as "The Killer Croc". Some of the newspapers wanted him to be a female. "The lady with the flashing teeth and sparkling eyes."

The reports of attacks and injuries to boats and outboard motors in Sweetheart's vendetta with noisy machinery naturally lost nothing in the telling.

Sweetheart's size was increased by degrees to over 20 feet (6.1 metres) for the benefit of readers. Ultimately his reported length reached seven metres (a fraction under 23 feet) in the Australian press.

One British newspaper unblushingly described the crocodile as "300 years old and 136 stone" and claimed Sweetheart's stomach contents included "crunched human bones and two motorboat engines".

In fact, Sweetheart had a perfectly normal diet for a 5.1-metre (16 foot 9 inch) and 780-kilogram crocodile. He was a very large bull crocodile, but neither a freak-size animal, nor a *Jaws* monster. His food included catfish, barramundi, birds, river turtles and wild pig, but not combustion engines or people. What set him apart from other large crocodiles was the fact that he detested outboard motors. He bit both the mechanical irritations and the boats that carried them from time to time as a demonstration of displeasure. But if he swallowed any metal fragments it was accidental.

The extraordinary thing was that he never harmed a single human being in the process.

He had plenty of chances to add his name to the list of man-killers. In his more vigorous attacks he turned boats completely upside-down, tipping equipment and occupants into the water willy-nilly. The up-ended fishermen flailed out in panic for the river bank with some wonderful variations of the Australian crawl. They must have seemed inviting targets to any red-blooded crocodile. But Sweetheart preferred to crunch the metal and plastic cowls of the outboard motors rather than sink his huge yellow fangs into soft human bodies.

There was another entirely human reason why all of Sweetheart's retaliations on the buzzing annoyances which disturbed the peace of his lagoon were not reported. He frightened the occupants of some of the boats so badly that they were embarrassed about it later. It was understandable.

People didn't wish to be reminded of a humiliation or to be laughed at by their fellows.

During the period of his depredations some of the visitors insisted on swimming in the lagoon in the area where the attacks took place. Sweetheart left them in peace.

Alas, his chivalry was not returned. There was an aspect of human behaviour Sweetheart could not have learned in his crocodile world down in the murky deeps of the lagoon. Human beings do not stand a loss of dignity well. They are also resentful of injury to property. Some victims complained bitterly about the damage to outboard motors and the loss of rods, rifles and fishing lines, and demanded the removal of the crocodile as a menace.

There was one other thing. Humans are so technically well equipped that in any total war between man and crocodile there could ultimately be only one ending. It was not a fair contest. But then it was never intended to be.

Sweetheart has a personal biographer. Colin Stringer, a Northern Territory fishing expert and wildlife enthusiast, became fascinated by the Sweetheart stories. He spent two years interviewing people who had been in boats attacked by the crocodile, or who knew the Finniss area from previous years. His book *The Saga of Sweetheart* is an account of almost everything known about the huge crocodile.

Would Sweetheart ultimately have become a man-killer, extending his vendetta against boats and engines to the people who controlled them?

Was it simply a matter of ego? People couldn't stand a crocodile who kept on winning?

Those questions are likely to remain unanswered. Colin Stringer sets down the story in a book which is as revealing about people as it is about the crocodile.

He believes that Sweetheart lived in the Finniss River system for years before he began his series of attacks on boats.

Stringer spoke to Aborigines who grew up near the Sweet's Lookout area. The Finniss was a prime location for crocodile shooters, and hundreds of salted skins were freighted out to Darwin in the 1950s and '60s. Sweetheart must have learned the tricks of keeping out of sight of the hunters. A painful experience, and some luck on his side, may have helped keep his caution sharp. For he carried two non-fatal bullets in his spine for many years.

However, he may also have enjoyed a certain amount of local immunity. Stringer believes Sweetheart was a totem animal of the Matngala-Weret tribe, a part of their Rainstone-Dreaming. If this was correct the Aborigines may have had the affinity to him which they termed a 'Ngirrwak'—they called him 'Old Man' and believed they were actually related to him. He was a totem creature, a part of their clan system.

His Aboriginal informants told Stringer that the presence of the crocodile in the lagoon was well known to all the tribespeople. Nugget Marjor was an Aborigine who was born on the Finniss in the early 1900s, and who grew up and later became a crocodile shooter in the area.

"We never had no trouble from the big 'gator," he said. "We always knew he was there watching us when we went to get turtles or barramundi. But he never go for us. Not even for our dogs. And we never try to shoot or spear him. I saw that big croc lots of times. But he just sat there lookin' at me. He never try to get me or my dugout canoe. I shot a lot of crocs, but we always left Old Man Sweet's Lookout alone."

In the 1970s saltwater crocodiles became protected in the Northern Territory—30 June 1971 was the official date. Something also happened which set Sweetheart against boats and outboard motors.

In later years he had a number of propeller scars around his head and neck—a natural result of combat with outboard motors up to 25 horsepower. But he also had an injured eye which seemed to have come from an earlier injury.

If he had been run over and had his eye injured by an outboard motor it might explain his abhorrence of the mechanical devils in his lagoon.

Another suggestion put forward was that the sound of an outboard, heard underwater in certain situations, is not unlike the growling-gurgling challenge issued by male crocodiles in the breeding season.

It was pointed out that motors made a sound most similar to a crocodile when they were just started, were idling, or had been put into reverse. However, in practical terms, these also were the times when a crocodile could most easily catch up with the buzzing annoyance.

Once, Sweetheart completely overturned (and chewed) a moored dinghy and outboard which had not been run for a fortnight, indicating that sound was not always a factor.

Most of the attacks did occur in the early breeding season— September, October and November. But they increased in the latter stages. In 1979 there were also attacks in May and June, though there was also a good deal of deliberate human provocation at that point.

However, Sweetheart must have been in the Finniss many years before he bit a boat. The first recorded attack occurred in 1974, at midnight, only 30 yards from Sweet's Lookout landing.

There was almost a sense of poetic justice about it because Boyne Litchfield, who owned the boat involved, was a former crocodile hunter who had shot and skinned hundreds of saltwater crocodiles since the 1930s.

It was near midnight on 14 September 1974, on a night of oppressive heat and thunderstorms.

Boyne Litchfield, his son Peter and Dulcie Pattenden were fishing for barramundi by the landing, when something huge struck the aluminum dinghy, almost capsizing it.

The enormous head of the crocodile—illuminated by flashes of lightning—appeared over the stern as it seized the outboard motor cowl in its jaws and shook the whole craft the way a dog shakes a rabbit.

Boyne Litchfield tried to reach an oar but was thrown over the seats to crash on his back. Dulcie Pattenden was actually thrown out of the boat but she desperately clutched a seat to drag herself back.

Litchfield managed to get back to the stern and grab the starter cord of the 7.5 hp Mercury outboard motor. But as soon as the engine fired, the crocodile transferred its attention from the cowl to the propeller and crunched the blades in its jaws. Water poured in over the side and swamped the craft.

Then, as suddenly as it had begun, the attack ceased. The crocodile, as though satisfied that it had sufficiently punished the source of its annoyance, swam silently away leaving the occupants of the boat quaking.

Foremost in their minds was the thought that only hours before—in daylight—they had all been in the water swimming only 100 yards from where they were attacked.

Boyne Litchfield was one of the few people in Australia who have actually witnessed a fatal attack. He told Col Stringer that in his early shooting days he had been aboard a lugger anchored off Bathurst Island. In the evening, a dugout canoe with two

Aboriginal men and a woman approached the lugger. Litchfield saw the head of a huge crocodile appear beside the canoe. Moments later it rose out of the water, put its forepaws on the side of the dugout and seized the woman in a flash of powerful jaws. Then it was gone, leaving only ripples behind.

"There was hardly a scream or a splash," Boyne Litchfield said. "It happened so quickly." Almost all the people who have personally seen a crocodile fatality use similar words.

He did not expect another confrontation with Sweetheart on the basis that lightning seldom strikes the same place twice.

But a year after the first Sweetheart attack in 1976, Litchfield was back again trolling for barramundi on the Finniss River at Sweet's Lookout lagoon, and a second attack took place in early evening, a kilometre and a half farther down river.

Again it came without warning—he thought at first he had hit a submerged log. Again the crocodile seized the outboard motor and shook it in fury, biting a piece out of the cowling. Then it bit the hull of the boat, leaving a series of thumb-sized holes in the aluminum below the waterline.

The fishermen had to paddle to land and plug the holes with rolled-up paperbark to prevent the dinghy sinking on the way back to their campsite. "That night we slept with campfires all around us."

Litchfield saw the crocodile a number of times after that but was careful to keep well clear.

The next encounter in November 1976 saw a graphic illustration of Sweetheart's strength. He came up below a 12-foot boat with a 15 hp outboard motor carrying two men and two children. They said that the crocodile lifted the boat clear of the water and swivelled it completely around to face in the opposite direction.

The owner of the boat was a policeman, Ken Phillips, of Darwin. With him in the boat were his friend Merv Allchin and Ken's sons Matthew, aged nine, and Michael, who was six years old. They had decided to spend the day barramundi fishing at Sweet's Lookout. Stringer records in his book that shortly before the attack, the two boys had been singing the song 'Never Smile at a Crocodile' from the musical *Peter Pan*.

It was the first recorded daylight attack, and after the crocodile had spun the boat around like a toy they had the unnerving sight of Sweetheart's head close enough to touch. "He lifted his head —it must have been three feet long—out of the water right along-side," Phillips recalled afterwards. "It was close enough for me to have reached out and patted him. He was huge!" He was embarrassed to find that, in the confusion, his fishing line had somehow become tangled around his neck.

The attacks began to increase in both regularity and severity.

In September 1978, Sweetheart tipped an unattended dinghy owned by station-owner Clyde Reborse completely upside-down. The dinghy had been moored by the bank and had not been used for a fortnight. Sweetheart left his personal signature with tooth-marks on the outboard motor and hull to show how it had hap-pened.

On 15 September 1978, he completely sank a hired dinghy containing Brian Cowan, George Tsakissiris and the five barra-mundi they had caught. The crocodile struck at 8 o'clock at night, the impact throwing the two fishermen into the water.

They swam over the top of each other in their panic to reach the bank and Brian collected so many pandanus spikes in his bare feet on the way back to camp that safari tour operator Max Davidson had to dig them out with a bush knife.

But they need not have worried in their overarm sprint for shore. The crocodile was not interested in them. It was happily engaged in mortal combat with its real enemy—the outboard motor of the capsized boat.

Sweetheart inflicted a satisfactory amount of damage to his metallic *bête noire*, crushing and ripping off the hood with vigor-ous bites, breaking in the sides of the lower cowling. Among the equipment lost were four expensive fibreglass fishing rods, a bucketful of barramundi lures, a shotgun said to be worth $1000 and the boat's petrol tank. Though the press credited Sweetheart with swallowing the tank (together with the outboard motor), the probable answer was that the fuel container filled and sank. There were no volunteers to dive and find out.

The next pair of swimmers, on a morning in May 1979, were Dick Gleissner and Carl Blumanis. They had a heavy-duty Clark dinghy and a 25 hp outboard motor, the biggest yet. They felt a jolt, saw a huge head rise out of the water, then Sweetheart flipped the boat right out of the water and upside-down, emptying out the two fishermen before the hull crashed back into the river.

More fishing rods, gear and another firearm—an expensive Brno rifle—went to the bottom of the river. However, Gleissner and Blumandis were tough in the Territory tradition. Gleissner swam the boat in to the bank where they righted it. Then he got the outboard going again and the two went fishing once more with what remained of their gear.

They actually caught another 15 barramundi. But by the time they tried to find their vehicle it was dark and they lost their bearings.

It took them until 3 a.m., blundering through pandanus thickets along the river's edge, before they finally located it. By that time they had been forced to jettison their entire catch. Their comments on the day's fishing remain unprintable today.

Other attacks on boats followed. When the official total reached more than 10 the Northern Territory Parks and Wildlife Commission declared Sweetheart a 'problem' crocodile. Ranger David Lindner was instructed to trap and relocate him. If this could not be accomplished the instruction was that the animal would have to be destroyed.

Dave Lindner told Col Stringer that he had not wanted to see Sweetheart killed. On the other hand it seemed likely that if the confrontations with boats continued, there was bound to be a human fatality sooner or later.

The possibility that the billabong should be declared a protected crocodile area does not appear even to have been considered.

Official policy of the time was that if there was a problem between fishermen and crocodile, the crocodile would have to go. Not the fishermen.

Most of the parties who were in boats which suffered Sweetheart attacks had firearms with them. Rifles and shotguns are listed among the toll of equipment lost in the capsizes. This indicates that most of the people concerned knew that they were in an area where an attack was at least a possibility and were prepared to shoot at the 'protected' crocodile in 'self-defence.'

Rangers who were sent to 'get' Sweetheart one way or another admitted that they went out on the river with firearms, hoping to deliberately provoke the crocodile into making an attack so that they could shoot it.

Problem people or problem crocodile?

The fact remains that, despite an evidently long sojourn in the Finniss River, and despite numerous opportunities, Sweetheart had never hurt a human being.

Nonetheless, the government order was given to move or destroy him.

Ranger David Lindner, who was put in charge of the assignment, said later that his own personal preference was to see Sweetheart caught alive, unharmed, and placed in a crocodile farm where he would be a tourist attraction.

However, despite this expressed wish, attempts were made to kill the crocodile. Hooks were set, baited with flying fox and dingo. This was an old and effective method of catching big crocodiles but since the crocodiles usually swallowed the bait, the hooks normally ripped up their stomachs and killed them in the most painful manner.

Sweetheart ignored the baits.

Efforts were made to catch him in a net.

But George Haritos, a former professional crocodile shooter who acted as adviser to Dave Lindner said, "That old croc was plenty smart. He just swam along parallel with the net, never went into it."

On George's advice a trap was set with a smaller crocodile (dead) as bait. But this too was a failure.

An attempt was made to lure Sweetheart into rifle range by hanging a dingo carcass in a tree. Crocodiles seem to prefer dogs —for reasons of their own—to any other kind of prey. The intention was to lure the big crocodile into a situation where a sniper with a .308 Brno rifle could get a shot from the branches of a forked tree on the opposite bank.

The target (as the old-time croc shooters knew well enough) was small, even on a huge animal. The bullet had to hit the hard head plate immediately above and behind the eyes to score a fatal shot.

Sweetheart could not resist the bait. He came at dawn and took the dingo. The sniper missed.

At this point there were few voices raised on behalf of the crocodile. But former crocodile hunter Stefan Sebasten, who operated a tourist safari company out of Darwin, spoke as a lone voice in the wilderness when he said that people were provoking the crocodile.

"They don't give him any peace," he said. "He should be left alone. Crocodiles just don't go around snapping at anything."

"It's no wonder one could get angered enough to attack. I just want to warn these fishermen to leave the croc alone."

Leaving the crocodile alone was not an option that anyone appeared willing to consider. The *Northern Territory News* of Monday, 18 September 1978 carried a 'Giant Crocodile Scare' headline and a subheading: 'We Will Be The Bait'.

The substance of the story was that two Northern Territory Parks and Wildlife Commission officials would go out on the Finniss River to try to duplicate the conditions of the previous attacks. The story said that after a hire dinghy had been attacked:

"The next day, when the boat was salvaged, the outboard
motor was bitten in half and the fuel tank was missing,
believed swallowed."

The reporter had evidently been misinformed or let his imagination run free. A quote from the Northern Territory Parks and Wildlife Commission was on more factual lines.

"A senior commission officer said today, 'We will have to
duplicate the conditions and arouse the croc.

'We believe it is probably attacking under territorial
instincts, not predatorial,' he said.

'We've investigated these reports and decided to take
this action as a matter of some urgency.

'But we are treating it as an isolated incident. Not a
frequent problem.

'Our first option is to see if the croc will come out. I repeat, if!

'If it does we'll attempt to shoot it and retrieve the crock,' the spokesman said.''

Who then, was provoking whom?

The 'human bait' effort actually proceeded rather more informally than was officially suggested.

Ranger Dave Lindner went out on the Finniss River with Northern Territory Police CIB Detective Denver Marchant, a cool and humorous customer. (In fact it was Marchant's expression 'Sweetheart' that Dave Lindner applied in the inspired name for the crocodile.) Marchant told Col Stringer, "Dave invited me down to the Finniss basically to give him a hand, I suppose. The whole object was we were going to shoot it. It wasn't an issue to catch it. That had been tried before and failed."

They had a choice of weapons on board, including a .375 Holland & Holland rifle, a short double-barrelled .557 double rifle and Marchant's service issue .357 revolver.

"The trick," Stringer quotes Marchant, "was to entice this thing into attacking and then poke the rifle down its throat and fire both barrels."

'The best-laid plans o' mice and men gang aft agley', wrote the poet Robert Burns. On anything like equal terms Sweetheart seemed to be more than a match. He made the attempt look ridiculous.

When Dave Lindner leaned over the side to unsnag a lure Marchant had caught on a submerged branch, Sweetheart ignored the opportunity offered.

At 9 o'clock that night Dave Lindner was trying all the annoyances he could to bring on an attack—stopping and starting the motor and reversing it.

"I was looking at Dave," Marchant told Col Stringer in an interview for Stringer's book *The Saga of Sweetheart*, "when suddenly there appeared this hideous apparition behind him . . . Bang! Dave shot forward, landing on his knees. I fell over backwards . . . It was the croc right at the top end of the motor . . ."

Sweetheart shook the motor and the rangers' boat angrily, so that water poured in over the transom and the two would-be hunters were thrown about inside like peas in a bottle. Then, as quickly as he had appeared, the crocodile let go and submerged.

By the time Marchant and Lindner regained their composure, found their artillery and got the spotlight functioning, there was nothing to be seen. The lagoon was dark, silent and perfectly still.

"We need a bigger boat," said Marchant thoughtfully.

Sweetheart had notched another victory.

A second attempt by Lindner in 1979, with Phil Hauser, had an identical result. Lindner had a theory that animal behaviourist Greer's recordings of crocodile aggression noises, which he had studied—"a low, burbling, gurgling growl"—sounded to his own ears most like an outboard motor in reverse.

He told Stringer that he was actually saying to Hauser at the time, "If my theory on reversing a motor is correct, we'll go right down Sweetheart's gob."

They did.

If ever there was a smile on the face of a crocodile, it should have been then. Sweetheart took the transom in his great jaws and went into the now-familiar routine of shaking the craft like a toy. He threw it about so violently that both the men fell over. The double rifle clattered to the bottom of the boat and Phil Hauser skinned his knees tumbling over the seats.

The attack lasted only a few seconds. It was cold and dark and 4.15 A.M. Sweetheart released the boat after giving it a thorough shaking. He surfaced again to regard them balefully from 50 metres away. Then he was gone.

It was to be his final triumph over Lindner.

An Australian Associated Press article from Darwin, datelined June 1979, summed up the situation as it was at that point. It also reflected the official attitude in clear terms.

"Darwin, June, AAP—A 17-foot rogue crocodile which stalks and attacks outboard motors at a popular fishing spot south of Darwin is defying all attempts to capture or kill him.

The huge saltwater crocodile has attacked dozens of

dinghies at Sweetman's Lookout on the Finniss River, about 80 kilometres south-east of Darwin.

The rangers, led by crocodile expert David Lindner of the Northern Territory Parks and Wildlife Service, were hunting the crocodile and were prepared to shoot him.

They had not sighted him and were ready to abandon the search when he loomed out of the murky water and clamped his jaws around the rear of the boat.

A spokeswoman for the Service said the crocodile shook the dinghy savagely and let go only to take a bite at the outboard motor. He then submerged and disappeared.

The rangers were hunting the big croc following an attack two days earlier on a fishing expedition.

Mr Lindner and a Darwin CIB Detective, Sergeant Denver Marchant, were fishing for barramundi on a day off when they were attacked.

'The crocodile surfaced without warning and bit the top off the motor,' Mr Lindner said. 'He disappeared before we could do anything about it. I wouldn't say I was frightened—I was more interested than frightened,' he said.

'I understood his motives, but I suppose the average bloke out fishing would see him as a *Jaws*-type monster.'

The Wildlife Service spokesman said the aggressive crocodile had attacked the boat of a safari operator in March and had been responsible for a series of attacks on fishing dinghies last year. He said rangers wanted to capture the crocodile but were prepared to shoot him if all attempts to do so continued to fail.

Rangers were camped at the spot trying various methods—including using other dead crocodiles as lures, tape recordings of territorial roars of crocodiles and sonic equipment to drive him into nets.

'We would like him alive for research purposes,' the spokesman said. 'We want to know why he is so aggressive toward outboard engines.

'Our theory is that he associates the sound of engines

with the roar of a crocodile trying to assert a claim on his territorial patch.'

The spokesman said there was no doubt the crocodile was clever.

'It's extremely evasive—the most evasive crocodile we've struck,' he said.

'He's never seen on the surface in daylight, he won't be drawn into a spotlight at night and he doesn't bask on the banks of the river because there are no basking tracks.

'Most crocodiles can be captured or shot at because they can be approached discreetly. But not this fellow. He submerges until he attacks and then he just looms out of the water.

'Plenty of other crocs have been seen on the Finniss but they're not our fellow because they're not big enough. He's really a wily one.'

The spokesman said the 17-foot length and six-foot width of the rogue crocodile had been established by sighting reports and by measurements of teethmarks on the outboard motor of the Wildlife dinghy attacked last Saturday.

He said the crocodile was about 40 years old and had survived through the hunting seasons of the '50s and '60s because of his cunning.

'He must have been a big croc even then, and to escape the hunters he had to be clever,' he said.

The crocodile had to be dealt with, the spokesman said, because he represented a potential danger to human life and because a tourist safari boat regularly passed through Sweetman's Lookout.

'I hope we don't have to shoot him,' he said. 'He could prove to be invaluable as research material if we were able to capture and move him to another spot.

'We'd also like to use him in any future crocodile breeding farm experiments.'

The spokesman said the crocodile had attacked an aluminum dinghy at the fishing spot last September and

had overturned it, forcing the two occupants to swim for
shore.

'But we are certain he is not attacking under predatorial instinct, but territorial,' he said."

In 1988 the attitudes of officialdom and the other human partici-
pants in the Sweetheart drama may seem open to question. But
they represented the thinking of the time.

Even the suggestion that the crocodile should be caught and
kept alive was an advanced concept for that era. It shows how
much and how rapidly our attitudes to wildlife have advanced
since then, thanks to naturalists like Harry Butler, Britain's
David Attenborough and David Bellamy. They have brought the
wild into millions of surbuban living rooms. Through their enter-
taining, informative and enormously popular television programmes, they showed wild animals as fascinating and alive.
Creatures with intense survival problems. Not mere targets to
shoot at, or potential trophies—heads to hang on walls.

Greenpeace and non-human rights in the 1980s claimed public
attention through vigorous personal intervention programmes
against whaling, sealing and forest felling. Their actions, whether
people liked them or not, gained headlines and television time,
and turned environmental matters into major issues.

While they earned the disparaging description 'Greenies' from
their opponents (and worse epithets) they did heighten public
consciousness on issues that had not previously been seriously
considered, and took the environmental cause a good deal farther
down the track.

But in the 1970s people in the Northern Territory had only just
accepted the concept of protecting crocodiles at all. Up to 30
June 1971 Sweetheart could have been shot by any passing igno-
ramus, his great hide salted and sent off to the skin market.
Protection of crocodiles was only maintained, against local reluctance and grumbling in some quarters, by the assurance of the
Northern Territory Parks and Wildlife Commission that 'problem' crocodiles would be promptly dealt with. People, in short,
would be protected too.

During this period the Wildlife Service was extremely anxious to avoid any human fatalities which might inflame public opinion against their conservation programme.

In the 1980s Sweetheart might have been seen as a kind of reptilian Robin Hood. A scaly folk-hero and a creature to be admired for his defence of his natural domain. He might have been protected from the undoubted provocation he received.

Forward-thinking tourist operators would probably have seen value in taking tourists to the spot and turning him into a living object of interest *in situ*, as happens on the Adelaide and south Alligator Rivers today.

But in 1979 he was an embarrassment to a department trying to win public sympathy for crocodiles. He was also an annoyance to barramundi fishermen. Most of these considered that God had given them natural rights to any piece of habitat where they chose to launch their noisy boats.

I had several such rigs in the 1970s myself and thought in much the same way. The times and my own thoughts have changed. There is no constructive benefit to be gained from apportioning blame for what happened in the past. Blame is not applicable. People in the Northern Territory in particular have come to terms with their wildlife in admirable fashion and have set an example to the rest of Australia and perhaps the world.

However, the change of attitudes has been progressive and did not happen overnight. We are now looking at the events of July 1979, and to understand them we need to be dispassionate and objective.

Ranger Dave Lindner was a man torn between the clear instructions and policies of his department, and his own personal admiration and respect for the huge crocodile which had outwitted him so often.

His own hope was to catch Sweetheart alive, though his reluctance to go near traps or snares made Lindner wonder whether he would ever be captured.

Meantime he arranged for a Wildlife Service heavy-duty aluminum dinghy to be given to the safari operators who were complaining about Sweetheart, and who had persisted (against all common sense) in hiring little boats out to their clients and sending them out on the Finniss.

Sweetheart obligingly bit the bigger boat. But those aboard suffered no traumas because it was too big to be overturned or even shaken thoroughly. There should have been a message there for the safari operators. Instead they scheduled a fishing competition which seemed likely to attract a dozen or more lightweight car-topper craft, and gave this as a reason for removal of the crocodile.

"So we had a priority," Lindner said later. "Get rid of Sweetheart. It was very disheartening because the very reason I provided the heavy boat to the safari operators was in recognition of Sweetheart's right to exist and inhabit the billabong. People should have adapted their fishing habits to accommodate him.

"However we hadn't been able to get the public to support Sweetheart . . . We realised that should a fatal attack take place we would have to take the brunt of public backlash. That was something we couldn't afford. If you lose your job because one croc project blew up, you wouldn't be able to help other crocodiles at other times."

It was a dead dingo which finally lured Sweetheart into the hands of men. Lindner found it dead on the road after it had been hit by a passing car. Crocodiles love dead dog more than any other bait—why is an unexplained mystery. It must have something to do with the scent of a dog, and on the same basis the deceased flying fox is also a reptilian delicacy.

On 18 July 1979, Dave Lindner set a snare with the dingo as bait. It was a simple device, not nearly as complex as the tunnel traps used successfully in the 1980s.

When Sweetheart snatched the bait at daylight next day he released a trigger spring which jerked the lassoo of the snare taut behind his forelegs.

The noose was made from industrial belting. Strong, broad and flat so that it would not cut into the crocodile. It was attached to a steel cable. The crocodile rolled and snapped and lunged. But he could not reach back to the loop around his chest, and the harder he struggled the tighter it held him.

Sweetheart was caught.

Crocodiles have an effective metabolism for their lifestyle. They can move more quickly than mammals in some circumstances, and are capable of awesome bursts of violent energy. In natural conditions their victories are usually gained quickly, the struggle soon over. But over an extended period a reptile does not have the stamina of a warm-blooded animal. Crocodiles in particular tire quickly. Once they lose their energy it takes them a long time to regain it. They hold their breath as a natural instinct while struggling. This can cause a build-up of lactic acid in their muscles which may prove fatal in a noose or trap if the struggle goes on long enough. Big crocodiles are particularly prone to dying after they have fought to the end of their energy reserves.

Dave Lindner was aware of this. Experiments in Rhodesia had shown that captive animals too big to be handled ordinarily could be quietened by using tranquilliser drugs. The tranquilliser was thought to prevent exhaustion and death from extended struggling. An anaesthetic called Flaxadil had proved the easiest and least dangerous of the various drugs to administer.

Dave had the drug, but he had no dosage rate for an animal as big as Sweetheart.

Sweetheart rolled and fought to the very end. But at last he was beaten. The huge jaws trussed and tied together, the tranquillising drug injected into his enormous body.

At that moment it seemed that the battle had had a happy ending. He would be transported live to a crocodile farm.

But as they towed his rope-bound body across the river behind a dinghy to Sweet's Lookout landing the steel cable attached to the noose caught on a snag in mid-river. It pulled his head down and he took in water. In his unconscious state the water ran into his lungs.

When they winched him out of the water onto a trailer on the other side of the river, Sweetheart was dead.

Even in death he had his own kind of triumph.

His huge body was mounted by the Darwin Museum. He provided a great deal of valuable information for science. His vital statistics showed that he was 5.1 metres in length, 2.3 metres in girth, 780 kilos in weight and was from 40 to 80 years old. His stomach contents included the remains of wild pigs, catfish, barramundi and two long-necked river turtles, but no 'crunched human bones' or 'motorboat engines'. His skull was 65.5 cm long and his testicles were sexually active, indicating that he was still breeding as head of the lagoon.

He had a number of old injuries, including two bullets in his spine, and several of his limbs had been broken, probably in past duels with rivals.

It took 14 months' work by the museum staff under the Curator of Natural Sciences, Graeme Gow, to clean Sweetheart's skeleton and complete the research. Taxidermist Ian Archibald mounted the huge crocodile in a unique display which includes murals of Sweetheart's lagoon below Sweet's Lookout—the beautiful stretch of water lined by pandanus palms and overhanging river gums where he ruled so long.

For a time the stuffed crocodile toured Australia, evoking admiration wherever it went.

Today Sweetheart is a centrepiece in the Darwin Museum, and more than 120,000 visitors a year come to gasp in awe at his size and his ferocious appearance. He is still Australia's most famous crocodile.

The crocodile who attacked outboard motors and never hurt a human . . .

Looking at the mural of the beautiful stretch of water Sweetheart defended so well, few visitors can resist a pang of sorrow for the grand old warrior who lost his final battle for the place he loved.

But for man, his great and magnificent bulk could still be rippling the lagoon in the Finniss River today.

FATAL ENCOUNTERS

▲▲▲▲▲▲▲▲▲▲

*T*here are statistics available on crocodile attacks on humans in Australia. One set, compiled from official records, states that there have been some 60 attacks, with 27 deaths, since 1876.

This makes an interesting comparison with the list of 185 shark attacks, and 93 fatalities—or it would if either list were accurate.

Unfortunately the documentation of both shark and crocodile attacks through the years has been so haphazard that the figures are almost meaningless.

Officially there are supposed to have been only two crocodile-caused deaths in Western Australia. Paul Flanagan at Wyndham in 1980 and Ginger Meadows at the Prince Regent in 1987. But I know of at least three others and there are certainly more than that still undocumented.

One of the pathetic unrecorded stories I found accidentally in the graveyard of the abandoned Benedictine mission at Pago, on Vansittart Bay near Kalumburu in the Kimberleys.

A large stone cross stood in a corner of the cemetery overgrown by shrubs and creepers. The legend on the face of the cross was spelled out clearly in brass lettering, in marked contrast to the graves of forgotten monks and brothers who had died in the work of the Lord, far, far from their native Europe. These last resting places were indicated only by uninscribed boulders of local stone. The graves themselves were so overgrown by jungle that they were hardly recognisable.

I was told that the Navy had built the cross, and in Royal Australian Navy tradition the materials used were designed to last forever. The grave contained the incomplete remains of Gunner H. Davies, Royal Australian Navy, who had come to Vansittart Bay in HMAS *Geranium* in September 1920.

Poor Gunner Davies was in high spirits when *Geranium* dropped her anchors with a splash and a rattle of chain out in the bay. When the ship reached Fremantle he was going to be married. His fiancée was already on the high seas, sailing on a passenger liner to meet him there.

Boats were lowered over the side and officers and men were allowed ashore for rest and relaxation. Some took fishing lines, others books. Gunner Davies, in an adventurous mood, set out to explore the surrounding country.

By nightfall he was lost.

In his eagerness to examine the new land he had not taken sufficient care to remember the way he had come. The rugged Kimberley country is treacherously deceptive. Even bushmen are careful to keep landmarks in sight, and it is all too easy for the inexperienced to lose their way.

Davies panicked. Began to run.

But as darkness set in there was still no sign of anything familiar. He spent a wretched night, and in the morning began walking again. By the end of the day he was suffering tortures from thirst, and his boots had worn through so that as he dragged his weary feet the marks of his blistered and blood-stained toes showed clearly through the patches of sand.

A creek barred his way at a place the Aborigines called Njana. For a moment he was overjoyed. It must lead to the sea. At last he thought he had his bearings. The ship would not be far away. What a relief! Grateful for the coolness of the water he began to swim. As he neared the far bank the crocodile surged forward. There was a flash of jaws and a swirl . . .

The diary kept at Kalumburu Mission records the sad progress of events. "On 28 September 1920 the distressed captain of the HMAS *Geranium*, Lieutenant Commander W.M. Vaughan Lewish, called for assistance. The officers and crew of his ship had gone ashore in Vansittart Bay for relaxation and in the evening one had failed to return. Could the missionaries—or rather the Aborigine trackers of the mission—help to find the missing man?"

The remarkable tracking skills of the tribal Aborigines pieced the story together as one scrap of evidence after another was found. They discovered the tracks and saw the pitiful evidence of the worn boots and the dragging footmarks. They found that the tracks went down into the creek but they did not reappear on the other side.

On 9 October there was an ominous entry. "M-yuron and Puntji arrived with the belt of the missing man. At Njana Matjeri had found one leg."

15 October: "We came with the mission lugger *Voladora* in front of Njana where Matjeri and Maramen were waiting for us with the body, minus head, arms and one foot." They said they had found the skull and arms. But they had been buried in sand and could not be found again.

16 October: "We buried the remains in the mission at Pago."

Captain Vaughan Lewish called again several times in HMAS *Geranium* and eventually brought the stone cross which was carried ashore and erected with a service by Davies' shipmates. It still stands in the corner of the now-abandoned graveyard.

It was a story of life brought abruptly to a halt, of a wedding which never took place. That was the end of it all for Gunner H. Davies, 67 years ago. Now all that is left is the cross over his grave.

Two other fatalities which are not recorded on official lists involved the superintendent of a mission, taken in Walcott Inlet, north of Derby, and a young policeman lost at Derby in the 1890s. The policeman was fond of fishing. He liked to sit on a lower landing on the town wharf and dangle a line, unaware, like Val Plumwood, that crocodiles could jump.

He went regularly to the same spot and sometimes the enormous tides that rise and fall 25 feet at Wyndham came very close to the landing. One day he did not return from fishing. When a large crocodile was caught some time later, his uniform buttons were found in its stomach.

One of the problems in recording crocodile attacks is to know that they happened at all. Witnesses almost always say the same thing. "It happened so quickly . . . There was just a great swirl of water . . . No scream. Not a sound . . ."

This is in cases where there are witnesses. Where someone sees the crocodile take the victim.

In other instances where people are missing in crocodile areas portions of the torn body are occasionally found, or sometimes remains are recovered from inside a caught crocodile.

But in many cases of disappearance people are simply presumed drowned. At Wyndham, in 1987, not long before we called through in the vessel *Kimberley Explorer*, three Aboriginal men had tried to cross crocodile-infested Cambridge Gulf in an overloaded dinghy on their way back to the Kalumburu district.

Some time later the overturned craft drifted ashore on the far side of the gulf. Two bodies were found—one minus a foot. But no trace was ever found of the third man.

Aborigines were convinced that he had been taken by a crocodile, but there was no proof and the Coroner's verdict was death by drowning.

In another instance at Wyndham, a British refrigeration engineer, John Thompson, disappeared from a freighter tied up at the wharf in 1948. The nearby meatworks was discharging blood and offal into the gulf, and in the red waters of the 'drain' at the mouth of the discharge pipe there was the greatest congregation of saltwater crocodiles to be seen in Australia at that time.

Because of the huge tides at Wyndham, ramps moving with the rise and fall were used for access from ships to the jetty. On the night Thompson disappeared, after a few drinks, a temporary ramp without rails was in place. He had evidently walked straight over the edge in the darkness and no one heard his cry as he splashed down into the black Gulf waters.

"They searched for him for a week and never found a body," Tex Boneham, a crocodile shooter, recalls. "Then I caught this real big fellow of a croc. He must have been 18 feet long. Inside

him was a gold signet ring with the initials J.T. on it. The ring
was sent to Britain and it turned out that John Thompson had
been wearing it on the night he died."

Did Thompson drown? Or was he taken by the crocodile as he
struggled in the tidal water?

In the absence of any evidence the Coroner decided that death
was by drowning. But the question about whether he was taken
by a crocodile remains open. It seems most likely that he was,
for the reason that crocodiles like to kill their own prey. Once
they have done so they will revisit a 'stored' carcass again and
again, and they will also attack prey killed by other crocodiles.
But it is a curious fact that the bodies of humans who drown in
crocodile waters (like the two Aborigines from the Wyndham
dinghy accident) are usually recovered.

One of the ironies of the Beryl Wruck case in the Daintree in
North Queensland was missed by the press in the drama following her crocodile attack. On the day after she was taken, an
Aborigine, Ned Fisher, suffered a fatal heart attack while rowing
his dinghy. He fell overboard and his body drifted up and down
the Daintree with the tide for a day and a half before he was
found. Despite the concentration of crocodiles in the area and
Beryl's tragic death—which might have been thought to stir the
crocodiles in the way that sharks become excited—no crocodile
touched Ned Fisher.

There must have been many instances through Australian history in the north of Australia where people on their own in lonely
places succumbed to crocodile attack without anyone ever knowing what happened to them. Val Plumwood would have been one
if she had not survived to tell the story.

But even if the toll ran into two or even three hundred victims,
it is still insignificant compared with the annual road toll. In 1987
three people were officially killed by crocodiles in Australia; 2572
died in road accidents; 23,000 had their lives terminated by
smoking-related diseases. The road casualty list on any one
weekend exceeded the total number of known crocodile deaths
for the past 10 years.

As crocodile numbers continue to rise in the north, and more
and more tourists flock to the Kimberleys, there must necessarily

be more crocodile-human contact. It seems logical to expect more attacks in the future, though theoretically increased public awareness as a result of publicity from attacks like those of 1987 should induce more public caution.

But there will probably still be the occasional tragedy, like the one which befell Kerry McLoughlin at Cahill's Crossing on the East Alligator River, Kakadu, in March 1987.

McLoughlin was a 40-year-old storeman who worked at Jabiru. He had been in the Territory 20 years or more and knew the East Alligator well. Perhaps too well. Familiarity created the unlucky situation which led to his death.

To understand what happened it is necessary to have a mental picture of the location.

Cahill's Crossing—named after the old King of the Territory buffalo shooters, Paddy Cahill—traverses the East Alligator river bed to the Oenpelli side and Aboriginal Arnhem Land.

It is a concrete driveway set over big, rounded river boulders and used at low water. At high tide it is flooded. The actual crossing is about 150 metres long and is comparatively narrow— 14 feet wide, or not much more than the width of a truck. At low tide, when it is exposed, it is plain to see. But when the tide rises above the level of the crossing it becomes invisible under the muddy waters. The concrete also becomes dangerously slippery. There are crocodile warning signs at each end, and these used to raise a smile from knowledgeable locals.

McLoughlin had gone to the crossing with his 17-year-old son on 17 March 1987 to go fishing. The crossing was a favourite fishing platform with local fishermen. The prized fish was barramundi—the fish everyone in the north wants to bring home—and a good time to catch them was on the rising tide when the water began to swirl back over the crossing from the sea. At weekends there would be a row of waving fibreglass rods as anglers cast their lines and wound in their reels hoping to hook into a fine fat 'barra'.

There were also crocodiles. They had a habit of congregating downstream from the crossing at low tide. On the rising tide some of them cruised up river.

Local fishermen knew about the crocodiles. They kept an eye

on them but did not regard them as a problem. Tourists were sometimes alarmed by the sight of the crocodiles visible only a little way downstream from rod fishermen up to their knees in water. The anglers thought this a bit of a joke.

The locals would laugh when concerned tourists shouted warnings. "We know all these crocs by their first names," they would reply.

On 17 March 1987, a crocodile came who was a stranger. A big animal more than 16 feet long. McLoughlin was unaware that it was a newcomer. He was regarded as a typical tough Territorian. A man who would dive to unsnag a barramundi lure from a sunken branch without a second thought, and who regarded crocodiles with a confident grin. He was also a friendly soul and when he saw the big crocodile passing upstream he told some visiting American tourists about it. He knew they would like to photograph the large reptile.

When he saw some friends across the river he had what turned out to be a fatal impulse. He waded over to say 'g'day' with his fishing rod in one hand and a stubby of beer in the other. It was a normal enough thing to do, except that maybe he had left it a little late.

Once on the Oenpelli side, McLoughlin did not stay a long time, and he did not have a lot to drink. They pointed out to him what he already knew—that the tide was rising fairly rapidly over the crossing.

So with a few parting cheery remarks he began wading back again. As he reached the centre of the crossing he found that the tide was higher and was running more strongly than he had thought. But at that point he saw it as an inconvenience rather than a danger.

Then—with a curse—he missed his footing and slipped over the edge of the concrete roadway. Now he was in a different situation. He was stumbling amongst the big rounded river boulders, difficult to walk through even at low tide. With the tide now swirling between waist and chest deep (the concrete was raised half a metre above the ordinary river-bed level), McLoughlin realised that he was in difficulties.

The tourists on the bank he was making for had started yelling.

From his point of view it didn't help. He knew he had a problem, and he was furiously aware that he was making a spectacle of himself.

He tried hard to return to the crossing and regain his footing. But the surging tide pushed him farther away. There was nothing for it now but to head for the bank, wet and bedraggled. Bloody nuisance! What were all those idiots on the bank yelling about?

The group of elderly American tourists he had spoken to earlier on the bank saw McLoughlin in the water. Having no local knowledge they couldn't understand why he was there at all. They had photographed the crocodile and knew how big it was. They could not comprehend the lack of concern of the local fishermen who said, "The crocs are always there. Don't worry, mate. They're OK."

But for once, it wasn't OK. The big crocodile, who had been causing some disturbances—'humbugging' the Aborigines called it—with the smaller crocodiles below the crossing, was new to the East Alligator system. Rangers later believed that he had been driven out from somewhere else and was looking to establish himself in a new territory. He was in a cranky mood.

As McLoughlin struggled, waist-deep, toward the bank the large crocodile became alert, attracted by the splashing. It began to cruise upstream to investigate the source of the sound.

Now even the locals became concerned.

The tourists began to frantically throw sticks and stones at the crocodile. As the crocodile passed McLoughlin people screamed and yelled. It went a little way past him, assessing the situation, then turned back purposefully towards him.

Now it became a race.

McLoughlin by this time had heard the shouts of "crocodile!" and understood the danger. As he splashed toward the bank, a man trying too hard and out of breath, it seemed to the horrified watchers to be a tragedy happening in slow motion.

"It was all so needless," said Everett Galbraith, a 63-year-old American tourist. "We saw the crocodile and yelled to the man to get out of the water. But he didn't."

In fact, McLoughlin was doing his best. But with his wet

clothes, the current drag and the rough bottom, it was hard to make progress.

The crocodile submerged. In what some people saw as a final gesture of defiance—but which may also have been an intelligent attempt to distract his tormentor—the hunted man hurled his stubby of beer at the spot where the crocodile had gone down.

Then, probably knowing how hopeless it was, he tried again to reach the shore. To the huge relief of the watchers he actually reached the bank by some rocks ahead of the crocodile and some distance above the crossing. Gasping for breath he began to pull himself up and out of the water by a branch.

But just when it seemed he might be saved the crocodile leaped, bursting through the surface. The tourists, who had been throwing stones and branches, stopped and stood appalled as the huge jaws flashed and closed across McLoughlin's head and shoulders.

"There was a hard slap," Galbraith said. "Then there was nothing. It was all quite still."

With that first bite and roll the crocodile tore his head off and decapitated McLoughlin. Then it seized the twitching body in the bloodstained water and swam away upstream to be lost to view around the bend.

The watchers (who included McLoughlin's 17-year-old son Michael, frozen with a can of soft drink in his hand) stood numbed in horror.

"It was all so fast," Galbraith said. "And yet so slow. I could just visualise what was going to happen. I had a three-metre stick and tried to get to him. But he was too far away and it all happened so fast.

"Afterwards, after all the yelling and shouting, it went quite still. Just nothing, as people realised what had happened. It was bizarre."

The rangers at the nearby Kakadu National Parks and Wildlife were called at once and a boat was launched at a ramp just south of the crossing and sent out after the crocodile.

It was found in the mangroves a little distance upstream, still with McLoughlin's limp body clutched triumphantly in its jaws.

The rangers fired and scored a definite hit, the animal convulsed, dropped the body and disappeared.

"Unfortunately we were never able to tell whether we killed it or just wounded it," said ranger superintendent Clive Cook. "It was disappointing.

"Usually, if they're wounded they go up on the bank and stay out of the water. If they're dead they float after four or five days. This one was different. We kept boat patrols out, but we never saw him again.

"You couldn't blame the crocodile. But we felt it was necessary to pre-empt local vigilante groups taking the law into their own hands as happened in Queensland. It wasn't a crocodile that had been seen in the area before, and if it survived it hasn't been seen since.

"Our main role in Kakadu," he said, "is to manage the people. The crocodiles look after themselves quite well. McLoughlin was a local. He'd been in the area a long time and had become accustomed to a prior situation where crocodiles were comparatively rare and there wasn't the kind of danger we have today.

"He was unfortunate. He was caught by a number of related minor things which went wrong and suddenly found himself in a situation he hadn't expected. Also he was obviously very, very unlucky that there was a big crocodile strange to the area which was hungry at that moment. Most times he would have got away with it."

Queensland has had the most recorded crocodile attacks on humans in Australia. This is not because it has the most crocodiles, but because there were more people in crocodile areas in the past, resulting in more interaction than in the Northern Territory or Western Australia.

The Beryl Wruck tragedy occupied national headlines at Christmas 1985, and in the early part of 1986. In February, eight weeks after her death, there were new headlines.

An attractive woman fisherman had been taken at the Staaten River in Queensland's Gulf Country.

It was another story of bad luck. Kate McQuarrie, a 31-year-old first hand on the barramundi fishing boat *Kiama*, had gone up the river in a dinghy with the skipper Bob McNeil to set barramundi nets.

The outboard motor refused to start for the return trip. They were forced to walk 15 kilometres along the river bank in steamy, hot conditions, back to where the *Kiama* lay at anchor. Then they had to swim out to the boat. They were aware of crocodiles —what barramundi fisherman wasn't? But they had no choice. Exhausted after the walk, lathered in sweat, there was no other way to reach the boat. The choice was to stay with the sandflies on the river bank or to swim out to the boat which was also their home. A place where there was a shower to clean off the mud, food and a cool drink. A cool drink . . .

So they said, "Here goes . . ." and swam side by side, with steady strokes, until they reached the *Kiama*. There was no indication that anything was wrong. The side of the boat was steep and Kate was exhausted after the long walk and the swim. Bob McNeil swung himself up and over the rail and turned to help Kate on board.

To his horror he saw a huge crocodile head appear behind her. The jaws opened. "It just grabbed her in a second. There was a huge swirl and she was gone . . ."

He ran to the cabin to grab a rifle but in the few seconds it took him to find it and get back on deck Kate and the crocodile had disappeared. "It was a monster," McNeil told his base at Karumba, 150 kilometres away, by radio. "At least 5.5 metres long."

Police came from Karumba with heavy-calibre weapons to search for the crocodile and at dawn next day, a fisherman sighted the crocodile with Kate McQuarrie's mutilated body in Vaon Rook Creek, a tributary of the Staaten River.

A group including Bob McNeil trapped the crocodile, blocking off its escape with barramundi nets. McNeil shot the crocodile, which sank.

Kate McQuarrie's mutilated torso was recovered. But the fishermen were never able to secure the dead crocodile, though they waited for several days for the huge body to float.

Kate's heartbroken parents at their farm in Murwillumbah, in northern New South Wales, said that she had discussed the danger of crocodiles with them only a month before she was taken. "It must have been an absolute last resort for her to go into the water," her Scottish-born father Archie McQuarrie told reporters. "She told us she would never swim in any North Queensland creek or river for fear of crocodiles. She was afraid of them," he said.

If Kate McQuarrie was taken despite her fear, or premonition, of crocodile attack, Paul Flanagan was at the other end of the scale.

Flanagan, a 26-year-old truck driver from Midland in Western Australia, arrived at the northern port of Wyndham, driving a big truck rig on 24 November 1980.

Wyndham had the highest temperature in the State that day— a searing 41 degrees Celsuis. Paul Flanagan and another truck driver arrived about 9.30 P.M. and parked their big trucks outside the hotel. Then they settled down to slake some of the enormous thirst they had generated on the hot and dusty road north.

At closing time they said they were going to roll out their swags on the beach to try to catch a cool breeze.

"Don't do it," the locals warned. "This is crocodile country."

Flanagan and his mate laughed. The more seriously the locals tried to dissuade them, the more determined they became.

Wyndham was famous for its meatworks and its crocodiles. The two went together. Cattle from the Kimberley hinterland were brought in to be slaughtered during the cool months, and the blood drained out into Cambridge gulf near the town wharf.

Where the blood reached the water at a point known as 'the drain', crocodiles lay row on row.

Killing had stopped at the meatworks for the hot weather period three weeks before Flanagan's arrival. But the crocodiles were still about and hungry because of the cessation of the blood which brought fish and birds as prey for them to catch.

A narrow belt of mangroves separated the beach on the Gulf, and the town dinghy ramp, from the town streets and the nearest backyards. Goats and dogs were sometimes taken by crocodiles in the mangroves. Wyndham people were always cautious using the dinghy ramp.

Flanagan and his mate took a carton of beer and their swags down to the ramp with some other drinks for some companions they had acquired. They were Aboriginal ladies who seemed happy to share a good time with the truck drivers celebrating reaching the end of the State's longest road haul—more than 2000 kilometres from Perth.

Midnight came and went. In a spirit of bravado Flanagan announced that he was going for a swim "to cool off". The Aboriginal ladies begged him not to. That was all the extra encouragement he needed.

He splashed around happily, a beer in his hand, calling for the crocodiles to come and get him. Fortune sometimes favours the foolhardy. He staggered out of the water, dripping and triumphant, and exclaiming loudly that the Wyndham crocodiles were "all bullshit".

Half an hour later he went into the water again. This time, instead of splashing on the edge, he set off for a swim about 30 metres offshore.

"There's a croc behind you!" one of the women screamed, seeing a vee of ripples on the dark shining water. Flanagan took no notice. Perhaps he thought they were joking.

Suddenly there was a huge swirl, familiar in most descriptions of crocodile attacks. Flanagan disappeared without a sound—no scream or shout. Not even a splash.

Constable Kevin Doy and Constable A. Mettam at the Wyndham Police Station, only a short distance from the landing, received an incoherent call from Flanagan's new friends at 1.20 A.M., and they and the district wildlife officer set off at once in a Fisheries Department launch to search the area.

Two hours later, at first light, they found Flanagan's body 800 metres from where he was attacked, dragged up on a mud bank. Two crocodiles lay beside it, one on each side.

The bigger crocodile, which was nearly four metres, was shot so that the body could be recovered, and the smaller one—not much more than two metres—slithered away and escaped.

The dead crocodile was well known to Aborigines in Wyndham. It had an injured leg, giving it a limping gait on land and a distinctive track. It had taken a dog in the mangroves not long before.

Another attack where alcohol impaired judgement occurred at the remote Northern Territory Gulf town of Borroloola, on 9 September 1986.

Rusty Wherrett (39), of Mareeba, Queensland, who had been working locally on fencing contracts, had been on a Saturday night drinking spree with his mate Dennis Vowken. They were accustomed to moving around. Police said Wherrett travelled under at least four different names and in all news reports he was referred to as "Lee McLeod". The two decided to sleep out in the open. "Starlight Hotel," the old swagmen called sleeping under the stars. The spot they chose was 500 metres from the pub on the river bank at the Rocky Creek landing, a popular fishing spot near the town, on the McArthur River. Before turning in they had a few more drinks.

When the mate woke on the bank next morning—considerably the worse for wear after the night's heavy drinking—Wherret was nowhere to be seen. His shirt was still there. But there was no sign of Wherrett. Feeling hung-over, disoriented and reluctant to approach the police, Vowken did nothing for the best part of Sunday. He said later he thought Wherrett might have "gone for a walk".

But by nightfall he reluctantly reported Wherrett missing. Constables Rex Grass and Mal Jensen began a search believing him drowned. But they changed their minds when they made the grisly discovery of two severed human legs 100 yards upstream from the boat ramp.

Inspector Maurie Burke, of the Northern Territory Police, later described the body search in a graphic article in the *Australian Police Journal*, edited by Phil Peters.

The dismembered legs immediately identified a crocodile attack and the prime suspect was a large local crocodile called 'Gus' who had taken up territory in that part of the river.

Wildlife officers who went out in a boat to search for Gus located him in an unusual way.

"It was highly likely that he was the culprit," Inspector Burke wrote. "And this was partially confirmed by the particularly putrid stench from his breath. Whilst patrolling for him the officers, whether they could see him or not, were aware of his presence by the stench of his breath.

"Even submerged the bubbles expelled were putrid enough to cause near-vomiting by officers if they were caught unaware leaning from the boat and having the bubbles burst in their faces.

"It appears that this is peculiar to the crocodile, especially if it has taken a human. Apparently the contents of a croc's stomach virtually ferment in a cocktail of powerful gastric juices and acids, giving rise to the crocodile's particularly foetid breath."

The officers from the Northern Territory Conservation Commission, Bryan Walsh, Phil Hauser, Bill Binns and Ross Bryam, harpooned and finally shot Gus on the Thursday night, five days after the attack.

An examination of his stomach contents proved that Gus was indeed the killer. He was a large crocodile. The end of his tail had earlier been bitten off either by a shark or in territorial conflict. But his estimated normal length was 16 feet (5.1 metres).

The remains of the unfortunate victim were found inside the crocodile. Inspector Burke reported: "The digestive juices had already reduced bone matter to the consistency of rubbery gristle, flesh to a jelly-like substance and skin bleached and rubbery in texture.

"From the bruising sustained to the hands and arms it was evident that McLeod/Wherrett was alive when taken. It would appear that he was taken from behind, crushed through the middle by the immense power of the jaws. Whilst struggling to escape his arms and hands were lacerated and punctured by the crocodile's teeth.

"He was carried upstream for 100 metres before the final 'death-roll' and flailing of the now-lifeless body severed the arms and legs, one of the legs being flicked high onto the river bank."

The pelvic bone was rendered vertically through. "The awesome power of the crocodile being evident in the fact that it was the flailing action which literally tore the arms and legs from the torso."

Identification was made by police forensic specialists. Senior Constable Dave Prowse of the Territory Police took skin tissue sloughed off in the stomach. This was washed, dried and dusted with black powder. When the powder was wiped off with methylated spirits the residue in the ridges of the skin showed the whorls and lines. Constable Prowse was able to place a thumbprint under a microscope. It matched perfectly police records for 'McLeod' (one of Wherrett's aliases) supplied from Queensland,

and completed one of the most bizarre and unusual identifications in Australian police records.

Ironically, crocodile warning signs had been placed at the landing only days before Wherrett and Vowken arrived there on that fatal Saturday night.

The luckiest man in Borroloola was a local who five months earlier had attempted to cross the river carrying a carton of beer. The crocodile grabbed him and then 'spat him out'. He was taken to Darwin for treatment for bruising and a severely lacerated right arm and shoulder. He also lost the carton of beer!

Inspector Burke's final summing up was: "It was a little sad that that chance meeting of man and beast resulted in a horrific exodus from this world by Wherrett and the final destruction of one of nature's relics of prehistoric times.

"Had Wherrett's judgement not been clouded by alcohol there would have been no cause to write this account."

There was a theory, for a time, that crocodiles did not attack divers. It was dispelled when Trevor Gaghan, a 28-year-old skin-diving enthusiast on holidays from Melbourne, went diving at Nhulunbuy, a mining settlement on the Gove Peninsula in the Northern Territory. With a Nhulunbuy friend Max Cumming, on 8 October 1979 he went to a spot called Rainbow Cliffs to dive for crayfish. While the two men were out in the water, Trevor's wife Christine sunned herself on the beach.

She watched their fins going up in the air and the disappearing underwater as they searched under rocks and ledges for crayfish. The hunt for the tropical 'painted' crays seemed to be going well.

Suddenly, there was a scream. Christine Gaghan looked up and was horrified to see that a large crocodile had appeared and seized her husband by his arm.

He shouted desperately for help but was dragged under in a boil of water. Christine, incoherent with shock, drove into Nhulunbuy to call the police. But when they returned to the Rainbow Cliffs with a four-wheel-drive vehicle, there was no sign of the crocodile or the diver.

"That night we used searchlights to go up into the creek," Constable Dave Benson said. "Soon after, Trevor Gaghan's body surfaced face down in the middle. He had a broken arm and had been bitten and badly bruised across the torso. But the thick wetsuit protected him from the teeth to an extent."

However, the wetsuit did not save his life.

Wildlife officers flew from Darwin. The body and the crocodile were located in a small creek about a kilometre away from the scene of the attack.

Rangers waited for the crocodile and eventually harpooned and shot the 3.5-metre animal responsible.

The carcass was put on show in the main park and in the school at Nhulunbuy.

"This was done to quieten local residents who were talking wildly about shooting all crocodiles in the area," Constable Benson said. "After the Rainbow Cliffs killing, people were talking about shooting them willy-nilly. We didn't want to see a lot of people running about recklessly with high-powered weapons."

Several days later Christine Gaghan, who had witnessed her husband's tragic death, was still being treated for shock in Nhulunbuy hospital.

Wildlife officers said that it was unlikely that Trevor Gaghan's bag of crayfish had attracted the crocodile. It had established a territory in the nearby creek. It dominated the area and it would have been attracted by any activity in the water.

In February of the following year another visitor to Nhulunbuy disappeared in mysterious circumstances while swimming in a local waterhole. On 1 July 1980 there was a confirmed fatality when a 30-year-old Aboriginal woman, Bukarra Number One Munyarrwun of Nhulunbuy outstation, was taken near where the Cato River joins Arnhem Bay, a place where there is an old wartime airstrip near the river.

She was a mother of two children living in a tribal situation, subsisting largely on bush tucker. She had been fishing waist-deep in the billabong of the isolated Dhalinbuy settlement, 50 kilometres from Nhulunbuy. Friends heard her scream and saw a crocodile, which they estimated to be five metres long, seize her and drag her under the surface of the billabong.

Police were called by radio and came bumping by four-wheel-drive down the dusty track from Nhulunbuy. Later Bukarra's torso, minus the severed lower half of her body, was found 500 metres away by Police Sergeant Bob Haydon. Her pitiful remains were taken to the mortuary of Nhulunbuy hospital with all the possessions she had—a shredded remnant of a cotton dress.

The Aborigines of her tribe said that all of them, Bukarra included, had known that the big crocodile was there. They called him 'Baru' and he was a religious totem, a 'grandfather', not only of their tribe but also eight other Aboriginal areas nearby.

Police and Northern Territory wildlife officers had intended to shoot the crocodile after Bukarra's death. Sergeant Haydon believed that the crocodile Baru had also been responsible for the disappearance of an old man and a boy near the settlement in previous months.

Tribal elders had at first agreed reluctantly that the crocodile could be shot. But then they changed their minds and vehemently shook their heads. Baru must not be harmed.

"Out there it is sometimes difficult to know what happens," Sergeant Haydon told a reporter from the Perth *Sunday Independent* newspaper when he was questioned about the missing people.

"The billabong is that crocodile's territory and he will stay around. But they told us that he's their religious totem. So that's it. Now he's safe."

The Aborigines' own answer was a series of 'sorry' ceremonies. Corroborees to appease Bukarra's spirit, and to persuade the crocodile, as an ancestor spirit from The Dreaming, not to attack again. The ceremonies went on for a fortnight after the death. Then what was left of Bukarra was flown back from Nhulunbuy for burial by the settlement with further mournful corroborees.

With five possible crocodile-caused deaths in the area, two of them confirmed and all of them occurring within 12 months of each other, it was natural that people in the mining town of Nhulunbuy became alarmed. With a population of 4500 people, including 1700 children, they had reason to be concerned. A number of townsfolk called for an end to the protection of 'sacred' crocodiles.

"Who will be the next victim?" the town newspaper queried in an article which demanded a 16-kilometre 'crocodile-free zone' around the town.

But as years went by the people of Nhulunbuy learned to live with crocodiles.

Perhaps the ceremonies of Bukarra's people were effective after all. In the 17 years since, there has not been another crocodile attack in the area.

The list of northern crocodile victims goes on.

In April 1975, Peter Reimer, aged 32, a plant operator for Comalco in Weipa, North Queensland, and formerly of Perth, was killed by an enormous crocodile in water that was little more than knee deep.

He had been on a hunting and fishing trip with two friends. After a pig hunt he had gone to cool off in a lagoon in the Mission River, in the Gulf country, 32 kilometres east of Weipa.

His two friends, Rodney Kirby and Douglas Goelener, both Comalco aluminum plant operators in Weipa, had decided to go fishing when they arrived at the river about 3 o'clock on a Friday afternoon. Reimer went off on his own pig shooting.

When he had not returned to camp with the vehicle by nightfall they became worried. They searched until they found their vehicle parked by a swamp not far from camp but there was still no sign of Reimer.

They spent all night lighting fires and firing shots in the belief that he was lost. But soon after daylight on the Saturday they found Reimer's hat, belt, rifle, watch, ammunition and clothing near a tree on the bank of the lagoon, and saw the ominous signs. Reimer's footprints led down to the water and nearby was the track of a huge crocodile.

Thoroughly alarmed by now, they called the Weipa police. "We saw the marks where the crocodile slid down the bank to get him," Sergeant Ron Rooks said. "The water was only 45 centimetres deep."

The police, Kirby and Goelener took up vantage points around the lagoon and sighted bubbles coming up to the surface where the crocodile was submerged. They blew it to the surface with a charge of gelignite and shot it while it was stunned.

When they dragged it ashore they found Reimer's body inside the crocodile which had swallowed him whole. It was an enormous beast—19 feet in length.

It was the largest crocodile of any involved in the fatal attacks. Most of the man-killers that were measured were over 11 feet 6 inches (3.5 metres) and most were in the 13 feet to 16 feet-plus (4 to 5 metres) size range.

The victims were usually taken by surprise. One or two had time to scream. But most often the attack was swift and soundless, culminating in the swirl of water which saw the last of the victim.

Though there were sometimes witnesses, the recorded attacks usually were completed so quickly that there was nothing which could have been done to help the victims.

One of the most remarkable escapes was that of Mrs Platner Chudualla, a 54-year-old Aboriginal woman from Kalumburu Mission, in north-western Australia.

On 8 May 1976, she was at a fishing spot about eight kilometres from the mission when she was seized by the arm by a five-metre crocodile and dragged into deep water. The bite crushed her forearm and shattered the bones.

Then the crocodile changed its grip. Taking her by the right thigh it swam off, dragging her below the surface for more than 50 metres.

Then, as she was sure that she would die, the crocodile— astoundingly—let her go. Bleeding and terrified she swam back to the bank. Later she was flown to the Derby hospital where she recovered after a series of operations to rebuild her smashed forearm.

The final fatal attack for 1987 was at the tip of Cape York Peninsula. Torres Strait Islander Cornwall Mooka of Mabuiag Island left his dinghy to walk to Cowal Creek on 27 June. Later, leg bones and clothing were washed up on the beach. A week later an 11-foot (3.3-metre) crocodile was shot by National Parks officers and human remains were found inside it.

In most cases the people taken by crocodiles were in the water when the attack took place. Exceptions to this were Val Plumwood, who was trying to climb a tree from water level, and Kerry McLoughlin, who had just dragged himself out of the water by a fallen tree at Cahill's Crossing on the East Alligator.

In all instances the unfortunate people killed were intruders in crocodile territory. But for every attack there must have been hundreds, perhaps thousands, of people who had been in a situation where they might have been attacked but who got away with it. Either there were no crocodiles at that point, or if there were they weren't hungry or weren't interested. The fact is that while some crocodiles, like sharks, attack humans, the majority do not. Statistically, those who became victims were desperately unlucky. The most remarkable thing is not how often crocodiles attack people but rather the reverse. It is surprising that with all the chances offered by humans, crocodiles attack so seldom. Nonetheless, for safety, it has to be assumed that any large crocodile may be attracted to human prey in certain circumstances.

When the attacks do occur they earn a nationwide notoriety for crocodiles which often seems to be out of logical proportion to the actual threat. The death of American Ginger Meadows at the Prince Regent, in 1987, for instance, became an international incident.

The instinct to protect—looking after our own—is strong in the human race. It is a desirable trait and one reason why *Homo sapiens* is the most successful animal alive.

But it does make for a difficulty in our relationship with other animals. We tend to see things only from one side.

The dislike of crocodiles as a creature which can eat people is understandable. We sometimes take this to an extreme where the fear of a man-eating predator amounts to a national phobia, as it does in the case of sharks and crocodiles. Perhaps it goes back to the misty shadow memories of our ancestors. A time when "things which went bump in the night" were no joke, but deadly and life-threatening. A time when the red eyes of hungry predators glowed in the darkness beyond the protective fire at the mouth of the cave. A reason, also, why a log fire still makes us feel so cosy and safe.

Human survival in the face of so many natural enemies must have been desperate indeed. Today there are few creatures left which eat people and confrontations with terror are no longer a part of daily existence.

But when an attack does occur, as in the case of Ginger Meadows, it revives all those ancient horrors. Perhaps this is why we react so dramatically.

Our thinking on the subject is more emotional than logical. While crocodiles may have killed somewhere between 50 and 150 people in Australia in the past 100 years, the numbers are a pinprick compared with our decimation of the crocodile population. Some 113,000 skins were shipped out of the Northern Territory in the 1950s and '60s, with other consignments from Queensland and Western Australia.

Similarly we call sharks 'man-eaters' regardless of species, and every shark caught and killed by 'sportsmen' is a death justified on that account. But hundreds of thousands of sharks are caught off Australian coasts each year in nets and set-lines, most of them to be eaten by humans as fish and chips.

In any such comparison it is man who is the major predator. A killer so technically efficient, that we have pushed whole species of animals to extermination. And while crocodiles and sharks kill simply to eat, humans have killed large numbers of animals large and small for amusement. For 'sport'.

Both sharks and crocodiles are interesting creatures. If we regard them merely as objects of irrational horror, we are depriving ourselves of an understanding of animals which evolved to a balance in the environment long before we came on the scene.

As Val Plumwood put it, a crocodile is not a creature you could come to love. Only another crocodile of the opposite sex could do that—and they do it very well.

But our tendency is to look at animals simply in terms of their use to humans. 'Good' animals are dogs which protect and love us, cats which eat mice and purr affectionately, hens which lay eggs, cows which provide milk and meat. 'Bad' animals are foxes which eat the hens, wolves which eat the sheep. Particularly 'evil' animals are those which have the temerity to eat people.

Crocodiles may one day become 'useful' to us in an industrial sense. When they are raised in artificial situations in farms or crocodile ranches they can provide skins for a lucrative world market. They have the potential to be a major tourist attraction and tourism has rapidly become one of Australia's most important industries.

Though they will never make cuddly pets, and would always definitely be of doubtful value for giving rides at a children's party, crocodiles have their own unique qualities and they were, after all, around long before man.

At Gantheaume Point, at Broome, the pearling port of Western Australia, there are a set of three-toed dinosaur footprints indented in the red rock by the sea.

The creature which made them, an individual of the species *Megalosaurus*, had a two-metre stride and passed that way 70 millions years ago when the rock was mud.

At that time there were crocodilians in the ocean and in the swamps. Today the dinosaur is long extinct and remembered only by the impressions left by its feet. The crocodilians are still with us. Alive.

ATTACK—EXPECT THE UNEXPECTED

▲▲▲▲▲▲▲▲▲▲▲

What makes a crocodile attack?

What should you do on finding yourself—despite all reasonable precautions—in the unenviable situation of a Ginger Meadows or a Val Plumwood?

In fact, there are a number of moves that can be made to effectively fend off or frustrate an attack. Knowledge of what to do in those most difficult circumstances might have saved poor Ginger Meadows' life at the Prince Regent on 29 March 1987.

It is easy to be wise after an event, of course. Much more difficult to make the right split-second decision when confronted by the terrifying sight of a hungry predator that has your measure. But when a situation goes sadly wrong the experience should not be wasted. We learn from mistakes—our own and those made by others—and the knowledge gained from one tragedy sometimes prevents others in the future.

Mankind, originally the weakest and most vulnerable species, has outstripped the rest of the animal world precisely because of our ability to learn and capitalise on past errors and defeats. Today that problem-solving ability is channelled into such far-out projects as space travel, 'thinking' computers and satellite communication.

Though the sabre-toothed tigers which once terrorised our ancestors are long since extinct (we found the answer for *them*), we still have a horror-struck fascination for large and dangerous animals which kill people. A fatal shark or crocodile attack is guaranteed nationwide headlines. An unfortunate person dying in a motor accident may rate only a couple of lines in the back pages of a local newspaper. *C'est la vie!* as the French have it. That's life.

But how could Ginger Meadows have been saved?

The answer must remain hypothetical. Nevertheless there were things the two girls, Jane Burchett and Ginger Meadows, could have done on that day which would have delayed the onset of the attack or perhaps averted it altogether. Buying time can be critical.

Remember that if they had only another 90 seconds or so of time Steve Hilton might have been able to reach them with the boat and either rescue them or frighten the crocodile off.

It can be dangerous to lay down precise rules for crocodile behaviour. Their method of operation, after all, is surprise and the only firm rule should be to 'expect the unexpected'.

But there are particular behaviour patterns that are characteristic of the crocodilians and we can benefit by studying them. Knowledge of what crocodiles can and cannot do, and their likely reactions to our own movements could only be of help to someone finding himself or herself suddenly in a bad crocodile situation. And it is almost always sudden.

"What do we do now?" were Ginger's last words. The same desperate question must have occurred to anyone faced with an imminent attack. The decision of what to do, or especially what *not* to do, becomes critical at that moment. "Forewarned", as the saying has it, "is forearmed".

The crocodile's reputation in attack is for ferocity and aggression.

This is because he is basically an ambush animal, preferring to attack from concealment. When the crocodile explodes out of the water—to the surprise and dismay of the victim—the elements of ferocity and aggression are certainly there.

But few people realise that in the preliminaries to the attack a crocodile is both cautious and wary.

He is careful to grasp prey (or try to) where it cannot hurt him. He grabs a bullock or a buffalo by the nose as much to avoid the horns as because it is a deadly grip. All predators display such caution. In the continuing struggle for existence, risks are unaffordable. A thorough knowledge of self-preservation is the only way a crocodile gets to be big at all.

There is also a second reason for the calculated and cautious approach to prey. If an intended victim is frightened by a crocodile and escapes, it has an unforgettable memory of the event. It becomes more difficult to catch in future and can communicate its wariness to members of its species in the area when the time comes to go down to the river to drink. This may make the other animals shy and hard to approach. Life becomes harder for the crocodile.

In the old hunters' terms the quarry becomes 'spooked'.

So it is in a crocodile's interest not to begin or to press an attack unless it is reasonably sure of success.

Crocodiles, like humans, will respond quickly to a random opportunity if it occurs. But because they don't need to eat often— one of the advantages of the reptile metabolism—their usual *modus operandi* is 'wait and watch'. They observe animal or human movements for some time before they manoeuvre into position to make a strike. When they do—watch out—because all the advantages will be on their side!

The old Territory bushman's tradition about crocodiles is that they watch for patterns. Most humans and animals are creatures of habit. If a traveller arrives at a river and goes down to fill his billy, or if a bullock ambles down to drink, the chances are that next time they will both go to exactly the same place. And the next time too.

"An old man croc sees you the first day," the old timers would say. "But you don't see him. Next day he moves closer. Third day—look out!"

Tradition has it that experienced bushmen never filled their billies or water-bottles twice at the same place when in crocodile country, though logically it would seem that if crocodiles developed a fear of people, the most-used places—fords and river landings—would be the safest.

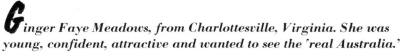

*G*inger Faye Meadows, from Charlottesville, Virginia. She was
young, confident, attractive and wanted to see the 'real Australia.'

*D*espite their remote location, many tourist and charter boats call at the Cascades. Until the tragedy of March 1987, visitors sometimes swam there.

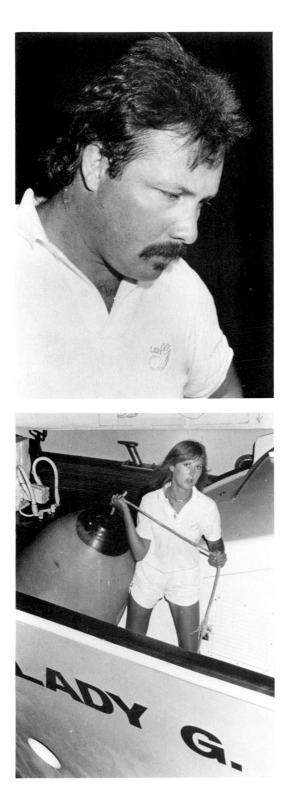

Skipper Bruce Fitz-patrick. He saw the crocodile first but had to watch horrified, powerless to help.

Madeleine Janes. "The crocodile seemed to go around behind Ginger. Then it got her."

*T*he search craft Penguin. Crocodiles leapt to snatch at the body carried just in front of the windscreen.

Baby crocodiles bite hard from birth but face an uncertain future.

(below) *Coquettish female crocodile in the submissive pose.*

*V*al Plumwood. Despite her shocking wounds, "I respect the crocodile's right to life."

*B*eryl Wruck. A
happy Christmas party
of friends at the Butter-
fly Farm was trans-
formed into a night
of horror.

*J*ohn Robb was
beside Beryl Wruck as
the crocodile lunged
from the darkness and
seized her.

Beryl Wruck's killer lies dead on the bank. In its stomach were human remains which stopped the evil stories.

*C*ahill's Crossing, on the East Alligator River, where a crocodile
decapitated Kerry McLoughlin.

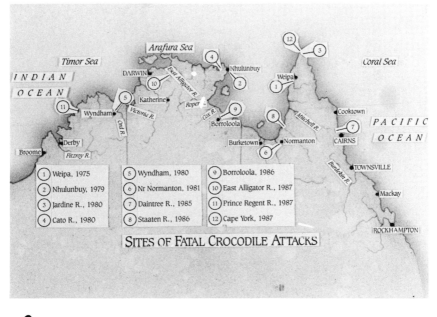

*S*ites of Fatal Crocodile Attacks

*C*rocodiles feed on kangaroos, pigs and large mammals, including buffalo.

CROCODILE DISTRIBUTION IN AUSTRALIA

Timor Sea

Arafura Sea

Torres Strait

INDIAN OCEAN

DARWIN

East Alligator R.

Nhulunbuy

Coral Sea

Weipa

Katherine

Roper R.

Gulf of Carpentaria

Cooktown

Wyndham

Victoria R.

Ord R.

Cox R.

Borroloola

Mitchell R.

CAIRNS

PACIFIC OCEAN

Broome

Derby

Fitzroy R.

NORTHERN TERRITORY

Burketown

Leichhardt R.

Normanton

Flinders R.

Burdekin R.

TOWNSVILLE

WESTERN AUSTRALIA

MOUNT ISA

QUEENSLAND

Mackay

ROCKHAMPTON

Saltwater crocodile

Freshwater crocodile

(above) **C**rocodile
Distribution in Australia

(left) **'G**ator, at the
Ballarat Wildlife Rep-
tile Park, shows how
high an agile croc
can go.

(above) *A man and his pet. Vic Cox and 'Henry' have known each other for 27 years.*

(right) *Two big crocodiles shot in pre-war days in the Territory. Note the formidable sex apparatus of male crocodiles.*

(above) *A 14 ft crocodile drowned in a barramundi fisherman's net, a current conservation problem. It also shows the remarkable crocodilian male organ.*

(left) *Dr. Grahame Webb, crocodile consultant to the Northern Territory Conservation Commission, ponders the future of this tiny porosus, only a few minutes out of the egg.*

*F*eeding time at the Broome Crocodile Park. Tourists watch entranced.

Regardless, it does seem that crocodiles prefer not to make an attack if they are at all unsure. They may back off at the last moment if the situation becomes unfavourable. This is where humans prepared in mental or physical terms can sometimes bluff their way out of trouble, in just the same way that a diver can sometimes bluff a shark out of attacking by a show of confidence.

We could learn a good deal from the Aborigines who lived with crocodiles in northern Australia for 40,000 years. In that time crocodiles ate many tribespeople—especially women and children. It was part of the cycle of life. Though Aborigines were sensibly afraid of large crocodiles they were an inseparable fact of life. Like the other creatures in the environment they were part of the Aboriginal 'family' and were included as honoured members in their mythology and ceremonial life. Aborigines also ate crocodile eggs and killed and ate small to medium-sized crocodiles if they found them in situations which were to their advantage—in a drying-out billabong, for instance. There was a natural balance.

In the course of everyday life northern coastal Aborigines spent a good deal of their time in or close by the water in areas where they were at risk from crocodiles. They speared fish or caught crabs in the shallows. Often they swam some of the more dangerous crocodile rivers. They paddled rafts and canoes on the estuaries and open sea.

How did they escape crocodile attacks?

The answer is that they didn't. But Aborigines lived by observation of the movement of animals. They had incredibly keen eyesight by white standards and could tell from a distance where crocodiles were and whether their behaviour indicated likely hunger. They were also usually armed. A man did not move without his spears and usually also carried a club or killing boomerang, depending on the situation or the day. If an Aborigine was surprised by a crocodile—an unusual event since they usually knew where the big ones were—they could often fight them off. Even a monster crocodile finds a jab in the eye from a spear most painful and inconvenient. An effective deterrent.

Women also carried digging sticks which were heavy and had

fire-hardened sharp ends. They could be used as formidable clubs or for eye-jabbing if need be.

When Aborigines crossed a crocodile river they preferred to do it as an organised group. In the Kimberleys they swam with small trees pushed under and ahead of them, spears and clubs at the ready on the branches. They could mount an effective defence. Kimberley dugong-hunters used to swirl many miles out to sea on outgoing tides, capture their dugong and drift back on the next intide. On the rare occasion of a crocodile coveting the blood-dripping red meat on the rafts, it could be beaten off with paddles and heavy dugong spears. Sometimes the hunters jabbed at eyes with a fire stick from the little fires they had on their rafts.

Big crocodiles—creatures which have been shown to learn quickly from experience—probably had painful encounters with Aborigines at some time in their life, perhaps when they were smaller animals. An angry tribesman with a club or a killing spear is something to remember. Crocodiles definitely recall such experiences and, regardless of size, would probably have been cautious about attacking Aborigines with weapons in their hands.

When shooters were hunting the big rivers and mangrove creeks of the north in the 1950s and '60s, they found that crocodiles learned about danger very quickly. After a day or so of successful shooting, the surviving crocodiles became so wary of the hunters that they disappeared at the first sight of a boat or the sound of human voices. Large survivors from that period are still wary of people.

But crocodiles which have grown to large size in northern Australia since 1972 have never had any reason to be afraid of people —black or white. Where once every man, Aborigine or European, went armed, today's tourists seldom carry anything more lethal than a 35 mm camera. Jane Burchett had only her running shoes. But—intelligently and courageously—she still managed to buy some time by throwing a shoe at the attacking crocodile. The fact that the crocodile stopped shows how little is sometimes needed to prevent or delay an attack.

However, the current time is perhaps the most dangerous in all history for potential crocodile attacks in northern Australia. This is because of a combination of factors. First, there is the lack of fear of protected crocodiles. Add to this the burgeoning increase in crocodile numbers and the lack of personal protection (weapons) and knowledge among the visitors. In the 1980s tourists in the Territory were increasing at a rate of 25–30 per cent a year. More people, more crocodiles.

Add one other consideration. People who have lived in the north, especially those in the Northern Territory, had become used to a situation where crocodiles were rare and timid. In 1977 they would wade in estuaries, fish for barramundi waist-deep in tidal rivers and go swimming safely in flood-plain billabongs— places where it would be utmost folly to venture in 1988.

But in some cases the thinking of the 'locals' has not yet caught up with the reality. "It was OK before, why not now?" they ask. A crocodile occasionally provides an answer.

In fact, a surprising proportion of the fatalities of the 1980s involved people who were northern residents. These included Aborigines. Though some in Arnhem Land still carry spears today, others are urbanised and have become as vulnerable a crocodile target as anyone else.

A comparison is sometimes made between crocodile and shark attacks.

For many years sharks were the national Australian phobia. Every popular beach has its surf patrol, shark tower and shark alarm siren. When a psychological test was run in the 1970s to determine the reaction of Australians to various words using 'lie-detection' equipment, 'SHARK' was the word which made the needle jump the highest. Shark attacks grabbed headlines each summer. Until 1987 when crocodiles overtook them in the monster stakes.

As a diver I spent a good deal of time filming and photographing sharks. Some of the comparisons between sharks and crocodiles are interesting. But there are probably more differences than similarities.

For example, there is only one species of man-eating crocodile in Australia, *Crocodylus porosus*. The only other crocodile in Australia, *Crocodylus johnstoni*, the freshwater crocodile, is harmless to man, though it can bite defensively if provoked. But several species of sharks—widely differing in temperament and physical characteristics—have been involved in human fatalities. Great White sharks, Tiger sharks, Whalers, Makoes, Hammerheads and Grey Nurse have all been named in attacks. Great Whites, Tigers and Whalers feature as regular man-killers. The pre-attack behaviour of each species is quite different.

Sharks are opportunistic feeders. They do not, as far as we know, wait around and plan attacks in the way crocodiles do.

Unlike crocodiles some sharks 'show' before an attack. Whalers and Tiger sharks circle a prospective victim often for long periods before moving in. But the Great White shark, *Carcharodon carcharias*, the biggest of all man-eating sharks, growing to 20 feet (6.1 metres) and 4000 pounds (2000 kilograms), disdains the preliminaries. Divers who have survived White shark attacks seldom saw the shark before they were hit. Whites come in hard and fast.

In 1963 Rodney Fox, one of Australia's leading spearfishermen and a favourite for the State title, was swimming in the South Australian Spearfishing Championships at Aldinga Beach. His account of the shark attack which nearly took his life compares with Val Plumwood's similar ordeal with the crocodile in the East Alligator River in 1985.

Late on the afternoon of the competition, when shadows were long in the water, he glided down for a shot on a big morwong. It was a fish which would have clinched the title for him. As his finger tightened on the trigger he sensed rather than felt everything go still in the water around him.

"It was a silence . . . a perceptible hush . . . then something huge hit me on the left side with enormous force and surged me through the water. I knew at once what had happened and was dazed with horror.

"I felt sick, nauseous. My mask was knocked off and everything was blurred. There was a queer sensation as though my insides were all squeezed over on one side. I reached behind and groped for the shark's eyes. At that point it let go of me and I pushed my arm down its throat by accident.

"With the release of pressure uncontrollable agony swept over me. But at least I was free. As I kicked for the surface I felt the shark under my flippers all the way. As I gulped air I felt the scrape of his hide and wrapped myself around him so he couldn't bite again.

"The shark took me back to the bottom. We rolled around, scraping weed and rocks, and I let go, desperate again for air. On the surface there was red everywhere. My own blood." And through it all the head of the shark appeared. Conical snout, great rolling body, like a rust-coloured tree trunk in the blood.

"Terror flowed through my body. But just before the shark reached me again, it veered away and I felt the tug of the fish float line on my belt. The shark had grabbed the fish on my float and suddenly I was jerked below again and towed nine or ten metres on my own line. It seemed ridiculous to die of drowning after all I'd been through. But my fumbling fingers couldn't undo the belt to release the line.

"Then it parted, perhaps on the shark's teeth, and I floated up to the surface . . . "

Fox was terribly injured. His lungs were punctured, rib-cage, lungs, stomach exposed, ribs crushed, arm ripped to the bone. Fortunately his wetsuit held his mutilated body together and, even more fortunately, a boat was close by as part of the competition supervision.

He was in a hospital in Adelaide within an hour on his last reserves of strength and almost on his last litres of blood.

He lived, through his fitness and determination and some gifted surgery, to go diving again. There was one added factor, an essential ingredient in Val Plumwood's survival too—courage.

I spent a lot of time filming Great White sharks at the Cheynes Beach Whaling Station in Albany, Western Australia from 1976 to 1978, when whaling finished. We had a camera cage moored alongside dead sperm whales tethered to a pontoon half a mile offshore from the factory flensing deck. Blood tinged the water around the cage and it was an eerie location, which set the scalp prickling under a rubber wetsuit hood even before a shark was sighted.

When a Great White did appear it was an experience to be remembered for the rest of a lifetime. With their wide pectoral fins, pale almost ghostly presence and their effortless movement, they looked like giant aeroplanes gliding past. Though the plan was to take minimum risks, there were considerable elements of danger. A story for another time.

We pushed things to the limits in the shark cage. But with some luck we got away with it. We got film and still photographs of Great Whites in their own environment which would have been impossible otherwise.

It would be equally interesting to take pictures of crocodiles underwater, and it is a challenge to be considered. Ben Cropp has taken some nice shots of freshwater crocodiles. But it might not be practical to use a cage with a half-metre camera gap for big saltwater crocodiles as we did with the white sharks. *Porosus*, I have a feeling, with his evil yellow eyes, would quickly work out how to get into the cage. Or how to get us out. Swimming with big crocodiles without a cage could be a short-term proposition. Apart from the immediate (and not inconsiderable) problem of being bitten, the dirty water and lack of visibility in most tropical crocodile habitats would pose difficulties.

As a final comparison with sharks, I think that crocodiles are equally formidable and more calculating. But they are also a cautious animal. Crocodile attacks, like shark attacks, could be deflected in the right circumstances if you kept your head. Given a choice of facing a crocodile or a shark I'd take the shark every time. But that is an old diver's view. A preference for the Devil I know.

How do you deflect a crocodile attack?

The feeding of crocodiles at the Darwin crocodile farm is an experience no visitor to the Northern Territory should miss. When I was there in 1987 photographing, it was most interesting to see how easily even big crocodiles could be turned away at the last moment if conditions did not exactly suit them. They were fed chickens twice a week, and in the winter, two chickens in this period seemed to be ample even for the largest crocodiles. Some captive crocodiles do not eat for a period of several months in cold weather and it is claimed (but not proven) that in certain circumstances a crocodilian can fast for a year.

Some of the crocodiles at the farm would make a slithering rush up out of the water, jaws open in the most alarming and threatening manner. But they would often balk at the slightest movement in the crowd watching, or be disconcerted by some minor and unexpected action by the feeder. If this happened, often as not, they would turn around and hustle back into the water. There they would lie watching and waiting with suspicious eyes before they tried again.

This was a confirmation of the theories about crocodile caution —the need to be sure of all circumstances before committing to an attack. It appeared to me that a stubborn man with a stout stick could have bluffed the crocodiles out of taking the chickens without much difficulty.

Of course they were well-fed crocodiles. Any of the rules about crocodiles in the wild can change if you meet one that is desperately hungry, or has been wounded and unable to catch prey. The time of the year I was at the farm was September, the end of the cool period. From November through to March in the hot summer months, male crocodiles become much more aggressive and active. The man with the stick would surely have to watch his footwork. But I still think that someone with skill and confidence could deflect an attack with a good pole. A small dinghy oar would be ideal and this is all that the Northern Territory Conservation Commission field workers use to keep angry female crocodiles at bay when taking eggs from nests in the wild for research.

There was another interesting phenomenon at the farm. I had arranged with Nick Robinson, the reptile manager, to photograph the feeding. Normally this was done on Sundays and Wednesdays. I suggested an informal session on a Tuesday when there was no crowd so that I could go inside the fence alongside the man handing out the chickens for close-up shots.

Nick went to the water's edge with a basket of dead chickens. The attempt was a total failure. None of the big crocodiles in the main pond would feed. A couple did come slowly up out of the water to eye the chickens dubiously. But at the critical moment they refused them. We felt particularly stupid. There we were, being eyed off by dozens of supercilious saurians, whose unwinking expressions plainly said, "Silly humans—they don't even know what day of the week it is. We eat on Wednesdays."

We came back next day—Wednesday—and the crocodiles fed with zest. Chicken after chicken disappeared down snapping jaws. Sometimes the crocodiles came out of the water at a rapid pace. Others were more cautious. But most took the food with that characteristic lightning sideways snap that makes human observers shudder.

Apart from insisting on being fed on 'their' schedule (like smart dolphins who often 'train their trainers'), they all followed a pattern once they had taken a chicken. They did not eat on the bank but took the chickens back into the water. There they submerged and 'drowned' the already dead birds, making them easier to swallow with wet feathers. Then they came back to the surface and 'showed', with their heads held high out of the water. They crushed the prey with a chewing-snapping motion to break up all the bones before they finally swallowed it all at a gulp, heads still high so that no water went down their gullet flaps.

Contrary to the legend, crocodiles do not prefer rotting meat. They will take their food fresh if it is small enough. If it is a bird —magpie geese are a favourite morsel—they eat it at once with apparent relish. With bigger animals, particularly buffalo with tough hides, they have no option but to wait for decomposition. Their teeth, as we have seen, are spikes for holding or tearing. They have no facility for cutting firm flesh like sharks feeding on a dead whale.

A hungry crocodile will feed on even putrid material. But generally, crocodiles in the wild have a good selection of food. Northern Australian waters abound in catfish, barramundi, turtles, stingrays, mullet and small sharks. Crocodiles also eat numbers of birds and are quick enough to occasionally snatch them on the wing.

Large mammal prey—horses, cows, buffaloes, wallabies, wild pigs and dingoes—all feature in the diet of big 'Old Man' crocodiles. But they are probably an occasional supplementary luxury and the main bulk is marine creatures. Just as the Great White sharks are especially fond of whale or seal or dolphin, their everyday diet is stingray or tuna.

Crocodiles sometimes capture prey which exceeds their own weight by skilful use of terrain. In 1939 a huge Suffolk 'draughthorse' stallion—itself weighing a ton and capable of a pull of two tons—was dragged into a Northern Territory river and drowned.

Horses, buffaloes and cattle are captured at known drinking spots at the foot of steep muddy banks. When an unwary animal comes down to drink the crocodile seizes it by the nose—a soft, painful area and vulnerable because when it is held closed the animal cannot breathe. Once the nose is grabbed the crocodile throws the animal ju-jitsu fashion by twisting itself violently in the motion called the 'death roll' in the popular press. It is an accurate description.

When the unfortunate animal is down, it is easy for the crocodile to drag the beast struggling down the slippery mud slope into the water to drown. An alternative—if the first grasp at the nose misses—is to flail at the animal's legs with the crocodile's heavy and immensely powerful tail. This can bring even a buffalo down, sometimes breaking legs at the same time.

All these ploys aside, the easiest way for a crocodile to capture prey is still to catch it in the water. A swimming animal or human makes by far the easiest target. Horses which persist in cooling off in hot weather are frequent targets in station country, especially if they have been bred in non-crocodile areas and don't know the local survival rules.

There is evidence that crocodiles are cautious about catching human prey. After all, from their perspective, we are both large and unknown creatures. With the crocodilian requirement for the odds to be in their favour it is interesting to note that in most of the known cases of Australian human fatalities the victims were in the water.

Crocodiles have plucked Aborigines and New Guinea tribesmen from dugout canoes. In the great river deltas of New Guinea, old people (especially mothers-in-law) have to sit at the rear of the canoe. Crocodiles traditionally take the last person sitting in the stern.

Despite their undoubted capacity to do so, crocodiles seldom take human prey off banks or beaches. Usually the victim is a swimmer.

Among the popular legends is the notion that a crocodile 'can run as fast as a galloping horse'. Small crocodiles, especially the freshwater Johnstones, can indeed move quickly over sandbanks. 'Freshies' cover ground in a distinctive galloping motion, up on their hind legs and have been timed at speeds as fast as 18 km/h. Even big 'salties' can slide down a muddy river bank to water quite rapidly in a wriggling, slithering, toboggan motion. Small *porosus* (up to 2.5 metres) are also relatively agile, and often do a 'high walk', bodies well clear of the mud while crossing over low-tide flats.

But the idea that the big saltwater crocodiles can get up on their hind legs and sprint like a 'freshie' or a desert goanna is disputed by most people who know crocodiles. They have too much weight and bulk. When coming up to bask they usually let the tide lift them up to where they want to go. Later they slide down again without raising their bellies off the mud.

However, the smell of a dead animal will readily bring big crocodiles methodically crawling up and over banks to tear at a carcass. The sight sometimes seen by helicopter pilots flying over the Ord River in Western Australia of several large crocodiles wriggling and riping at a dead bullock is like a scene from primeval days.

There is a story of a hungry crocodile which marched up out of a river to a campfire and made off with a roasting pig—to the dismay of the intending diners and terrible language from the cook.

Territorians tell tales of waking to find the star tracks of crocodiles around their tents in wilderness camps. During the war a monster crocodile was supposed to have waddled up out of a river and seized an army cook who had set up his camp stretcher on the coolness of the bank. The story says that the crocodile picked up the cook complete with stretcher and mosquito net. The cook's cries brought the guards running. The crocodile was dispatched with a volley of .303 shots. The quality of the food in the mess at the time left something to be desired and the rescue was not popular in all quarters. Thereafter in the mess, when some particularly disgusting offering was served up, the troops would all chant "Who shot the crocodile?"

Chris Burchett, the Aboriginal liaison officer for the Northern Territory Tourist Commission, once had a crocodile go between himself and his children to snatch a dog on a river bank.

But generally, the crocodile's first preference is to capture his prey swimming. His second, to grab it on the edge of the water and drag it quickly in. They are essentially predators of the water's edge designed by nature to take prey either on land next to water or when swimming.

Crocodile handlers say that the safest place to be with a crocodile is right in front of it. Crocodiles do not move forward quickly from a standing start. They can swim out of the water and carry the impetus some metres at a sliding, slithering rush. But on shore their most effective move is a lightning sideways lunge which sometimes spins them completely around. It is far quicker than human reactions.

Often they spin the opposite way to what you might expect, with tail whirling to increase momentum. This can also confuse prey and throw it off balance.

What should you do if you are attacked?

The days when all Territorians carried a revolver on the hip, or a Winchester or .303 rifle slung casually over a shoulder, are gone. Visitors to national parks are sensibly not allowed to bring firearms in. But a good stick (or staff) is a convenience when walking and scrambling up and down hills, and it is also an excellent defensive weapon.

Besides crocodiles in the north, it is possible to strike the odd maverick and dangerous land animal of other species. Scrub bulls, wild boars, a cranky buffalo and snakes can all cause their particularly individual problems. Down in the desert fringes even bull camels in season can be dangerous. A stout stick of selected thickness greatly increases the chances of escaping unhurt should you ever be 'bailed up' in a close-quarters confrontation. As a last resort, the prod or bayonet jab, incidentally, tends to be a more effective means of keeping belligerents at a safe distance than baseball swings or whacks.

Coolness and determination, of course, help considerably. Natural commonsense says that the animal should never be poked, prodded or hit unless in dire emergency. You may simply goad it into going for you.

But all animals are very much aware of confidence. The main use for the stick is to keep that important space of distance between you and them. Not all the aggressors are males. Never underestimate a scrub cow with a calf nearby, or a female buffalo, or a mother crocodile with eggs.

When pressed, surprising things make effective weapons. Even a 35 mm camera, hurled or swung like a flail on the end of its strap, can deliver a hefty wallop.

It has been suggested that if there is more than one person involved, it is better to stay close together. Predators dislike having to handle more than one object to attack. Sharks seldom attack two divers together. Eye interaction plays a part. On the few occasions I have had real problems with sharks as a diver, I found that they tended to charge when I took my eye off them. Eyes indicate intentions and animals (like boxers and card players) watch them closely. Having two pairs of eyes to watch at once is a confusion for the attacker.

You may have noticed that your dog or cat dislikes the direct stare. In animals it usually precedes an attack. Crocodiles themselves have eyes which are conspicuous in attack—a trait remarked on by people like Val Plumwood who have survived such encounters.

Most crocodile attacks are made on single persons. If there is more than one, then the last to get out of the water or the individual on the edge of a group, is usually most at risk.

Kate McQuarrie, the 31-year-old deckhand taken by a crocodile while swimming out to the prawn trawler *Kiama* in the Staaten River in February 1986, was seized only after the skipper Bob McNeil had climbed out of the water to help her aboard. The crocodile, a huge beast, had probably trailed them both for some distance as they swam side by side from the shore. But while there were two of them together it did not attack, preferring to wait until there was a single target.

If Ginger Meadows had stayed with Jane Burchett instead of swimming off on her own she might have been alive today. The two girls standing with their backs to the rock were in a situation which would have made it very difficult for the crocodile to attack them effectively. He would have been pondering how to split them up or get them away from the rock wall.

While Jane splashed water at him, screamed defiance and threw her shoe, the crocodile held back, unsure what to do. She did naturally what was absolutely the best thing to do in the circumstances.

But when Ginger tragically made a break for it, she presented the crocodile with the situation he most preferred—a single swimmer target.

It is easy to be wise after the event. But if Ginger had stayed still with her back to the wall just a little longer, or perhaps joined Jane in throwing shoes at the reptile, Steve Hilton might have reached them in the boat in time. Another minute might have done it. Who knows? At this late hour we can only join in her family's sorrow for Ginger Meadows.

Experts do agree that movement is a trigger with crocodiles. This is true of most predatory wild animals including sharks. Run and they go for you.

In a marginal situation, pause to assess. If you can make ground, do so. But try not to panic. And never take your eyes off their eyes.

You can often 'eyeball' a dangerous animal into backing away. If you appear confident and aggressive, the animal's own doubt grows. You can use the crocodile's natural caution against it.

There are no medals in the animal world. In the jungle demonstrations of courage, for the sake of it, would be simply foolhardy. A wounded animal may be unable to catch prey and can become a target for other aggressors. Attackers choose to kill without risk. Most big predators in unfamiliar situations—and man is unfamiliar prey—tend to err on the side of caution. When in doubt they back out. But be careful not to block their escape route.

Everyone has met, at some time, an aggressive dog. Muzzle drawn back, teeth bared, he growls and barks at you. If you run, nothing is more sure than that you are going to be chased and bitten.

But if you hold your ground, talk to the dog calmly and firmly, he will most often back off, though he still growls and barks at a distance. Saving face is important even in the animal world. Sometimes you have to look angry and menacing, as though you are going to bite *him*.

I have used the angry-dog technique on sharks, to induce a

'Mexican stand-off' in which the shark threatens but finally backs away. When it is all you have left, bluff often does the trick. But you have to convince yourself to be convincing. It helps—silly as it may sound—to actually growl yourself as you put on your best threat display.

Even when only one person is involved and the odds have been seemingly hopeless, there have been miraculous escapes. Val Plumwood's sheer persistence was one example.

But others have jammed their thumbs in crocodiles' eyes and succeeded by other desperate means. One unusual method recommended by Africans (who should know since crocodiles eat more people in Africa than anywhere else) to make a crocodile let go of someone in its jaws is to bite its forefeet. Others have hammered on horny heads or broken the grip by main desperation.

In May 1986 a Zambezi River crocodile seized Jeremy, the 13-year-old son of South African tourist Hugh Lloyd, aged 45, while they were getting into a canoe. Lloyd jumped into the river and, plunging his arm down the reptile's throat, broke the gullet seal, forcing it to let go.

Lloyd's arm was bitten off below the elbow before a tour guide hit the reptile and finally forced it away. But Jeremy was saved, with injuries to his arm.

One of the things to remember is that a crocodile has limited reserves of energy and quickly exhausts itself. If you can persevere in trying to save yourself or someone else it may eventually tire and give up the struggle, as the crocodile did with Val Plumwood.

A surprising number of attempted rescues—where another person can get hold of the victim or harass the crocodile—are successful for this reason.

In 1981 Peta-Lynn Mann showed that even a 13-year-old girl can tip the scales in a battle with a 13-foot (4-metre) crocodile.

She had been out in an airboat on the Daly River with Hilton Graham, a 23-year-old employee in the safari camp operated by her parents Rob and Wendy Mann 110 kilometres south of Darwin.

As they came in to the mooring point Hilton leaned over to pick up the anchor line and the revolver he carried for emergencies fell out of its holster into the water, which was a little more than knee deep.

As he knelt in the muddy water, feeling for the firearm, a huge crocodile surged in and grabbed his arm. The grip was so powerful it broke his forearm. As it spun him around the crocodile tried to drag him back into deeper water. But Peta grabbed his other arm and refused to let go.

Three times the crocodile opened its jaws and seized Graham again, trying for a more effective grip. At one stage it tore out a big section of flesh from his right buttock. But Peta-Lynn—later awarded the Royal Humane Society's highest award for bravery —kept hold in a tug of war that eventually brought them to the bank and saved Hilton Graham's life.

Even then the crocodile left the water and followed them. But Peta-Lynn's persistence won out and they reached their vehicle and locked themselves inside. The girl then drove the dazed and bleeding man 10 kilometres back to camp to raise the alarm.

But for her determination and all of the 13-year-old strength she could muster, Hilton Graham would probably have been another statistic in the file of crocodile-caused mortalities.

Never, *never* give up.

Of course, by the time you have got yourself in a position of peril, things have obviously gone much further than they should.

The Western Australian Government Department of Conservation and Land Management (CALM) puts out a pamphlet on crocodiles which contains most of the essential advice in a nutshell.

It gives the following sound advice:

- Observe the warning signs.
- Seek local or expert advice about crocodiles before swimming, camping, fishing or boating.
- There is a potential danger anywhere saltwater crocodiles occur. If there is any doubt, do not swim, canoe or use small boats in estuaries, tidal rivers, deep pools or mangrove shores.
- Be aware. Keep your eyes open for large crocodiles. Children and pets are at particular risk in the water or at the water's edge.

- Do not paddle, clean fish, prepare food or camp at the water's edge. Fill a bucket with water and do your chores at least 50 metres away. Returning daily or regularly to the same spot at the water's edge is dangerous.
- Do not lean over the edge of a boat or stand on logs over-hanging water and don't hang articles over the edge of the boat.

One point which is not covered in most of the official warnings is the fact that many people are confused by the name 'saltwater crocodile'.

They think that—like the saltwater fish which cannot live in fresh water—*Crocodylus porosus* are found only in salt water. Not so. *Porosus* can be found many miles upstream in northern rivers. In Queensland, some travel hundreds of kilometres from the sea, and in the Northern Territory (and New Guinea) by far the highest densities of *porosus* are in freshwater swamps.

In fact, many of the biggest and therefore most dangerous 'saltwater' crocodiles live in inland freshwater lagoons because of the rich environment. The swamps teem with birds, barramundi and turtles. Wallabies, wild cattle and buffaloes come to drink there. Most 'saltwater' crocodile nesting also occurs in freshwater areas, or at least in areas that are fresh water a good part of the year.

Some of the areas of most risk are the picturesque Northern Territory floodplain lagoons with prolific bird life and water lilies covering the surface. The scene is so pretty that the casual observer would not expect to find anything more deadly than a dragonfly there. On the contrary, the floodplains are the very place where you may find a big crocodile in a virtual pond or even a buffalo wallow.

Saltwater crocodiles have been known to travel as much as 20 kilometres overland. Big crocodiles can sometimes be found hidden in creeks so small that they are virtually rivulets or drains off a main waterway. They lie there in unlikely places to trap a hapless pig or wallaby. A tourist might do as well.

Former shooters advise that people should be especially careful in riverbank or shore areas at night, where crocodiles may be out of the water, invisible amongst vegetation. Don't get between them and the water. Watch out for tracks and slides in crocodile country.

Finally crocodiles are nocturnal and most active at night. In warm weather they spend most of their time avoiding the sun and are difficult to see.

When you look around on a sunny afternoon and see an apparently empty and innocent sheet of northern water, it could be dangerous to assume that there are no crocodiles about. Concealment is a crocodile's particular trait. They can submerge an hour at a time and breathe under water-lily pads or floating vegetation. Big ones are specially wary and most adept at disguise and their approach along the bottom toward a point on the shore is stealthy and usually impossible to detect.

Expect the unexpected.

SEE YOU LATER ALLIGATOR— IN A WHILE CROCODILE

▲▲▲▲▲▲▲▲▲▲▲

A nyone looking at a map of tropical Australia could be excused for thinking that it is alligator territory.

The Northern Territory has the West Alligator, South Alligator and East Alligator Rivers. In Western Australia there is an Alligator Hill on the Fitzroy River and Alligator Creek at Beagle Bay. Queensland has a couple of Alligator Creeks and an Alligator Swamp.

Despite all this there are no alligators in Australia.

Alligators do exist in North and South America, and China. They are especially plentiful in the United States in the swamplands of Louisiana, Mississippi and Florida.

One real alligator did cause a temporary flurry of excitement in Perth, capital of Western Australia, some years ago, when a sighting was reported in a suburban lake. However, police and wildlife officers who hurried to the scene found that it was only a sad and long-deceased corpse. It turned out to be a preserved specimen which had been exhibited for years in a carnival sideshow. Finally, terminal decomposition set in and the appalling smell drove away more patrons than the long-suffering alligator attracted.

The wilting remains were dumped, and the practical joker who found them saw a marvellous opportunity to set up a 'crocodile' scare.

This kind of confusion between crocodiles and alligators has gone on for many years.

In the Northern Territory the leather-tough old bushmen who pioneered the river country called the big and hungry saltwater crocodiles which they encountered 'alligators' or often simply 'gators'. This distinguished them from the smaller, harmless freshwater or Johnstone's crocodiles usually called 'freshies'.

'Alligators' ate men, cattle and horses, and were damned dangerous. Freshwater crocodiles were all right—that was all the bushmen needed to know.

In the same way, Australians called the cheerful *Tursiops* bottlenose dolphins, so common in our estuaries and coastal waters, 'porpoises' right up to the 1970s.

The porpoise, a small Northern Hemisphere member of the whale family *Phocoeidae*, is related to the dolphin. But it is quite different in appearance, having a blunt head, unlike the familiar beak and cheeky grin of *Tursiops*. More importantly (like the alligator) porpoises are not found in Australia.

Nonetheless, there is a Porpoise Bay at Rottnest Island in Western Australia, where a true porpoise never finned, and doubtless other 'porpoise' features around the continent. Like old bushmen with the 'alligators' many old fishermen still stubbornly call dolphins 'porpoises' and will do until they (not the dolphins) die.

The 'alligator' of northern Australia, of course, is *Crocodylus porosus*, the estuarine or saltwater crocodile. Even the name 'saltwater' is a misnomer because saltwater crocodiles travel upriver hundreds of kilometres from the sea at times and do quite well in freshwater zones. In fact, there is a higher population density of *porosus* in northern freshwater swamps than in the tidal rivers traditionally considered their 'natural' home. Some of the bigger (and most dangerous) 'old man' crocs live in fresh or brackish billabongs of the floodplain country of the Northern Territory. In places like Kakadu, they find a satisfactory menu of birds, barramundi and the occasional young buffalo from their waterlily ponds.

Crocodiles and alligators are related but there are some essential differences. The most important practical difference for humans is that crocodiles readily eat people. Alligators seldom do.

Ogden Nash, the American humorous poet, penned one of his delightful verses on the subjectt.

THE PURIST

"I give you now Professor Twist
A conscientious scientist,
Camped on a tropic riverside,
One day he missed his blushing bride
She had, his guide informed him later,
Been eaten by an alligator.
Professor Twist could not but smile.
'You mean,' he said, 'A crocodile.' "

Ogden Nash

Both crocodiles and alligators are part of the same family, the crocodilians, found in warm tropical latitudes throughout the world.

Crocodiles, alligators and the rest of the crocodilians have been around a long time. They evolved with the dinosaurs and the other great reptiles. But they survived when the giant running lizards, which once terrorised the planet, became extinct. Why the dinosaurs died out, nobody knows. It is one of the great mysteries of Planet Earth.

Not all the crocodilians made it to the present day. Some of the prehistoric beasts, similar in form to present crocodiles but 50 feet long, would have posed definite problems in our own age. Scientists believe that there were once 108 species of crocodilians. There are arguments about the numbers. Some researchers say that logically there would have been many more.

Today, 22 species of crocodilians survive. They are one of the four remaining orders of reptiles. Twelve other reptile orders, including the dinosaurs, are believed to have perished in that ancient scaly catastrophe at the end of the Cretaceous Age.

Compared with the 3000 species of lizards and 2700 species of snakes, the 22 species of crocodilians may seem an unimpressive number. But before the arrival of that impudent upstart *Homo sapiens*, modern man, the crocodilians did very well.

They were found around the world in significant numbers wherever the habitat and climate were suitable.

As with most other large wild animals, man has been their nemesis. The soft, scant-haired, two-legged humanoid, who arrived so late on the scene—100,000 years for *Homo sapiens*, with only 10,000 years out of the caves, against 200 million years for the crocodilians—has wrought untold destruction on the habitat and wildlife of the planet.

The sobering thought is that a major part of the man-made damage, most of it irreversible, has occurred in the past 100 years. In that perspective the question of where we will be another century on from now is one we hardly dare ask.

Crocodiles may yet have the last laugh—or the final grim grin. Tests have shown that rats, reptiles and spiders are the creatures most likely to survive an atomic holocaust. At Hiroshima and Nagasaki aquatic animals survived better than terrestrial ones.

When I was at the Monte Bello Islands in the 1970s we found with geiger counters that after more than 20 years there were still patches with dangerous levels of radiation. This followed the British tests of atomic weapons which devastated the islands in 1952 and 1956. It was considered a political necessity at the time, but judged as environmental vandalism by later generations.

There were other interesting features. Birds, normally prolific on offshore islands, were absent. Native mammals like the spectacled hare wallaby had been killed off. That curse of the north —the bush fly—was notably absent. Man himself would not have survived the radiation. But turtles and monitor lizards, the reptiles, were in abundance. So was *Rattus rattus*, the common rat. Despite the lack of flies, spiders proliferated.

Perhaps other life forms may, in the future, have a second chance. A life without the influence of us bumptious bipeds. A gloomy view is that history (if anyone survives to write it) will record that the latter end of the 20th century saw the out-of-control growth of population, genocidal wars and atomic irresponsibility. A cumulative threat to all life on earth, with the final and most devastating effect on the cause of the problem, *Homo sapiens*.

I believe, as a natural optimist, that there is a brighter alternative to this picture of terminal madness. Man will simply have to learn to live better with his neighbours, including crocodiles. Adjusting for survival is one of our talents and this 'happy ever after' solution is so obviously what most of us want, and what the world must have, that it seems strange that it appears to be so difficult to achieve.

Perhaps our somewhat arrogantly self-chosen scientific appellation *Homo sapiens* (meaning 'wise') is as much a misnomer as those Alligator rivers in the Northern Territory?

Confusing crocodiles and alligators is less dramatic than turning continents to dust. Nonetheless scientists regard correct identification seriously. William Shakespeare asked the famous question "What's in a name?" and we may agree with him that in the context of Romeo's lovely Juliet, "A rose by any other name would smell as sweet." Whether he would have included crocodiles and alligators in the proposition is open to question.

It is essential for scientists to know what species they are dealing with to effectively study their behaviour. The information they derive (viz. crocodiles eat you: alligators don't) has both practical and academic interest for the rest of us.

Where do the names come from anyway?

'Alligator' derives from the Spanish *conquistadores* who first encountered crocodilians in the Americas. They called them 'el lagarto' meaning 'lizard', which seems logical enough.

'Crocodile' originates from the Greek. Naturalists like Herodotus were familiar with the Nile crocodile, *Crocodylus niloticus*, which was once found not only in Egypt but also in the Mediterranean as far north as Palestine. One school of thought claimed that 'crocodile' came from the crocus flower because of the creature's colouring of yellow and green.

But a Greek term for lizard is 'krokodeilos' and while the term for saffron (and maybe the colour of the lizard and later the saurian) is 'krokos', it seems most likely that the Greeks, like the Spaniards, simply saw crocodiles as giant lizards.

Lizards traditionally do a lot of basking in the sun, and so do crocodiles.

Humans do not have a great opinion of lizards. 'Lounging around like a lizard' is an expression of disapproval usually aimed at a member of the species *Homo sapiens* considered to be in a state of undesirable relaxation. My mother, a busy woman herself, used the phrase often, though not always to great effect. To her the desirable condition for members of the human race (and especially me, her son) was one of activity.

It did not seem to matter much what the activity was. Or even whether it was useful. The important thing was to be 'doing something'.

Lying late in bed (the defence of "thinking" always contemptuously dismissed) evoked images of lizards and an eventual but inevitable bad end. I had better watch out. If I kept on with lizard-like behaviour it seemed that there was little hope for me.

Crocodilians obviously do not look out on the world with similar thought processes to humans. But if they were to waste their time with some of our kind of perceptions they would undoubtedly take an opposite view of activity.

For a reptile stillness would be a virtue. Jittering about like a human, wasting energy for no good purpose, could very well be viewed as a reptilian sin.

Unnecessary expenditure of effort for a crocodile not only serves no good purpose, it can even be dangerous. It makes a crocodile tired, for one thing, and a tired crocodile is more vulnerable to rivals and enemies. Less equipped to capture and hold prey. Less likely to win a fair crocodile maiden.

When you consider it, we humans are, in contrast, incessantly active. We are always doing something. Even when we are sitting down we tap our feet, drum our fingers, or generally fidget. We twitch in our sleep. Crocodiles, if they thought about it, would be bewildered by our restlessness.

For instance our idea of 'relaxation' is often tennis, jogging, cycling, wind surfing, or other physically demanding pastimes.

But when a crocodile relaxes he is literally as still as a stone. Crocodiles spend a good part of their day apparently doing absolutely nothing.

This is one of the reasons why reptiles need to eat less often. Why they can convert 30 per cent of their food into body mass, as against only 3 per cent for humans or birds.

It is the difference between the 'warm-blooded' mammal and the so-called 'cold-blooded' reptile metabolisms.

In fact the crocodile very carefully keeps his blood temperature close (say within 3 degrees) to a warm 30 to 32 degrees Celsius. He does this by bringing his temperature up, basking in the early morning sun. Cooling it in the water in the heat of the day. Keeping it up in the constant temperature of the water at night when land temperatures ashore drop considerably.

Temperatures are very important to crocodiles. They influence most factors of their lives, including eating, courtship and breeding. It follows that they are most active, hungry, aggressive and sexually interested, in the hot months of the tropical summer, from November to March. This is the time when attacks on humans usually take place.

Temperatures determine the limits of crocodile habitat. They can swim vast distances. One traveller once appeared at Cocos Island out in the Indian Ocean 1200 kilometres from the nearest land, and another drifted a similar distance in the Pacific to the island of Palau. But they can only live and breed where they are comfortably warm.

Humans, with a constant mammalian temperature of 98.6 degrees Fahrenheit, or 37 degrees Celsius, inhabit the earth from the Arctic Circle to the Antarctic wastes. But we do need clothes, buildings, and either artificial heating and warmth or air-conditioning and refrigeration to survive. Temperature is as important to us as it is to crocodiles. If our blood temperature varies a degree or two, we are sick. A large variation kills us.

Crocodiles are capable of explosive bursts of energy. They can move with astounding speed, considering their bulky bodies. When humans and crocodiles are seen together on slow-motion film (of crocodile captures, for instance) the reptiles' sideways thrusts are still almost quicker than our viewing eye can follow.

But reptiles frequently die from exhaustion (lactic acid build-up in the muscles) when they are trapped or snared and struggle for a long time. This, indirectly, led to the death of 'Sweetheart' at the Finniss River, in 1979. The 16 foot 9 inch (5.1 metre) crocodile, exhausted from struggling in a dingo-baited snare, was injected with huge amounts of a tranquilliser, and drowned while being towed.

However, crocodiles are wonderfully well equipped by nature for the amphibious life they lead.

It is more important for them to have speed of strike (quick as a rattlesnake) and initial power to overwhelm prey rather than stamina. If the attack goes on too long then something must have gone wrong with the crocodile's plan.

Man, in contrast, needed stamina. He had to keep doggedly on the track of large prey, once he had wounded it, gradually wearing it down. A different requirement.

In most other comparisons of natural physical attributes the crocodiles are markedly superior to humans. Their ability to drop their heart rate from a normal 15 to 30 beats per minute to an incredible one beat every three minutes while resting underwater, is only one of their remarkable accomplishments. But it was man's very weaknesses and the necessity to solve the problem of his survival that resulted in his eventual overall superiority. This stemmed not from speed or strength but through that most awesome phenomenon of the animal world, the human brain. Able to think, to outwit, to invent, man—the unprotected creature—has outstripped all animals everywhere. However, we are discussing the crocodilians, not *Homo sapiens*—who does seem to have a habit of stealing the limelight.

Returning to our original point, what *are* the essential differences between crocodiles and alligators?

The most important method of cutting through likely confusions is geographic—any crocodilian you sight in Australia is going to be a crocodile. Either *Crocodylus porosus*, the 'saltie', or *Crocodylus johnstoni*, the 'freshie'. In Texas, Louisiana, Mississippi or the Florida Everglades swamps, your Saurian subject would without doubt be *Alligator mississipiensis*.

If you had a specimen of both *Crocodylus porosus* and *Alligator mississipiensis* at your feet you would notice an immediate physical difference between the two in the head area (the bodies are not so dissimilar).

The head of the alligator is rounded somewhat like the toe of an old-fashioned shoe, and the skin lumpier than the crocodile. When the mouth is shut most of the teeth are hidden and the alligator actually looks quite affable in repose.

Not so the saltwater crocodile. His teeth are exposed all the time in that permanent jagged grin which looks so menacing to us humans. To use an entirely human expression, he looks more evil. For once our emotive judgement is right. The crocodile *is* meaner.

In fact in the hypothetical situation of you having the two reptiles at your feet, both you and the alligator had better watch out —the croc would be likely to kill either of you.

Saltwater and African crocodiles generally grow bigger and are more aggressive than alligators, though worldwide there are large and small species of both groups, even 'dwarfs'.

The size of large crocodilians is a subject of constant contention. There are supposed to have been crocodiles in Australia over 30 feet in length. One shot in the Pioneer River in Queensland was quoted by Ion Idriess in his book *In Crocodile Land* as having been 32 feet, with a portion of its tail bitten off.

The biggest *Crocodylus porosus* ever taken in India was claimed to have been 33 feet long. It was caught at Bengal in 1840 and its head was sent to the British Museum.

Beasts of that size are outside our comprehension. They must have weighed several tons, if they existed at all.

Did they exist?

I am reminded of the figure of 36 feet in length for a Great White Shark, *Carcharodon carcharias*, which stood as the official world record for the species for very many years. The specimen was caught by net fishermen in Port Fairy, Victoria, in 1852, and the jaws were sent to the British Museum.

I always viewed that figure of 36 feet with incredulity myself because I had never been able to find an authenticated record of a white shark (a creature I personally know reasonably well) more than 19 feet 6 inches in length (and that was big enough).

Comparatively recently someone in the British Museum thought to measure the famous jaws and found that the tooth sizes were compatible with a white shark a mere 16 feet or 17 feet long.

Another legend bites the dust . . .

I had a feeling, an instinct, that it might be the same with crocodiles. After speaking with many people with vast experience of the saltwater crocodile I have never found anyone who could personally prove a capture, or any authentic record, of a complete specimen of *Crocodylus porosus* that was more than 21 feet long, let alone 30 feet, though Old Charlie in the Northern Territory may have been an exception. His decomposing carcass without the head was 18 feet, according to the ranger who measured it, and it was a careful measurement. With his head Charlie was more than 20 feet, the largest recorded crocodile in Australia.

Tom Cole, who is quoted in Col Stringer's book *The Saga of Sweetheart*, is an authority in point. He was preparing his own book, *Spears and Smoke Signals*, at the time of speaking to Stringer.

"A lot of nonsense has been written, and much more talked, about the size to which they (crocodiles) are supposed to grow," he said. "Thirty and even 40 feet being freely mentioned. This I find hard to believe. I first hunted crocodiles professionally in 1935 and have personally shot several thousand. I have been deeply involved in importing and exporting skins in large quantities. I introduced commercial hunting to New Guinea and over a long period of time I have handled in the vicinity of 50,000 skins.

"The largest crocodile I ever shot myself was on the Victoria River in the Northern Territory, which measured 18 feet 9 inches. I shot one in the Kikori Delta of Papua which went 18 feet 6 inches. Another, which lived in the Gogol River until it met me, was 18 feet 3 inches.

"The largest skin I have ever seen was from Borneo. A portion of its tail was missing, but I believe that had it been complete it might have made 20 feet.

"I think it's reasonable to assume that of 50,000 skins, if crocodiles had generally grown much longer than 20 feet I would have seen at least one.

"A big crocodile is as easy to shoot as a smaller one. Perhaps easier because the target is bigger."

Sweetheart, of Finniss River and Darwin Museum fame, is a very big crocodile. Cole's 18-feet 9-inch (5.9-metre) specimen— nearly two feet longer, or 10 per cent bigger must have been a monster indeed.

The authoritative research volume on crocodiles is *Wildlife Management: Crocodiles and Alligators* edited by Grahame Webb, Charlie Manolis and Peter Whitehead and released in

1987. In general it is cautious on crocodile sizes. But in a section dealing with the distribution and status of world crocodilians, Brian Groombridge of the Conservation Monitoring Centre, Cambridge, UK, states that *porosus* is ". . . the largest extant crocodilian, reported to have attained around 9 metres in length. A few individuals of 6 to 7 metres still occur, notably in the Bhitarkankia Sanctuary at Orissa" (Indian east coast).

Groombridge, of course, is only quoting figures which have been generally accepted by both scientists and laymen for years.

But there seem to be no scientific measurements—the proof positive—to confirm crocodiles in the seven- to nine-metre (29-foot) size range. Certainly the species does not ordinarily grow to anything like that size.

George Craig, at Green Island off Cairns on the North Queensland coast, has a huge *porosus* named Cassius which he is certain is the largest captive crocodile in the world. Prior to the arrival of Cassius, his other big crocodile, Oscar, was listed in the *Guinness Book of Records* as the largest. There is only a few centimetres difference. Both are massive animals.

George is a former crocodile hunter of vast experience in the river systems of Papua New Guinea and northern Australia. As a crocodile shooter and exporter he handled more than 29,000 skins.

He agrees with Tom Cole that he has yet to see a skin or verify a record of a saltwater crocodile exceeding 21 feet.

Cassius has suffered damage at both ends. He has lost a section of his tail and some four centimetres off his snout. Even with these limiting physical impairments what is left measures 17 feet 4 inches. But George believes that if he were intact the battered Cassius would measure something over 18 feet.

George has established 'Marine Land of Melanesia' on Green Island, the famous tourist island on the Barrier Reef. He also has a passion for crocodile facts and truths. In his travels around the world searching for big crocodilians, or records of them, he has run a number of myths to ground.

"You wouldn't believe some of the stories I've heard," he told me sadly. I agreed that I had heard some whoppers myself.

George says that he has long ago learned to discount popular versions of the overall lengths of crocodiles. They usually tend to be estimates, and the error is (to be kind) invariably on the generous side. It is in fact extremely difficult to guess the size of a crocodile larger than 16 feet. "Longer than my boat—and that was 21 feet," is a frequently heard story. I used to hear it myself about sharks. I have had whaling harpooners—men who have to estimate whale sizes as part of their livelihood, and get a huge fine if they guess wrong and shoot an undersized whale—swear on their sainted mothers that they have seen 30-foot Great White Sharks off Albany.

They honestly believed it and it was tempting to accept the figure because of their professional capability of observation. With reluctance I have to say that there is no actual proof of 30-foot white sharks in the cold waters off Albany. Are there any 30-foot crocodiles in the tropics?

It is surprising that when exaggerations are checked out and reduced to actual size they seem to run fairly consistently at about 30 per cent.

Why? The sighting of a big creature is an important event. The bigger, the more important. Some of the importance rubs off on the observer who reports the sighting. There is an incentive to exaggerate and it is most often done unconsciously.

An honest tape measure is a great leveller of legends.

"With crocodiles the most scientific method is to look at head measurements," George Craig says.

Cassius has a head measurement of 67 centimetres in length, and 46.1 centimetres in breadth.

"But he's had the end of his snout knocked off," said George. "Intact he would have had a 71-centimetre head."

Cassius was named for the scars of adventurous living.

Breadth of head, says George, perhaps gives a better indication of age and size than length.

He happily reels off figures on big crocodile skull sizes. "I've been everywhere around the world tracking down legends of these so-called giant reptiles that don't exist."

But of the ones which *do* exist, he found the biggest crocodile skull in the world was in India. It came from the Coringa region south of Calcutta and measures 78 by 52 centimetres. That crocodile, George concedes, could have been over 20 feet. But Cassius, at 71 and 46.1 is not a lot smaller. Seven centimetres difference is only the breadth of a hand.

The biggest skull in the British Museum—an Indian animal, and perhaps the reputed 34-footer from the Bay of Bengal—is only 71.5 and 47.8.

There is a skull of 74 and 51.6 in a museum in Leningrad, one from the Philippines in Massachusetts, USA of 67.4 and 44.8. A Sarawak skull is 71 centimetres long. An 'Orinocho' skull from South America, now in New York, is said to be 73 centimetres, but George hasn't been able to verify it.

The biggest skull in Australia is 'Charlie', a Northern Territory *Crocodylus porosus* killed in the Mary River by barramundi poachers, one of whom was later jailed for the offence. Charlie's head is 66.1 centimetres in length but 48 centimetres in breadth, which made him a very big crocodile indeed. His corpse, as previously mentioned, was 18 feet, or 5.5 metres. Add the 66.1-centimetre (2-feet, 2-inch) skull and you do indeed have a crocodile of just over 20 feet.

The biggest crocodile skull George was able to find in New Guinea—a legendary haunt of monster crocodiles and the area where George spent many years as a shooter with his river boat *Janis B*—was a respectable 73 and 43 centimetres. But, "They told me it was over 23 feet," says George with an air of injury. "There was another from the Fly River which was 72 by 44. Big croc, yes. But not so big as they said it was. They claimed 6.2 metres. That's over 20 feet. But when I measured the skin it had somehow shrunk to 5.08."

Big Cassius has one advantage over the skulls gathered painstakingly by museums over a century and more. He is still alive and taking in regular tucker.

"He may grow a bit more yet," said George optimistically. "I reckon he's about 80 years old now and he's probably got at least 20 years or so left. Maybe we'll give that Indian head a shake yet."

Unlike humans who stop growing at maturity, crocodiles seem to keep adding weight and length through their adult years. One advantage this affords is the regular replacement of teeth.

Cassius has particularly large teeth. One of his discards measured 3.4 centimetres in diameter, or nearly one and a half inches in thickness.

He is covered in scars from years of duelling with rivals and George believes he lost the end of his nose to a boat propeller.

"In fact I think he's the original Sweetheart," he said, when I visited him at Green Island in May 1988.

"But surely," I protested, startled at the idea, "Sweetheart is stuffed and tanned?" The recollection of the big crocodile, frozen in a pose of permanent aggression in the Darwin Museum, was strong and clear.

George shook his head. "That croc isn't big enough—only 65.5 cm by 46 cm in the skull, and 5.1 metres," he said. "More importantly he doesn't have the scars that should go with all those encounters with propellers. This guy does. He's a much bigger animal, he's from the same area and fits the picture better. Have a look yourself."

When I looked in his pool Cassius was indeed scarred as George said. And he was massive, immense. His broad back and incredible loins made the stuffed creature in Darwin look a lesser beast in comparison. "God knows what he weighs," said George. As a mortal I could only shake my head. It must have been more than a tonne.

An 18-foot crocodile is not just two feet longer than a 16-footer. He is about 30 per cent heavier in weight. His muzzle was of particular interest, with the end sliced off at an oblique angle as though by an axe. It was not the kind of wound likely to be suffered in a fight with another crocodile. Crocodile bites do not have clean edges. They are jagged.

But Cassius's white-scarred wound did fit perfectly the concept that it may have been caused by a propeller.

"It would be an easy mistake to make," George explained. "A big croc is caught at Sweet's Lookout. Naturally everyone assumes it's *the* crocodile. They want it to be. But maybe the real Sweetheart was laughing at them?"

George conceded that the attacks on boats ceased after the capture of the crocodile.

"But probably the real Sweetheart just moved up river," George says. "They were harassing the hell out of the crocodiles there, shooting at the big ones and trying to trap them. They killed the croc now in Darwin in that pool. Cassius—Sweetheart, whatever you like to call him—just got fed up and left. Those old man crocs are very wary with it all. Caution is how they get to be big, and remember that the real Sweetheart was never seen in ordinary circumstances. If he had lost the end of his nose to a propeller, or if some of the other long scars on his back were caused by props, or if the bit off his tail was chopped off by a boat, then it would explain his aggravation and hostility towards outboard motors. I'd feel the same myself."

I have to admit that I was sceptical when he first made the suggestion. But I left Green Island thinking that George Craig very likely *did* have the real Sweetheart.

Cassius was caught within a mile of Sweet's Lookout where Sweetheart gained his notoriety. Aside from the right kind of disfiguring scars conforming to propeller injuries, there was one other piece of possible proof.

When the new hovercraft made a run out from Cairns and circumnavigated Green Island it made a noise like a high-pitched outboard motor engine. All George's other captive crocodiles, more than 30 in number, ignored it with saurian disdain.

But Cassius went berserk, throwing his scarred body around his enclosure in foam-lashed anger until the noise had receded. The same reaction that had made the original defender of Sweet's Lagoon notorious among boat owners.

There is, all things considered, something appealing in the notion that Sweetheart's persecutors may have got the wrong reptile.

That the grand old warrior may have survived, to reappear years later in a kind of crocodilian resurrection.

The possibility is naturally vehemently denied in Darwin. But probably only the huge animal in George Craig's Green Island pond knows the real answer. His unblinking yellow eyes are not likely to let us in on his personal secrets.

One of the problems about checking crocodile sizes—apart from the obvious difficulty of getting a big one in a situation where you can safely run a tape measure from nose to tail—is that they come in all shapes. This makes it hard to get an accurate length when you only have a part of the beast. Humans have long heads, round heads and square heads. There are small men with big heads, big men with small heads. Crocodile and alligator heads also vary. 'Old Charlie', for instance, had an extremely wide head. If his length had been calculated on a width-to-length skull ratio, the formula would have suggested 15 feet, when he was obviously considerably bigger. Indian saltwater crocodile heads, on measurement, tend to be longer and slimmer than Australian ones.

Have there been freak beasts in the past, outside all normal bounds of accepted dimension?

Dr Grahame Webb, consultant to the Northern Territory Tourist Commission, interviewed many former crocodile shooters and took note of all available statistics, including sizes. Checking this chapter over in Darwin for accuracy he noted "Overall I agree that crocodiles over 20 feet have always been extremely rare. Ron Pawlovski, who shot many crocs in the Gulf of Carpentaria—and who really started the first crocodile farm in Australia—reportedly shot a crocodile at 28 feet. The next biggest he shot was around 18 feet. There are, of course, no parts of the large animal remaining as verification. But it always nags at me that I spent three days talking with Ron and everything else he told me about crocodiles turned out to be very precise indeed. I can't imagine him fabricating something like this. One way or the other it would be nice to think that there was still one really large one out there to surprise us all."

Who could say more than that?

Perhaps Malcolm Douglas, adventurer, film-maker and owner of the Broome crocodile park, knows of one such beast. It swims in a northern river and Malcolm describes it as "bloody enormous". He tried to capture it alive in 1987 and failed. The monster was too clever for his traps.

Malcolm hesitates to put a size on it for fear of disbelief.

"We call him 'The Hippo'," he said. "He dwarfs everything else I've ever seen. Compared with him, the 16-foot 4-inch croc we did catch looked like a 12-footer."

Could he guess a size?

"Almost impossible from the bank. But once we did have him alongside a net. The corks were three feet apart and his length covered eight corks along the net. Maybe a little more."

The other area of crocodile lore, almost as unsatisfactory as the stretching of sizes, is the age to which crocodiles live. We humans know our own ages to the month and sometimes the day. We like to know about animals too.

It is traditional that crocodiles live a long time, like the unlikely traditional trio of elephants, parrots and tortoises. But exactly how long *do* they live?

The British newspaper which quoted Sweetheart as "300 years old" was obviously maintaining its hallowed traditions of unprincipled exaggeration. But it is often difficult to establish ages for wild animals.

It is generally accepted that the saltwater crocodile grows about a foot a year in its early life. But the growth rate can vary considerably even in animals fed the same diet.

One of the world's biggest overseas crocodile farms (with 14,000 captive crocodiles) is the Samut Praken crocodile farm in Thailand.

There it was found that specimens of *Crocodylus porosus*, the saltwater crocodile, reached 3 metres or about 10 feet in length and 100 to 150 kilograms in weight in 10 years. This is about the size the species begins to become dangerous to man. A male *porosus* matures and breeds at about 16 years. Females become fertile after about 10 years.

Vic Cox, who was the expert brought in to look for Ginger Faye Meadows' body at the Prince Regent in March 1987, had a pet crocodile called Henry for 27 years.

In that time Henry grew from a pre-adolescent of one metre in length, to nearly 14 feet (4.27 metres) and probably 300 kilograms in weight.

George Craig estimates Cassius's age at about 80 years. But he would be the first to admit that this is a guess. The age of 'Sweetheart' in the Darwin Museum is said to have been 'between 40 and 80 years'. This is not especially satisfactory—there is a world of difference between a human of 40 and one of 80 years.

The oldest crocodile in captivity in Australia is 'Charlie', at the Hartley Creek Zoo, in North Queensland. Charlie is said to have been caught in the nearby creek in 1934. Since the animal is still small—less than 4 metres after 53 years—it has either had a bad diet or it should be called 'Charlene' because it is undoubtedly a female.

Australian researchers, including Professor H. Messel and Dr Grahame Webb, have used a capture/recapture technique researching crocodile growth. Wild crocodiles are caught, tagged and released. When they are caught again some time in the future their growth rate over the intervening period can be checked.

In Zimbabwe, where there is an advanced programme of crocodile management, experiments have been carried out on determining the age of wild crocodiles from growth rings in the bones (skeletochronology) and in the horny keels on the crocodile's back called the dorsal osteroderms, which also have seasoning rings.

Jonathan M. Hutton contributes an interesting section in the book *Wildlife Management: Crocodiles and Alligators* on the subject and Grahame Webb, already quoted, one of the book's editors and the major authority on crocodile research in the Northern Territory, has used similar techniques in Australia.

Crocodile ageing is still something of an open question.

Dr Webb explains. "We know a great deal about crocodiles' early years. Initial growth rates have been determined from fieldwork and captives in crocodile farms. But the age of mature specimens is still an area of uncertainty.

"What we *do* know is that crocodiles lay down seasonal layers of bone in rings similar to trees. One 18-foot crocodile from the Victoria River had 65 rings in its long bones, which means 65 years in our terminology.

"But we still don't know the extent of a full lifetime. It could be as long as 100 years. But I doubt that it would be much more than that."

What about crocodilians worldwide?

Porosus is the largest. The Black Caiman *(Melanosuchus niger)* of South America also grows to a considerable size. There is said to be a 73-centimetre 'Orinocho' skull in New York, which is probably a Black Caiman, and claims for 23-foot individuals have been made. This seems to indicate that some specimens may grow as large as *porosus*.

The African Nile crocodile and the Indian Mugger or Marsh crocodile *(Crocodylus palustris)* are both rather similar to the Australian saltwater crocodile in appearance, and Nile crocodiles, in good conditions, achieve almost the same size. The Mugger is smaller, growing to about 12 feet (3.6 metres).

Crocodylus porosus is not only the biggest crocodilian, he has the distinction of also being the world's largest non-marine carnivore. The biggest overall flesh-eater is the bull Sperm whale at 60 feet and 60 tonnes. It follows that the saltwater crocodile is also Australia's largest animal.

However it is by no means as exclusive to Australia as the kangaroo or the duck-billed platypus. The range of *porosus* territory extends to Sri Lanka, India's east coast, the Bay of Bengal, Burma, New Guinea and the Solomon Islands, as well as northern Australia. A cosmopolitan gent.

A hundred years ago there were large numbers of *porosus* in all these areas. The advent of man, with his technical advantages of outboard motors, spotlights and the high-powered rifle—along with a fashion for crocodile leather shoes and handbags—proved disastrous for the saltwater crocodile. By the 1970s *porosus* was facing extinction through most of its range.

Protection has resulted in a recovery in Australia in the 1980s and the New Guinea population is sustained with both captive animals (23,000 in one PNG crocodile farm) and in the wild. But there is serious concern for *porosus* elsewhere.

Crises for the crocodilians have occurred with species in many parts of the world.

The American alligator was prolific and well entrenched in the vast southern swamp systems of the USA when the first Europeans came.

Their skins were used first to make boots for the armies in the Civil War. Then alligator and crocodile leather became fashionable for shoes, handbags and accessories late in the 19th century. In Florida, as many as 2.5 million alligator skins had been taken by 1893. In Louisiana about 3.5 million skins were taken between 1880 and 1933.

The hunting pressures were severe and alligator numbers fell to a degree where some people feared that the species would follow the bison on the road to extinction.

Controls were introduced in the United States at state and federal levels in the 1970s and proved so successful that alligator numbers—now estimated at 800,000—are approaching those of the last century.

Louisiana was probably the best example of the effectiveness of controls. Alligator numbers reached a low of about 26,000 in 1957. By 1987, following a period of protection and controls, the population had increased to more than 300,000.

In Florida the recovery was so successful that wildlife authorities are receiving up to 5000 alligator 'nuisance' calls each year.

The slaughter of crocodilians in South America, mainly for the French skin market, had devastating results on vulnerable populations. In some areas, though belated protective legislation does exist, it is largely ignored on the distant reaches of the jungle rivers. In other areas there is careful management and very effective controls. Venezuela, for instance, expects to harvest 150,000 Caimans in 1988 from a base population estimated at five million.

Alligator mississipiensis is fortunate in being resident in a country where universities and colleges proliferate and where there are ample funds for research. It has also been probably more widely and sympathetically studied than any of the other crocodilian species.

It is an interesting animal. It is claimed that at some time in its life an alligator will eat everything living that comes within reach of its jaws. Man is such an occasional victim that obviously every alligator doesn't have the pleasure. The manatee (American cousin to the Australian dugong or sea-cow) is probably another rare treat for *mississipiensis*.

Nonetheless the dietary range is widely varied from blue swimmer crabs, fish, crayfish, birds, muskrats, nutria and even snakes.

Alligators prefer the fresh or brackish water of swamps, rivers, lakes and ponds. They can tolerate much colder conditions than African and Australian crocodiles. When the US winter comes on they burrow in the banks and hibernate.

The biggest alligator recorded is supposed to have been 19 feet 2 inches (5.84 metres), in 1935. But occasional lengths of 18 feet (5.5 metres) and 17 feet (5.18 metres) have been claimed—though there are the usual difficulties in getting corroborative evidence. These sizes, if true, would be exceptional and the normal maximum is very much smaller. Females do not exceed 10 feet, or about three metres.

Alligators vocalise a good deal, bellowing during the breeding season. They are ardent lovers and attentive parents, the female spending a long period of tender care with her hatchlings. They can be bred successfully in captivity and the chance to study them at close quarters in alligator farms has produced some interesting observations.

For instance young alligators fed on a fish diet tend to be shy and wary. But those fed on red meat are markedly active and much more aggressive.

Could it be that a similar change occurs with *porosus*, when the saltwater crocodile grows big enough to begin taking mammal prey?

Though there have been alligator attacks on humans and some fatalities (less than a dozen up to 1988), such incidents are rare. They are usually territorial demonstrations that went wrong.

Alligator handlers say, ironically, that they are confident with alligators in the wild, but often cautious about large beasts in captivity and over-familiar with humans.

If there is a chance of being mauled, they say, it is with an alligator which has lost its fear of humans and knows our habits.

Alligators prefer not to venture into saltwater. The ocean edge of their habitat used to be occupied by the American crocodile, *Crocodylus acutus*. This is a moderate-sized animal whose range once included Mexico, the Caribbean and the northern coastal sections of South America.

Probably there were never many *acutus* in the United States and numbers there are now down to as low as 20 breeding females in Florida. *Acutus* was once abundant in Mexico, the Caribbean Islands and Dominica. But the creature is now threatened as a wild animal through skin hunting and destruction of habitat.

Also threatened are the other family of alligators which exist— oddly enough—in China. The Chinese Alligator, sometimes called the Yangzi Alligator or Tuo-long by the Chinese, is scientifically known as *Alligator sinensis*. In the 1980s it was regarded as critically endangered. It is a small, two-metre animal restricted to the lower reaches of the Yangzi valley. Like its American cousin it hibernates in winter. Anhui Province has the biggest number, but the population there was still only 300 individuals in 1987.

The African crocodile, *Crocodylus niloticus*, is the most famous (and notorious) crocodilian man-eater. Though it is smaller than *porosus* it is both active and aggressive. Crocodiles kill more humans than all other large wild animals combined in the African continent.

There are probably at least 100 crocodile-caused deaths per year in Africa. Tribal people living by lakes and rivers who go down to draw water from the banks are most at risk. There were 10 deaths in Zimbabwe alone in 1984.

The Nile crocodile's range once extended from the Mediterranean to South Africa and Madagascar. Today numbers are enormously reduced. But there are still healthy populations spread throughout South Africa, Botswana, Sudan, Tanzania, Cameroon, Congo, Zambia and Mozambique.

There are two other lesser-known African species. The long-snouted crocodile with the marvellous scientific name *Crocodylus cataphractus*, a freshwater species which seems to be the counterpart of the Australian Johnstone crocodile, and a tiny, timid species from the tropical rainforests of West Africa, *Osteolaemus tetraspis*, the African Dwarf Crocodile. Both species are in decline from hunting for skins and destruction of habitat.

South America, mysterious land of steamy jungles and giant river systems, was a paradise for crocodilians until the advent of modern man.

Not surprisingly it has the most number of species (10) and boasts the highest number of variations.

These range from the biggest South American crocodilian, the Black Caiman, locally called Largato Negro and scientifically designated *Melanosuchus niger*.

There are also eight other varieties of Caimans—two kinds of Spectacled Caiman, the Brown Caiman, Yacare Caiman, Broad-nosed Caiman, the Rio Apaporis Caiman and two subspecies of dwarf Caiman (Cuvier's and Morelets). Most of these animals are smallish, in the two-metre range, with the two dwarf varieties of about one and a half metres. The Orinocho crocodile is a moderately large freshwater species found in Venezuela and Colombia. The American crocodile, *acutus*, is also common in Mexico, Panama and the northern sea fringes of the South American continent.

North and South America, in fact, account for half the world's species of crocodilians. But while the US alligators are secure, some species in South America, according to Groombridge, are endangered by illegal hunting for skins and destruction of habitat.

Other interesting world species include the formerly threatened and long-snouted Indian Gharial or 'fish crocodile' found in the Indus and Ganges rivers and throughout northern India. India has a strong conservation programme on crocodiles, with the three species of *porosus*, Mugger and Gharial. The wild population has increased 10 to 20 per cent with controls. There is also a related Gharial in Malaysia.

Thailand has its own crocodile, *Crocodylus siamensis*, somewhat similar to the Indian Mugger or marsh crocodile. Numbers are low and crocodile stocks in Thailand (formerly Siam) are only preserved through the Samut Praken crocodile farm. Their hybrid crosses between *siamensis* and the larger *porosus* have been found to produce the most satisfactory results in captive crocodiles bred for skins.

Cuba also has its own crocodile, *Crocodylus rhombifer*, a moderate-sized beast. Cuba has a number of large crocodile farms. The Philippines crocodile, *Crocodylus mindorensis*, a small, shy, freshwater species, is regarded as being in serious danger of extinction. There may be no more than 100 individual Philippine wild crocodiles remaining.

Prospects are better for the small New Guinea freshwater crocodile, *Crocodylus novaeguineae*. *Porosus*, the saltwater crocodile, was severely depleted in Papua New Guinea through shooting for skins and many skins of the freshwater species were also taken. But recovery is taking place. Because of the huge areas of permanent swamplands and their secretive habits, the crocodilians have survived the period of indiscriminate shooting and appear to have a secure future.

Last, but not least, on the list of world crocodilians is the little

Australian freshwater or Johnstone River crocodile, *Crocodylus johnstoni*. The name (author Jack Green tells us in *GEO* magazine) comes from Sub-Inspector Johnstone who collected the original specimen in the Herbert River in Queensland. It was first described by Gray in 1873 and he misspelled Johnstone's name and called the animal *johnsoni*. It has also been spelled *johnstonei* as well as the generally more accepted *johnstoni*.

The 'freshie' is consistently overlooked in references and writings about crocodiles in Australia. The bigger and more aggressive 'saltwater' species gets all the headlines because—of course—it occasionally includes specimens of the species *Homo sapiens* in its diet.

The 'freshie' does not eat people. It is a small, shy creature and prefers to stay out of the way when people are around. But it can deliver a good bite on occasion and can vigorously defend itself when caught in a net or accidentally trodden on.

Quite a number of people in Australia's northern regions have had to have wounds stitched after encounters while swimming or netting (which incidentally is now illegal in most areas).

But basically the Johnstone crocodile would much rather be left alone. It lives in freshwater lagoons and rivers and does its best to keep out of the way of hungry *porosus* cousins. It lives on fish, insects, freshwater crayfish and turtles. Like all the species, it lays eggs (up to 24 in number) and incubates them in a sandbank in summer before the floods of the Wet. The 'freshie' is usually about two metres but there are believed to be specimens of nearly three metres in Lake Argyle.

So much for the list of world crocodilians. Creatures which receive little favour or understanding from humans wherever they are found.

"A most maligned animal group, widely loathed, little understood and surrounded by myths. Crocodiles, like snakes and spiders, enjoy low public esteem," said Australia's Dr H. Robert Bustard, a world reptile authority, in the 1960s.

In South America people are as uncomplimentary about crocodiles as they are anywhere else. Stefan Gorzula, researcher from Venezuela, provides us with two examples.

A poem in a primer for schoolchildren takes a typical view:

"Ferocious, warty and ugly
Sleeping on the beach he shows
His two rows of teeth.
And every time I see him
Stretched out and sunbathing
With chills I think
Of the innocent beings
That this monster has eaten
By the riverside."

Gorzula's second instance is the South American naturalist Father Gumilla, who wrote (with unscientific lack of detachment):

"What definition could be found that would adequately
embrace the frightful ugliness of the Caiman (crocodile)?
It is the very same ferocity and the clumsy abortion of
the greatest monstrosity; the horror of all living beings;
so formidable that if the Caiman looked at itself in a mir-
ror it would run away trembling. The most lifelike fan-
tasy could not paint a more appropriate Satan than by
portraying itself with those characteristics of the Caiman."

Poor Father Gumilla. In our arrogance we humans tend to view all other creatures from our own selfish standpoint. But beauty lies in the eye of the beholder. Crocodiles undoubtedly find each other attractive and spend long periods in active or languorous lovemaking.

I am always reminded of a cartoon which hangs on the wall of Val Plumwood's study at Macquarie University in Sydney.

The drawing shows two crocodiles in a river viewing two human tourists walking on the bank.

"They look disgusting," says one crocodile to the other. "But they taste quite good!"

What would we do with our self-centered notions that only humans are beautiful, if God should prove one day to be a crocodile?

BITING THE HAND THAT FEEDS

▲▲▲▲▲▲▲▲▲▲▲

Queensland cane farmer Alf Casey got his pet crocodile from a professional shooter in 1963.

The tiny creature, not long out of the egg, came from the Proserpine River and was barely 11 inches long. A striped and speckled hatchling more like a timid lizard than a potential man-eater.

By 1986 the crocodile had grown to be nearly nine feet in length and was considerably heavier than a grown man. The original name of 'Charlie' was hurriedly changed to 'Charlene' when it laid a batch of 34 eggs.

In the intervening years Charlene amazed everyone who thought they knew about crocodiles. She was a pet in every sense of the word. The Caseys took her for rides in their car, she slept in their bedroom when they travelled. Sometimes she was taken to the bar and sat up with the drinkers. She appeared on television and on newspaper front pages. A saurian celebrity.

Charlene would shake hands on cue and enjoyed being scratched, stroked and cuddled. She had a variety of basic tricks including lying on her back until being told "Roll over, lazybones," whereupon she obliged by turning right side up. She seemed to be a living contradiction to accepted belief that a crocodile could never be trained.

On 2 November 1986—a date Alf Casey remembers with pain —she bit his left arm so badly that surgery had to complete the near-amputation between the elbow and wrist.

"Told you so!" said all the 'experts'.

Some people were for shooting the crocodile at that point. But from his hospital bed, 69-year-old Alf Casey begged wildlife officers not to shoot her.

"You can't blame the crocodile," he said bravely. "It was an accident and it was all my fault."

It was a particularly cruel blow for Casey. Some years before, in an accident with a circular saw, he had lost the three main fingers of his right hand. He was left with a virtual claw—thumb and little finger—and his left was his 'good' hand.

So now Casey had lost his good hand as well as having the earlier crippling injury.

"You can never trust a crocodile," said the experts. "This proves the point."

But Casey shakes his head.

He is a man of generous spirit. But he says that it is not a case of forgiving the crocodile. He believes that there was no hostile intention on her part and there is nothing to forgive. It was all a mistake. Alf Casey just wants Charlene "back home where she belongs".

What happened on that hot November day to make Charlene bite the hand that fed her for 23 years?

"It should never have happened at all," Casey repeats. "I was overtired and I did something I should never have done in any circumstances."

It was the final crushing of the cane season. The North Queensland air was heavy with smoke, the cane workers blackened, grimy and covered with sweat. They were also understandably in a mood for celebration.

A happy group of workers was gathered on the Casey farm. When Alf Casey went down to feed the crocodile about 4 P.M. some of them went down to the pen with him to watch the event.

Charlene was now mature. Much too big to be riding in cars or placed on the bar. But she was still a pet and would stand at the fence and put her paw out to shake hands when requested. She still loved to be scratched around her chin and to have her belly rubbed.

Hot weather always makes saltwater crocodiles hungry and restless. Ordinarily Casey would have noticed the danger signals and been cautious. But he was a tired man. There had been days of pressure with the cane harvest and at 69 he was no longer as young as he used to be. Nor, with the relief of the final crushing and the distraction of the visitors, was he as careful as he might have been.

He set down a bucket of frozen fish thawing in water by the gate of the pen.

Charlene, restless and hungry, came up to the door of her pen at once, smelling the fish. Alf opened the door and gave her a scratch and a pat.

Ordinarily he fed her on cue. At the word 'FISH!' she would stand up on her hind legs and would be fed.

"I always determined I would never use that word 'fish' except when I actually had one in my hand and was going to feed her," Casey recalls. "That day I broke my own rule."

Watched by the cane cutters, he said to Charlene, "Do you want a fish?"

Immediately the crocodile became excited. Perhaps for the benefit of the visitors he handled her, resisting, back into her pen.

Then, without shutting the gate, he went to the bucket of fish. In a moment Charlene was out again and once again he tried to put her back. Whether she mistook the movement of his hand—which smelled of the fish—for an actual fish, we will never know.

But as he put his hand out to turn her around she snapped and next moment Alf Casey was struggling with his hand in her jaws.

By natural instinct she retreated into her pen, hand firmly clamped in those terrible teeth which all crocodiles have. A pressure of several tons on the agonised hand and wrist.

Immediately the horrified watchers rushed to Alf Casey's aid. They thought the crocodile was going to drag him into the pen and tear him apart. With the best of intentions they tried to pull him back, not knowing the terrible injury they were about to cause him.

"That was what did it," Alf Casey says. "They meant well, but it was absolutely the wrong thing to do. They frightened the crocodile and she reacted instinctively to the attempt to pull away what was in her mouth."

He believes that, on his own, he could have talked Charlene into opening her mouth and releasing his hand. He had done it previously when she had picked up a poisonous cane toad.

"But with everyone pulling and yelling and the crocodile scared and backing off, there was only one thing that was going to happen," Casey says. "That was the worst thing possible. She went into a death roll. They wouldn't let me roll with her. My elbow locked and that was the end of my hand. If they'd only let me turn with the roll and handle it on my own it would have been all right. Though I'm bound to say they meant well. They thought they were saving me."

Eventually she did let go. But by then the bones of the forearm were broken, the flesh almost cut through, the hand and wrist a ragged remnant hanging by a ribbon of skin.

The accident, at that age, would have been a catastrophic blow for most men. It didn't sink Alf Casey.

In 1987, the year after coming out of hospital, he built a caravan park, and a new pen for Charlene. In 1988, aged 71, he was still driving a tractor on the farm and mending water pumps, despite his disabilities.

He does feel badly about the accident.

He believes that he put the crocodile in a bad position through his own mistake and it was unfair to her. His injury was pain enough. But on top of that—the cruellest blow from his point of view—he lost the crocodile. His son signed a release form for the Queensland National Parks and Wildlife Service rangers while he was in the hospital, and they gave Charlene to a crocodile farm as 'a dangerous animal' to be relocated for use as a breeder.

Now Alf wants Charlene back. He says that his son only signed the release conditional on Alf himself confirming it when he was well. But the crocodile farmer is resisting returning Charlene. Female *Crocodylus porosus* are in short supply and valuable.

However, Alf Casey has not lost hope. He believes that Charlene will come home one day and that he will still be able to handle her in the old way.

"She was amazing," he said. "It just shows how little we know about crocodiles. They're smarter than we think, and they've got feelings too."

He intends to go on feeding and petting her just as he did before.

For a man already so terribly injured, that shows a mountain of faith.

Vic Cox of Cockatoo Island had a similar experience—though on a less severe scale—with his own pet crocodile Henry.

Vic was a crocodile shooter in the early days and a painter for Broken Hill Pty Co. Ltd at Koolan and Cockatoo Islands. In 1987 he was brought in to advise police searchers looking for the body of Ginger Meadows at the Prince Regent River.

On a crocodile-catching trip in 1960 he harpooned a small crocodile in Barramundi Bay at Koolan Island. The barb made a tear in its belly skin, spoiling its commercial value and saving it from becoming a handbag.

Vic, a kind-hearted man, felt sorry for the little four-foot-long (1.2-metre) reptile. He decided to keep it and feed it until it got better. Twenty-seven years later he still had him and Henry had grown into a monster of impressive proportions.

No one could get into the pen (with a guarantee of getting out again) to run a tape measure over him. But in 1987 he was about 14 feet long (4.27 metres), perhaps 300 kilograms in weight. A big beast.

I saw Henry at Cockatoo Island that year. Observing his impressive set of fangs through the bars of his cage I remarked with some lack of sensitivity that crocodiles were mean-looking creatures.

"I think he's beautiful," said Vic, looking offended and regarding Henry with a gaze that showed that beauty does indeed lie in the eyes of the beholder.

And as crocodiles go, Henry was without doubt a superb specimen. He had brilliant green and yellow markings, and toothpaste-advertisement teeth.

At the time Vic had a dilemma. BHP had closed Cockatoo Island down and the workforce had departed. Soon Vic would have to go too. What would happen to Henry?

"He can't live with me," Vic said. "And he can't live without me. I doubt he'd get a living in the wild. Those big bull crocodiles in established territories won't tolerate a stranger."

Eventually Henry wound up in a happy compromise in Malcolm Douglas's Broome crocodile park.

But those 27 years of association had some eventful times for both Vic and Henry.

Once Henry, like Charlene, snapped up the hand that fed him.

"He fastened onto my hand," said Vic, "as well as the fish I was holding. He took all the skin off and shredded the back of my hand. I was only just able to drag it through his jaws because of the fish, and just before he pulled me over the fence. If he'd grabbed me higher, above the wrist, he'd have dragged me into the pen and done some real damage."

As with Charlene, the problem was caused by a moment's inattention and an over-familiar approach. "I was looking away at the time." Vic never made the same mistake again. "But I was lucky to get the second chance."

Henry never became tame like Charlene because he wasn't handled continuously by humans. But he was an affable resident in the pen by Vic Cox's house on the hill at Cockatoo Island for 27 years. He lived in a concrete pond which had originally been Vic's kids' swimming pool.

Once, in 1982, he escaped and threw the whole island population of 160 people into turmoil.

"He saw a couple of ducks on a neighbour's swimming pool down the hill," Vic said, "and he fancied himself as a hunter. He didn't have a lot of trouble getting out because the wire netting was rusty and he just pushed through it.

"But freedom wasn't too exciting, it seemed. The ducks flew away and the pool was too small—he sort of coiled around and overflowed out of it."

The Cockatoo population were put on crocodile alert overnight. But Henry solved the problem himself in the end by toiling home up the hill. After getting nervously jammed under the side of the house for a time, he made it back into his pen, where Vic had obligingly left the door open, and slid into his pond with a happy sigh of relief.

Though Vic (by popular request of Cockatoo residents)

strengthened the pen with iron bars, Henry never tried to venture out again.

There's no place like home, even when you're a reptile.

In fact crocodiles do have strong homing instincts. In the Northern Territory, Conservation Commission rangers 'relocating' crocodiles which had inconveniently showed up in Darwin Harbour, found that within a few weeks of removing them somewhere else, they often reappeared again where they had been originally caught. Back in their old haunts.

One large specimen actually walked 20 kilometres overland—a very weary and footsore *porosus*—to tragically perish in a grass fire when nearly 'home' once more.

In crocodile farms in Zimbabwe it was found that captives which broke out of their pens and escaped back into the wild often enough returned and 'broke' back into their old pens.

Even the little freshwater crocodiles have a homing instinct. As an experiment Dr Grahame Webb, in the Northern Territory, moved a group of 16 adult *Crocodylus johnstoni* a distance of 39 kilometers up the McKinlay River. Despite the fact that the new pool was bigger, and theoretically better territory, seven of the originals were back in their old home next season and one was half-way between. Some of the others may have been on the way.

"Great leaping catfish!" was a Mark Twain expression deriving from the Mississippi and not a saying we would normally associate with crocodiles.

Yet *Crocodylus porosus*—as we have observed in earlier chapters—is one of the more spectacular leapers of the animal world. The more dramatic in effect because the transformation from the seemingly somnolent horizontal to the jaw-snapping vertical is so unexpected (as Val Plumwood can testify) that it always takes us by surprise.

On the Northern Territory's Adelaide River, 60 kilometres east of Darwin, tourists aboard river craft like the *Adelaide River Queen* in the late 1980s were able to watch crocodiles making spectacular high leaps alongside the vessel.

Crew hands dangled chunks of buffalo meat on a gut line from a rod on the upper deck. Wild crocodiles became accustomed to swimming out and making a jump for the blood-dripping meat.

Customers were cautioned not to show themselves or have any part of their bodies outside the cabin of the vessel, and told to keep the windows shut. Some of the 'trained' crocodiles exploded vertically out of the water to a point where their hind legs were actually clear of the surface. Such leaps provided an awesome example of crocodile power and the tourists flocked with their cameras to see it.

The phenomenon was not without its critics. Some crocodile experts in the north warned that having saltwater crocodiles leap like dolphins beside boats might one day cause a tragedy.

"They can't be trusted," said Howard Young, a crocodile tour operator of Kununurra. "They are the most violent creatures on earth."

NT authorities said that while they agreed the principle of having crocodiles associate people with food carried some risks, the spectacle was attractive to tourists, particularly visitors from overseas.

Tour operators were licensed, and licences were restricted to suitable glass-enclosed vessels like the *Adelaide River Queen*.

Perhaps the highest crocodile leaper in Australia is not in the steamy rivers of the tropical north, but in Ballarat in Victoria. Ballarat is a place where snow falls in some winters and a town which is regarded as cold in Australia's coldest mainland State.

But the 11-foot (3.35-metre) crocodile, dubbed 'Gator' by the press, at Greg Parker's Ballarat Wild Life Reptile Park regularly makes leaps which take his snout two metres and more out of the water. The accompanying crash of jaws sends thrills and shivers through the crowds watching the feeding from behind glass windows.

Greg Parker stands on the edge of the water while the crocodile makes his jumps to take fish out of his hand. But he is the first to admit that he does not trust his charge for a moment.

"If he comes toward me or does something unusual, I know he's in a crook mood and I'm extra careful," he says. Despite their close relationship through 'Gator's entire lifetime (he began as a 13-inch [33-centimetre] hatchling living in a box by Greg's bed), Greg is under no illusions about what would happen if he fell into the pool.

"He'd eat me," he says simply.

'Gator—a name given by the press, and not especially approved by Greg—is a classic example of a hand-reared saltwater crocodile.

He is a magnificent animal, 11 feet long and probably somewhere between 200 and 300 kilograms in weight. Weighing a large, healthy, male crocodile is such a difficult exercise that Greg can only guess. "You'd need a tranquilliser to really find out." 'Gator is now 12 years old and was originally given to him when Greg was 23 by 'a mate in the north'. 'Gator has grown at a varying rate of about a foot a year since, though at the five foot stage he added 18 inches in one year.

The crocodile is strikingly marked with a beautiful yellow-and-green pattern and cream belly, which is shown to best advantage when he leaps. He lives in an artificially controlled water temperature of 28 to 30 degrees and eats a balanced diet of fish, chicken and rabbits. "Always whole dead animals," Greg says. "He began with dead mice as a tiddler." His intake is now about three to four kilograms a week in warm weather, less in the winter.

"Our theme here is conservation," Greg explains. "We aren't in the business of circus tricks. But leaping is something crocodiles actually do in the wild and it is a spectacular demonstration of crocodile power. It's also good exercise for him."

Greg has a regulated programme with the crocodile. "I haven't given him a name myself but the press always want animals to have names." He gives an address on the functions of the crocodile. "I concentrate not so much on the savagery as on their unique design by nature and what wonderful animals they are." Over the years the routine has become almost formalised and 'Gator appears on cue when he hears Greg with the microphone, opens eyes, closes nostrils, sinks, rises and finally leaps to make a spray-soaking fall.

Greg also has six freshwater crocodiles and two female *porosus*. He hopes that 'Gator will one day become a father. "He's doing all the right things at the moment. But he's a bit over-aggressive and gave our first female a hard time."

He admits there is an element of risk in the hand-feeding, but says that it is a practical way of doing it and he is very careful to keep to routines. Once he slipped while window-cleaning and ended up with his feet in the pond. "The crocodile swung toward me but I was quicker."

Cleaning out is something of a problem and Greg uses a broom like a matador ("He's broken four of them"). The park also includes a range of other reptiles and animals like Tasmanian devils, and wedge-tailed and sea eagles. But 'Gator the high-flier is the undoubted star of the show and the attraction most visitors come to see. If he ever escaped into Ballarat's chilly natural atmosphere he would undoubtedly get a severe culture shock.

But at the moment he's one of the most pampered crocodiles anywhere with two wives, regular tucker and the kind of applause ordinarily accorded to rock-and-roll stars.

"It will be interesting to see how long it takes him to reach maximum size," Greg says. "And to see how big he does get."

An 18-foot leaping crocodile would be spectacular indeed. Will Greg still be hand-feeding him at that stage?

Numbers of people have kept 'pet' crocodiles in northern Australia through the years for varying periods. Hugo Austla at Wyndham, for instance, has two large saltwater crocodiles named Bismarck and Rasputin, and a freshwater specimen named Aggie.

Bismarck is a huge animal, 16 feet or nearly five metres long, and probably more than 400 kilograms and with an uncertain temperament. "He eats half a donkey at a time in the hot weather," Hugo says. "But that lasts him a while."

However, few people have had the time or patience to handle small crocodiles as Alf Casey did, and Charlene continues to be the outstanding example of cordial relations between human beings and crocodiles in Australia.

Her friendship with Casey demonstrates what can be done.

But there are many other examples in history. Crocodiles were venerated in ancient Egypt.

There was actually a priest-city called Crocodilopolis (*Out of This World*, Michael Page) dedicated to their worship.

The main temple had pools, with crocodiles, and the chief sacred crocodile was richly decorated with jewellery.

The Greek historian Herodotus wrote that in parts of Egypt each household had its own pet crocodile. In important houses pet crocodiles were adorned with jewels, and when they died they were embalmed and placed in family tombs.

All through Africa crocodiles were linked in religious ceremonies with fertility and water—floods, and the life-giving rain.

In Madagascar it was believed that the spirits of ancestral chiefs took up residence in crocodiles, and acted as intermediaries between the gods and mortals. Requests to the gods for favours had to go through crocodiles. At Lake Itasy there was an annual ceremony in which humans promised not to kill any crocodiles, on condition that no tribespeople were taken. If a human was killed a crocodile had to die in return.

Australian Aborigines in Cape York and in the Northern Territory had strong religious bonds with crocodiles. On Cape York Peninsula there are still actual 'blood-brother' ceremonies between young boys undergoing initiation and small crocodiles. Blood is passed between them and the crocodiles are then released to grow large and become 'spirit people' of the tribe.

In the Northern Territory the fact that the huge crocodile named 'Baru', believed to be responsible for a number of human deaths, was a tribal totem animal saved him from being shot by rangers. The Aborigines refused to allow it.

There are a number of references in early records of active association between Aborigines and 'spirit' crocodiles, including some ritual feeding.

There are also a number of curious legends of Aborigines actually handling and even riding crocodiles. These may seem too far-fetched to be true, but the myth is persistent. Dr Stephen Garret, writing in the Australian *GEO* magazine, repeats a traditional Aboriginal story.

"Between the old man and the settlement was one of those slow, muddy rivers that wander to the sea all along the Gulf Coast of Queensland. He didn't want to swim. It was too deep and wide and there were too many sharks—he took up his woomera and beat the surface of the water. Moments later there was a ripple and a five-metre crocodile swung in under the bank—the old man climbed on its back and was carried to the other side. He left two fish in payment and continued on his way.

"Just a story? Perhaps. But it is told with great conviction by

Aboriginal people on the west coast of Cape York Peninsula. To the old man the crocodile was the reincarnation of his uncle—all the big crocodiles in the area were reincarnations of ancestors."

The legend is repeated from other sources.

R. A. Moncrieff, in a chapter of *Australian Walkabout* (1968) —a compilation of articles from the famous magazine—wrote about the 'Marauders of the North' in the same vein.

"Another (crocodile) belonged to an Aborigine at Aurukun on the west coast of the Cape York Peninsula. That beggar had a croc trained to ferry him across the river. He had his own call-sign, and when the croc came the Aborigine mounted it, sitting facing not the head but the tail. Another bit of jabber and away they'd go with the Aborigine stroking the brute's sides as they went . . ."

Moncrieff claimed to have been an eyewitness, a circumstance I would regard as extremely doubtful. But it shows that the story was well established and it surfaces occasionally in Territory tall tales like 'The Adelaide River Ferry'. Whether it is simply a myth, like our tale of Jonah and the whale, or whether there was ever any actual basis of fact is, of course, impossible to tell.

If Aborigines had their traditions and crocodile legends, the 'characters' of the north in earlier days certainly had theirs.

Some were pure and outrageous invention, others had a basis of truth.

The men who told the tales were larger than life themselves. There was Freddie Blitner, of Borroloola, who could supposedly use a spear or a waddy as well as the local Yanyula Aborigines. He won himself the nickname 'The Freshwater Admiral' when, in a rum-inspired haze one night, he attempted to launch an 18-foot crocodile into the McArthur River in mistake for his dug-out canoe.

Another identity at Borroloola in the post-war period was Harry Blumantels, a bearded Latvian crocodile shooter who scorned wearing clothes when out in the wild. "The side of me that is away from the sun is in the shadow," he told Douglas Lockwood. "A man doesn't need more covering than that."

He used to write 'cheques' for tobacco and rum on pieces of paper titled 'Riverbank Unlimited, H. Blumantels proprietor', redeeming them in fish and crocodile skins at uncertain periods.

At Borroloola he lived in an old upturned 25,000-gallon tank in the Wet, with holes cut in it for doors and windows. In the Dry he and his Alsatian dog slept under the stars.

He and his neighbour Tom Leahy, who lived a few hundred yards away, once had a disagreement about the boundary between their blocks. Unlike modern landowners they did not immediately brief their lawyers. They settled the matter in more traditional Territorian fashion.

On an appointed day they sat in their respective homes and each drank a bottle of rum. Then—at an agreed time—they went outside and lurched toward each other.

The spot where they met was henceforth considered to be the boundary. Leahy crawled the last few yards on his hands and knees.

With true stories like that it might be wondered why there was any necessity for invention.

But in the north storytelling, particularly the outrageous kind, was a developed art. The north, with its buffalo, wild tribesmen, scrub bulls, taipan snakes, pigs, sharks and crocodiles, provided a natural source of material. The climate also contributed to the yarntelling because in the Wet there often wasn't a great deal else to do. In the annual monsoon the rain poured down, sometimes deluging several inches in a night, for days and even weeks at a time.

Roads, never more than ruts at best, in February and March became streaming quagmires. Rivers brimmed their banks and spread in shining sheets over the floodplains, mirroring the black clouds overhead. Major movement by vehicle, or even on horseback, was so difficult it was usually only attempted for a life-or-death reason.

It was the season of make-and-mend. A time to stitch up split saddles, to oil old and trusty rifles, to clean and repair. Yarns came naturally when old-timers gathered together at Christmas and New Year. The storytelling was often aided by a case of overproof rum, thoughtfully ordered before the Wet 'in case of snakebite or exhaustion', or classified as 'medical comforts'.

Some of the yarnspinners were artists. As time went by they had naturally heard all of each others' stories and visitors were looked forward to eagerly.

There was always the possibility that they might bring some 'new blood' in the way of jokes or tales. But the old-timers' greatest delight was to find some gullible new chum who hadn't heard their stories before and pull his leg outrageously.

Innocents abroad also served another purpose. There was the natural joy of 'catching 'em all alive-oh!' and they were usually good for a few rounds of drinks while the veterans 'bashed their ears'. The better the story the more bountiful the liquid reward.

Territory grog shanties came in all shapes and sizes. They were places for lonely men from cattle stations, to buffalo shooters, prospectors, drovers, horse-breakers and horse-stealers, as well as travelling blacksmiths and saddlers (the last two both much in demand). In addition there were surveyors and 'government men'.

Another type of traveller, more frequent than might have been expected in the early days, were well-to-do young Englishmen, young bloods sent to patronise the colonies for 'colonial experience'. Or older gentlemen with a shrewd eye out for mining or pastoral investments.

Because of their own ingenuous and not-entirely-hidden convictions of social superiority, these were often favourite targets of the tall-tale tellers, especially those of Irish descent, who took a delight in pricking pomposity.

Some shanties were simply a pandanus roof and central lock-up section with the walls open to the four winds. But most were corrugated iron general stores which acted in all capacities. They were 'banks', and issued their own 'shin-plasters' or cheques which were always honoured even when all but illegible. They were meeting places, dance halls on occasion, churches (even more occasionally). And of course they served the store's purpose of supplying the necessities of life—including grog.

In view of the huge amounts of beer consumed today in the hot and thirsty north, it often surprises people to learn that before the Second World War there wasn't a great deal of beer drunk. There were no refrigerators and no way of cooling bottles except by throwing a wet hessian bag over them. Beer took up ruinously expensive space on the teamsters' wagons coming inland from the port.

A bottle of rum occupied a fraction of the space of a crate of beer and did the same job. Rum was cheaper, viewed in this context, was definitely more powerful and was much in favour. Wine ("plonk") was viewed with contempt and considered a drink for Aborigines who consumed it cheerfully and illegally.

The shelves of the store, besides the ever-popular rum, also carried Scotch whisky, bottles of 'square-face' Dutch gin and sherry for station owners' wives. Sometimes there was an attempt at decoration. Buffalo horns hung on the wall, with a story to go with them. Maybe a few crossed rifles of ancient vintage (1890 or thereabouts), wired to the bush timber uprights, which may have done unofficial battle with the local tribes. Perhaps a crocodile skin, or a skull of huge proportions. Often enough the floor was pounded anthill earth, which became as hard as concrete and took a polish of kerosene mixed with linseed oil.

Other standard items on the shelves would be ammunition; stockmen's elastic-sided boots and broad-brimmed hats; saddles and bridles; tins of fruit and bully beef; sacks of rice, sugar and flour; a wide range of medical 'comforts' ranging from pain-killer and liniment to corn-plaster and oil of cloves for toothache. There would be tins of treacle (guaranteed to bring on toothache) and even a few jars of boiled 'lollies' on the chance of a passing child who seldom had to pay.

A group of leather-faced old-timers would be gathered lounging in broken cane chairs near the stained counter. One or two would be rolling parsimonious cigarettes from what was left of their tobacco, or pulling thoughtfully at their whiskers and wondering whether the storekeeper would allow them more credit for another drink.

His purse-mouthed expression as he wiped the bar with a rag, showed plainly that he would not.

At that moment the newcomer arrives, British by his monocle, wealthy by the fact that he wears a coat and fob watch despite the heat, which has given him a somewhat purplish complexion. He shakes the rain off his back and stamps the mud from his well-cut boots. It is raining outside. Naturally, because it is the Wet.

The eyes watch him as he goes to the counter and orders a

drink. "Rum?" inquires the storekeeper, and slides him a bottle and a glass.

The newcomer's start of surprise as he gets a whole bottle causes smirks and shows he has not been long in the Territory. He takes off his hat, mops his brow with a bandanna and fans himself with the hat. A Trilby.

The eyes gleam at the sight of the well-padded wallet. A mining engineer? Gold investment advisor? Pastoral purchaser? Who knows?

Surreptitiously the first bets are laid.

"How do you do?" says the newcomer, feeling the stares.

"G'day!" reply the locals, shadowed faces under broad-brimmed hats.

"Wet, isn't it?" remarks the newcomer by way of polite conversation.

"Hell, no mate," says the chief storyteller. "This is just a sun shower. When you wake up an' find there's a shark chasing barramundi under your bed THEN it's wet!"

"Oh . . ." says the newcomer, only mildy disconcerted and not at all discouraged. He spots the giant crocodile skin nailed to the wall. "So you have crocodiles here?"

"Alligators mate," says one of the other old-timers. "Hundreds of the green-and-yellow bastards. If they'd only keep still and stop gnashing their teeth you could cross that river on their backs without getting your feet wet."

"Which puts me in mind of a story," says the storyteller, sliding easily into the opening. "Crocodiles . . ." He tosses his own shot of rum straight down between tobacco-stained teeth, and with two fingers delicately pushes it toward the newcomer.

"Did yer ever hear about the Adelaide River Ferry?" he asks him. The monocle turns toward him with a gleam of interest.

The glass is filled generously to the brim. "By your leave . . ." the storyteller takes a fingerful of tobacco from the newcomer's pouch and tamps his pipe. An advance against the entertainment to come. "Help yourself, old boy!" . . . "Ta . . ."

The pipe is lit, the glass appeciatively sipped. The story commences.

"Not heard of the Adelaide River Ferry? No? Well, there was

this old blackfellow had tribal land on both sides of the Adelaide and no way of getting across, 'cept by swimming. There wasn't much future in *that* because the river was solid with sharks 'n' alligators, bank to bank. You could hear the snapping of teeth and the slapping of the tails 10 miles before you got there on a still night.

"No sir! You didn't put even so much as a little toe in that muddy ol' Adelaide River. Those critters were so hungry they'd make a meal out of your shadow. You see a joker without a shadow, he'd been on the Adelaide River. But that's another story."

The glass is drained and filled again.

"The Adelaide River Ferry. Yairs . . . Well, that ol' blackfellow, cunning ol' sod, found a way around it. Takin' the easy way out like they always do. 'Stead of walkin' 50 miles around, he trained this big alligator to carry him on his back. He started by holding a barramundi out on the end of a spear like a carrot in front of a donkey. The alligator, which he claimed was his 'uncle' in some sort of tribal mumbo-jumbo, would paddle off after the fish. The old bloke would hop on his back and before you knew it they were on the other side of the river.

"Once he tried using a catfish instead of a barramundi. The croc got disgusted and just to show him, it sank in mid-stream. Gave the old blackfellow a hell of a fright—he had to practically walk on water to get back! No sir, he didn't try cheap-skatin' with a catfish no more!"

Here the old-timer pauses, wipes a hairy paw across his mouth and looks with exaggerated surprise at his glass which has mysteriously emptied once more. If there is no appropriate response from the visitor, the storyteller draws his attention to the situation by remarking on the extraordinary local rate of evaporation.

When the glass is refilled yet again and some more of the newcomer's best Havelock ready-rubbed tobacco tamped with a blackened thumb into the storyteller's capacious pipe bowl— "You wouldn't happen to have a match?"—the story can continue.

"Well, I used to see them down at the river often. We'd have to ride right around to shoot our buffalo. But not the old blackfellow. He'd give a funny sort of high-pitched call and slap the water, and the alligator would appear. Then off they'd go. 'The Adelaide River Ferry', we called it. But strictly a one-man show.

"After a while the alligator seemed to enjoy it even more than the old bloke, and he didn't need a fish any more. It was quite touching to watch them go off together. Mind you, I never dared tell a soul.

"Why not?" The new chum inquires innocently.

"No one would believe it, now would they?" The old-timer, deadpan in expression, shoots a swift glance out from under the shadow of his battered hat, checking to determine the level of credulity of his listener. Satisfied, he goes on.

"Well as I said, off they'd go together. The alligator swimming along, proud as Punch, the old guy facing backwards . . ."

"Facing backwards?" the newcomer inquires, taking the bait at a gulp.

"Yairs. Didn't I say? He always faced the tail. Never went any other way."

"But the fish?"

"Oh, he had that over his shoulder. Long spear you see."

"Backwards?" the newcomer asks again. The first seeds of doubt suddenly forming in his mind.

The critical moment is approaching. Skilfully the old-timer sets the hook.

"Guess you're wonderin'," he said. "Useter puzzle me a bit too. In fact one day I went down an' asked him straight out. He wouldn't give me an answer at first. Mumbled something in tribal lingo and went off on the alligator again, one skinny black leg dangling each side, stroking its great scaly back. Pretty to watch they were. But I never dared tell anyone. Especially when I found out the reason. Yairs, backwards . . ." He looks significantly at his glass. Empty once more.

The visitor takes his monocle and polishes it, the purple hue of his complexion visibly increasing. But really he has no choice. He has already invested two-thirds of a bottle of rum and a substantial portion of a pouch of tobacco. If he ignores the empty glass and the remark, "burns quick this new-fangled tobaccer" at this point, he will lie awake at night wondering about the end of the story.

"All right then. Why did he face backwards?" The old-timer takes an even more appreciative sip of the new glass and charitably ignores the note of testiness in the question. A lingering draw on the glowing pipe. Through the blue curling smoke, "I dunno that I can really tell you."

A murderous look from the new chum. This time the monocle falls out of its own accord.

"No, no, it's not I don't *want* to tell you." A sincere hand on the arm. "But I made this promise, see?"

In extreme circumstances, the story could be drawn out almost indefinitely. But the old-timer has shrewdly judged his run and the end of the bottle is in sight. He prepares for the *coup de grâce*.

"That old blackfellow was a bit ashamed, you see. We all thought he was a hero riding on that alligator, and he didn't want to let us know the real truth of it. But I got it out of him in a weak moment one day."

"So why did he ride the crocodile—sorry, alligator—facing backwards?"

The old-timer drains his glass with a throaty rattling sigh. "Nectar of the gods, it is!" Turning to his audience, "You'll never believe it when I tell you . . ." He pours the final glass himself this time and his rheumy old eyes, wrinkled as an old parrot, roll toward the row of bottles behind the bar in just the faintest hope.

"Go on, man. Go on!" The new chum's voice is now harsh and impatient. His right hand remains clenched in his pocket and there is obviously no further chance of another bottle or even a refill.

"He told me he didn't want to see . . ." says the old-timer sadly.

"Didn't want to see?" A bewildered expression crosses the new chum's face.

"Yairs. He didn't want to look at the alligator."

"But good God man, why ever not?"

"He was afraid of alligators, don't you see?"

One of the local coroners once declared that he could see a basis for a verdict of justifiable homicide in such circumstances. But the audiences were always hugely amused and the victims usually took it all in good part. They had little alternative.

Some of the leg-pulls had their origins in real events, or Aboriginal legends.

Many of the stories—like the policeman's buttons and the signet ring found in the stomachs of the crocodiles at Wyndham—were true and needed no embellishment.

There was no shortage of stories about croc shooters or their mates who dived in to tie a line around the leg of a 'dead' crocodile only to find that the crocodile was still very much alive, or they had the wrong crocodile.

Or the lady taking a skinny dip by moonlight in a billabong and feeling a very familiar touch.

"Ooh! Is that you Roger?"

To hear a slightly surprised Roger announce that he is on the bank towelling himself . . .

Vic Cox was one of the shooters who dived after a 'dead' crocodile that had rolled belly up, to find that the beast had been simply stunned. It became furiously alive when he put his arm around its neck to tow it to the boat.

He still carries the scars of its indignation on his head and chest, and regards it as one of the most dangerous situations.

"Not from the croc," he says hastily. "That was all in the day's work. But what was worse was the young chap on board the boat. I yelled at him *'shoot!'* not knowing he'd never aimed or fired a gun before. He grabbed the rifle and bloody near got me first shot. Luckily he only had five rounds or he'd have killed me! The croc got away of course . . ."

There was the young man from Cairns, in 1983, going home from a nightclub about 2.30 A.M. when he saw something strange in a gutter. He said, "Jeez—that looks like a crocodile!" and unwisely prodded it with the toe of his boot.

It was.

The crocodile's reaction was to take the leg off his trousers, and he was lucky that was all he lost.

When the police, summoned by local taxi drivers, hurried to the scene to apprehend the trouser-snapper it slithered down a stormwater drain and eluded capture.

There was the fisherman at Kalumburu caught by the tide, who was sleeping on the center seat of his dinghy, with his head overhanging one side of the boat, his feet protruding out over the other.

During the night he awoke with a yell of fright to find a crocodile had seized his foot and was trying to drag him overboard. Grabbing his rifle (and commendably taking care not to blast his foot) he managed to shoot it. But not before the crocodile's jaws had done considerable damage to his foot.

At the airstrip waiting for the Flying Doctor aircraft to take him away to the hospital, a sympathiser suggested he had been unlucky.

"Unlucky hell!" he exclaimed. "I'm the luckiest man alive! The bastard could've grabbed me head!"

But the crocodile story to end them all—fact or fiction—is the true tale about the crocodile in the East Alligator River which attacked and turned over a Toyota utility truck.

The incident occured in March 1987, only a few days after the tragedy in which Kerry McLoughlin was decapitated by a crocodile at Cahill's Crossing.

Naturally everyone in the area was very conscious of crocodiles. Even if they hadn't been the approach to the crossing was now studded with signs—'Beware of Crocodiles'.

A Toyota Landcruiser utility with a tray back and with several Aborigines jammed into the cab (because it was raining) approached the crossing intending to go over to the Oenpelli side.

"Conditions were marginal," said Ranger-Superintendent Clive Cook. "There had been heavy rain and there was about a metre of water over the crossing."

Part way across the Toyota encountered a large crocodile on its way upstream.

Whether the crocodile collided with the Toyota in a disputed right-of-way situation, or whether is was the other way about, is still unclear. But the crocodile scored a decisive victory.

After the impact it spun furiously and slammed the four-wheel-drive vehicle with its tail.

The 'iron horse' pitched off the crossing and fell ignominiously over on its side. The wheels spinning, fan belt whirring water briefly, before the motor coughed and died.

Inside the cab—naturally enough—there was pandemonium

as the water rushed in. Driver and passengers struggled and clawed to get out of the half-sunk vehicle.

But when they eventually scrambled through the window they found the triumphant crocodile circling the vanquished Toyota, with an expression of challenge indicating that he plainly wanted to continue the fight.

The terrified Aborigines sat 'bailed-up' in a row on the side of the upturned vehicle, legs around their ears, while the crocodile circled and 'eyeballed' them until the boat from the nearby Kakadu National Park ranger station came to the rescue.

One of the rangers—with absolutely no hint of racism intended —reported that the Aborigines who normally had happy and healthy ebony countenances, were a whiter shade of pale.

And the crocodile? To this day he believes Toyota trucks are sissies.

MANAGEMENT OF CROCODILES

▲▲▲▲▲▲▲▲▲▲▲▲

*U*ntil the end of the 1960s crocodile 'management' programmes in Australia were usually carried out with a .303 rifle. While most reptiles are notoriously hard to kill, it was discovered that a lead slug striking a crocodilian just behind the eyes was particularly effective. Crocodiles, like elephants, had their vulnerable spot.

There were variations. Sometimes a shark hook on a length of chain or wire rope was baited with a hairy and well-aged haunch of wild pig. Or a bullock carcass was liberally 'dosed' with strychnine.

This usually collected a few scavenging dingoes in addition and since the scalps were worth money, poison was regarded with some favour.

The basis of early management, in short, was the widely held belief that the only good crocodile was a dead one.

The first settlers held this view because they lost horses and cattle to crocodiles from the time they arrived in the north in the 1890s. Like the marauding dingoes, the big reptiles were shot wherever they were encountered and considered vermin. If nests were found the eggs were routinely destroyed.

There was no protection afforded any wild animals in the early days, and the suggestion of anything of the sort would have been laughed at.

The supply of wildlife was generally considered to be inexhaustible. If there were dangerous wild animals in your area, or creatures that were a nuisance, you just got rid of them. It was as simple as that.

Because crocodiles were labelled dangerous and 'ugly brutes' they were natural targets for anyone who felt inclined, long before their skins became marketable. Station owners and managers encouraged visiting 'sportsmen' to shoot at crocodiles. The bodies were left to rot.

Though there was a demand for alligator leather in the United States from the 1860s onwards, it was not until the 1930s that there was any market at all for Australian crocodile skins. However, before the Second World War sales of skins in Australia were sporadic and shooting was not well organized. In addition the most effective equipment—spotlights and outboard motors— were not generally available.

Daylight shooting on the banks or from oared dinghies did not make much of a dent in the population.

But after the war it was a different matter. Spotlights allowed night shooting which was enormously more effective. Outboard motors gave access to creeks and tributaries previously untouched. The crocodile skin business boomed. There was a high world price for crocodile leather. Ex-army rifles and ammunition were cheap. Adventurous souls returning from the war found that the routines of civilian life, in contrast to bullets and air-raid sirens, were dull indeed. Crocodile shooting sounded like a glamorous occupation. The north was definitely frontier country with something of the romantic aura of the Wild West about it.

In fact there was little glamour about croc shooting. It was just damned hard work, as Douglas Lockwood described it. Lockwood was for many years the Melbourne *Herald*'s man in Darwin. He used to jokingly call himself 'our crocodile correspondent' because so many of his Northern Territory stories seemed to involve crocodilians. " 'Crocodile Bites Man' was news," he used to say with a grin.

"Hunting crocodiles was a serious business for men who lived with danger," he reflected in an article written in retirement in 1980. "It was a tough, austere life of back-breaking work and sleepless nights.

"There was little sleep by day either, for it was then that the skinning was done." Lockwood had several trips with professional shooters like Jim Edwards, George Haritos and Don McGregor.

"I've known shooters to go three weeks without taking time off for a decent wash. They were then red-eyed from lack of sleep," he recalled.

"After a crocodile-hunting expedition the hunter's clothes stink of the dried scrapings of flesh and scale on arms and legs. Backs ache from the constant stooping while skinning. Heads throb from the weight and glare of spotlights, lacerated hands sting from the salt rubbed into the hides.

"Shooters are sunburned by the tropic sun and tormented by flies during the day. When the air is chilled at night the flies are replaced by myriads of mosquitoes and sandflies.

"Oh, great fun . . ."

The money made it all worthwhile. At least for a time. Ion Idriess himself wrote: "Apart from the incentive for hides it was great sport, ceaselessly alert for those ugly knobbed things that any second might rise beside the boat. A thrill to take the quick sight and see the death throes of this thing that otherwise might have lived to take to a horrible death a horse or a bullock or a buffalo or even a human being. I've long since lost the lust for killing things except for food, other than crocodiles and sharks." It was typical of the attitude of the times.

But the shooters themselves were surprised to find how soon it all came to an end. How quickly the rivers and creeks of the north were shot out.

Crocodile numbers dropped so alarmingly that, long before protection was introduced for saltwater and freshwater crocodiles, crocodile shooting had stopped being a full-time occupation for professionals.

In fact in the Northern Territory the first calls for protection came ironically from shooters anxious to see a continuation of their livelihood.

How many crocodiles were killed?

Some extraordinary figures have been quoted. It is sometimes claimed that 30,000 skins were taken from the Adelaide River alone.

But careful investigation has shown that there were far fewer professional shooters than is popularly imagined. While many old-timers in Territory bars may now claim to have been the original 'Crocodile Dundee', few of them really ever lived off their skill with a .303 Lee Enfield rifle, or the educated flick of a skinning knife.

Dr Grahame Webb (who runs a scientific research team as a company consulting the Northern Territory Conservation Commission) has interviewed surviving genuine shooters and checked back through sale and export records, following a patient trail of investigation. He has yet to find evidence that any more than 113,000 skins were ever taken from the Northern Territory, the most prolific area. He calculates (*Wildlife Management*: *Crocodiles and Alligators*, Sydney, 1987) that 87,000 skins were taken between 1945 and 1958 when shooting was at its peak. In the period when the industry was in decline, 1959 to 1971, only 26,000 skins were taken. There are no figures for Western Australia or Queensland. But some of the Australian professionals like George Craig were forced to move their operations to Papua New Guinea when Australian crocodile numbers ran low. Some went as far afield as Borneo.

The decline in crocodiles was matched elsewhere in the world, as the fashion demand for crocodile skins resulted in a plunder of American alligators, African crocodiles and South American caimans alike.

In fact most big wildlife was under threat during the same period—a threat which became increasingly critical in the 1980s with poaching pressure and habitat destruction. Elephants have been slaughtered, legally and illegally, for their tusks, leopards and tigers for their skins. The hunting followed the same ruthless and unthinking patterns as the prior slaughter of seals and whales. Before the 1970s the word 'conservation', as applied to world animal species, was largely unheard.

As far as crocodiles were concerned, in the north of Australia there was no legislation on a state or federal level to protect wild animals and no means of enforcing regulations if they had existed.

Western Australia was the first State to protect crocodiles following a commissioned report from the Australian reptile expert Dr H. R. Bustard, who warned that the two crocodile species were seriously endangered in WA. Western Australia protected the freshwater crocodile, *Crocodylus johnstoni*, as early as 1962, and the Northern Territory in 1963. Unfortunately, because there was still 'open slather' in the Territory and Queensland, poachers were able to run the skins across the border.

In 1969 WA took the further step of protecting *Crocodylus porosus* as well. The Northern Territory followed suit in 1971, with Queensland coming into line in 1974 after a 1972 federal government ban on crocodile skin exports. This closed the gate on poached skins going out through Queensland.

Protection by statute, of course, was just a beginning. Wildlife experts in State bodies realised that the legislation was necessarily a mere preliminary to a much heavier involvement.

Research was an important back-up to regulations to find the most effective practical means of protection. Knowledge of crocodilian numbers, the extent of their habitat and their nesting and breeding habits, were prime requisites in dealing with animals no one had previously much cared about.

Before 1970, in fact, little was known about crocodiles, except as raw material for handbags. From the 1970s onward important research studies were implemented. Among these were the field research programmes in the Northern Territory carried out by Sydney University teams under Professor Harry Messel, a former Canadian physicist who had previously researched polar bears as a scientific side interest and now became a flamboyant and major pioneer of protection for Australian crocodiles.

'Conservation' became one of the emotive words of the 1970s. The conscience of people around the world was awakened to the plight of all wild creatures, including crocodiles. The Northern Territory Parks and Wildlife Commission (now the Conservation Commission) was established. Queensland and Western Australia established their own similar bodies, CALM (or the Department of Conservation and Land Management) in WA and the Queensland National Parks and Wildlife Service.

An old word was given a new meaning in relation to wildlife. 'Management' was now understood to mean protecting and caring for wild animals rather than just eliminating them. It also involved controlling the interaction between animals like crocodiles and humans for the benefit of both parties.

The fact that crocodiles occasionally ate people did cause problems. Fatalities at Nhulunbuy in the late 1970s provoked a good deal of local Northern Territory concern and demands for culling. The Daintree incident in North Queensland at Christmas of 1985 aroused particular public emotion in that State. The Queensland government of the time—despite the legislation for protection on the statute books—was sympathetic not only to groups calling for the removal of large crocodiles from populated areas but it seemed to tacitly approve crocodile killing by people not approved under legislation. Ginger Meadows' death evoked similar calls for culling in WA from people in the Ord River and Kununurra areas, who feared the possibility of attacks.

Through the years from 1971 to 1987 protection proved outstandingly successful in terms of a recovery of the crocodile population.

An initial difficulty for scientists was that there were no figures for the original level of numbers to use as a measuring stick for comparisons of recovery. Scientists could only guess. This made it hard to assess the significance of the new crocodile figures.

As Dr Grahame Webb of the NT Conservation Commission Crocodile Research Unit put it: "You could go down the Adelaide River and say 'Gee, there were 574 crocodiles!' or 'There were *only* 574 crocodiles.' You needed to know how many there were originally to assess the significance, and those figures—regrettably—just aren't available."

Webb and Professor Harry Messel, of the University of Sydney, were the two most prominent research scientists in the field.

Unfortunately they publicly disagreed on original population levels and recovery rates.

Professor Messel was instrumental in having Australian *Crocodylus porosus* placed on Appendix I of the Convention on International Trade in Endangered Species of Wild Flora and Fauna (CITES). This effectively prohibited any trade in skins or crocodile products. Professor Messel CBE, an articulate and widely published scientist, believed that prior crocodile numbers had been generally underestimated.

In an article in the magazine *Simply Living* he wrote, in his characteristically challenging style:

"How large were the original numbers of crocodiles? We can never know for certain, for as usual this Australian resource was neither inventoried nor studied until it was virtually extinguished. (An excellent example of the same process is now being seen with the barramundi, being netted and poached out at an alarming rate before its extent or biology have been sufficiently studied.) However, reports from hunters' figures on the skin trade and, above all, the innumerable documented statements and journal entries by the early explorers, attest to the fact that the original numbers must have been huge. Explorers such as King, Stokes, Cadell and Searcy refer time after time to the very numerous crocodiles on northern Australian rivers, and to the problems created by them. It appears that the saltwater crocodile population in northern Australia was well in excess of a million; but, as we stated above, we will never be able to prove it. Using this figure, which in my opinion is probably an *under*estimate, it will be seen that the present population of non-hatchling crocodiles is probably no greater than 1 or 2 per cent of its former extent. Thus, what probably took millions of years to achieve, was wiped out by voracious hide-hunters in less than two decades.

"Because of exclusion from breeding rivers, there would have been many more crocodiles than now in less-desirable habitat, such as along the coast, around islands and in hypersaline systems. We believe, however, that it could take hundreds of years for the present population to recover to its former level.

"What, then, is the population of *Crocodylus porosus* in northern Australia?

"We have made estimates, based upon our detailed

surveys of over 5168 kilometres of tidal waterways, for
the populations of non-hatchling saltwater crocodiles in
the Northern Territory, the Kimberleys of Western Australia and northern Queensland. Only figures for the tidal
waterways surveyed may be deemed to be reliable—the
remainder are probably upper limits and may be overes-
timated considerably. Only surveys of the waterways can
yield accurate figures. With this warning in mind, our
upper estimates for the non-hatchling *C. porosus* populations now are:

NORTHERN TERRITORY	12,000
THE KIMBERLEYS	2,500
NORTH QUEENSLAND	3,000
TOTAL	17,500

"Our above figure—i.e. less than 20,000 animals—
stands in stark contrast to that given in the *Northern Territory Conservation Commission Technical Report, Number 21*. In that report, the authors produce an estimate of
some 40,000 to 50,000 animals for the Northern Territory. However, they include hatchling *C. porosus* and in
addition give what we feel are inflated estimates for the
very poorly studied freshwater populations of *C. porosus*."

Dr Grahame Webb, presenting the Northern Territory Conservation Commission point of view, with co-researchers Peter J.
Whitehead and S. Charlie Manolis, in the book *Wildlife Management: Crocodiles and Alligators*, disputes the professor's figures.

He believes that statements supplied by other people to Messel
on original crocodile numbers were—with the best of intentions
and honest belief—greatly exaggerated.

"Australia is a dry and arid country," he said. "Even if man
had never existed in Australia there isn't the amount of habitat
to support a million crocodiles. We just don't have the wetland
situations for breeding like the vast swamps of Papua New
Guinea, or the alligator swamps of the Mississippi basin in the
United States.

"When you take an unemotional look at the diaries of the pioneers, talk to men who lived in northern Australia before there was any serious shooting, it becomes clear that there never was a huge crocodile population."

He quotes Ion Idriess, author of 25 books and a prolific writer about northern Australia before the Second World War.

Idriess, previously quoted in this chapter, made a number of trips with crocodile shooters in the Territory in the 1930s. He sets down his experiences in his book *In Crocodile Land* (Angus & Robertson, Sydney 1946).

Idriess wrote: "Do not imagine that all the Northern Territory rivers and tidal creeks are swarming with the estuarine crocodile. Although in occasional localities along the length of the Territory coast crocodiles are numerous, in most areas they are not nearly so plentiful."

Webb's view is that the saltwater crocodile population was never as high in the first place as many people believe because of natural limits. These included a scarcity of breeding territories, the mortality of juveniles and the territorial nature of large crocodiles. The species, by cannibalism and territorial conquest, kept its own natural check on numbers, he believes.

"There just never were back-to-back crocodiles in the north," he says.

He says also that the figures for skins taken were overstated in later years. The recovery of *porosus*—particularly in the Northern Territory—has been much better than anticipated. He places the increase at 6 to 8 per cent per year, with an especial increase in the number of large animals. He estimates a total NT *porosus* population of 40,000 to 50,000, against Messel's estimate of 17,000 for all Australia.

He disputes Messel's more pessimistic view that saltwater crocodiles are still under threat in Australia, or that it may take 'hundreds of years' for the population to recover. In fact he believes that by 1987 *Crocodylus porosus* was back to within 40 to 50 per cent of its original numbers in the Northern Territory.

The war of words between Australia's two most-published crocodile research scientists was watched with interest and some awe by other scientists and students in the field.

A dry humorist likened it to a territorial clash between two five-metre bull crocodiles sending the water flying in a river reach. One had to lose.

In the case of the two scientists the disparity in the figure projections meant that not only was one of them wrong, the loser looked liked being wrong by a big margin.

The situation was not helped by the fact that, in his early years, Webb had worked under Messel in his University of Sydney–sponsored crocodile programmes. Or that Messel was later charged by Northern Territory authorities with having dead magpie geese in the freezer of his crocodile research vessel *The Harry Messel*.

Messel said that he had the geese for crocodile feeding habit studies. The wildlife authorities said it was illegal to catch them. The case dragged on for several years, through various courts, at considerable expense to the University of Sydney, which met the professor's legal costs. It was finally quashed in 1986, the year of Messel's retirement.

Another possible source of friction was the fact that Professor Messel had been instrumental in having the Australian *Crocodylus porosus* placed on the world CITES Appendix I, in 1972, as a species in danger of extinction.

Representations from the Northern Territory Conservation Commission, on the basis of data provided by Webb and his co-researchers, succeeded in having *porosus* transferred back to CITES Appendix II in May 1985.

The move, which was supported by the Australian Council of Nature Conservation Ministers, the International Union for the Conservation of Nature, the Crocodile Specialist Group of the Survival Services Commission, as well as CITES, had great significance.

Effectively under Appendix I there could be no export trade at all in Australian crocodile products. With the more flexible Appendix II, which allows limited commercial exploitation, skins could be exported under specific controls because the species was no longer considered actually endangered.

"Appendix I is for critically endangered animals that are indeed on the verge of extinction," Webb says. "The Tasmanian tiger is the type of animal that's on Appendix I. If there *is* one then we really want to look after it. To have animals that are not in real danger on Appendix I is to 'cry wolf' and risk damaging the whole CITES system. Saltwater crocodiles were on Appendix II. They went up to Appendix I in 1979 and after a huge expenditure of money there were finally put back on Appendix II where they rightly belonged, relative to other animals, in 1985."

This was more than just an academic triumph for Webb. It had far-reaching ramifications, because it allowed the development of crocodile farms in the Northern Territory which could have a future profitable export trade in skins from captive animals raised within the farms. These would compete with similar farms in Africa and Asia.

Webb's down-to-earth personal view—which will be examined in more detail in the concluding chapter of this book—is that the best guarantee for crocodile survival is to make them an asset instead of an annoyance. The two obvious sources of crocodile dollars are tourism, and farm-bred skins and meat.

"When enough jobs and income are tied up with crocodiles— when they become a valuable resource instead of vermin—then, and only then, will they have a permanent place in our world," he says. "Something that is worth money is always well looked after."

Taking the opposing view that crocodiles are still endangered, Messel openly disputes the findings of Webb and his co-researchers in the Northern Territory. He told writer Sorrel Wilby on 3 March 1987, for the national magazine *Australian Geographic*: "No man alive knows these northern Australian waters better than I and I tell you crocodiles need to be protected and carefully controlled. I've got the figures and I can only go by what they say.

"The Northern Territory is trying to do a good job. It took me long enough to tell them how to do it, too!

"This dispute with the figures . . . sweetie, I am the scientist. I have the facts. Saltwater crocodile populations haven't increased at all since 1979 in certain areas. They're still at extinction level in some areas such as the Gulf of Carpentaria."

The magazine balanced this by also carrying Grahame Webb's viewpoint. He is inclined to be impatient with the numbers debate as sidetracking the main issues. I spoke with him in Darwin.

"Of course there are more crocodiles," he says. "Every fisherman, every person who lives in crocodile areas in the north will tell you that and our counts confirm the trend. But the actual head count has to be approximate and must contain estimates in many areas. Logistically you can't count every crocodile—an animal whose main trait is concealment—in every river and swamp in northern Australia.

"What *is* important is not so much the actual numbers but the increase—the population dynamics. When you have an animal population increasing at a rate of 8 or 9 per cent per year, it creates all kinds of other pressures. The expansion has certainly put pressures on humans in the Territory by limiting previous recreation opportunities—swimming, fishing, diving, that sort of thing. It has necessitated all kinds of other adjustments.

"The change for Territorians from days when crocodiles were rare to the present time when they are all over the place, has imposed a major change in lifestyle. I'm proud of the way they've coped."

Webb is right that the numbers disagreement has probably taken up too much scientific and public attention, perhaps to the detriment of recognition of the many positive research discoveries.

The public loves a scrap, particularly when the opponents are heavyweights. But it would be a shame—an absurdity, even—if future generations were to remember only the opposed views of Messel and Webb on crocodile counts.

This would be entirely negative. For all their disagreement on numbers there are a great many other points on which they are in accord. What should be recognised is the immense contribution both men have made to knowledge on Australian crocodiles in widespread areas of research, aside from the controversial counts.

Messel was the most active Australian pioneer in crocodile research. His efforts in securing protection in the early 1970s stopped poaching and removed dangerous pressures on a failing crocodile population. His research was on a grand scale and he tapped widespread sources of funds. The Sydney University equipment included a 21-metre, 125-tonne ocean-going vessel *The Harry Messel*. His 12 years of fieldwork and his training and bringing other scientists (including Webb) into practical research have resulted in a widening spread of research into a previously little-known but important animal. He has contributed an enormous amount of knowledge and stimulated important public awareness.

"No man has spent more time or money than Harry Messel," Webb acknowledges.

Webb himself has been researching Australian crocodiles, *porosus* and *johnstoni*, for more than 15 years. He has published more than 70 scientific papers on his findings and largely co-edited and contributed to *Wildlife Management: Crocodiles and Alligators*, as well as a novel, *Numunwari*, which is to be made into a film titled *Dark Age*.

Time will tell which man is right on the issue of crocodile numbers. But in terms of the overall task, history should applaud the efforts of them both.

Meantime public and scientific attitudes in the rest of Australia vary, like regional politics, from state to state.

In 1988 Australian modern crocodile management came under three separate state authorities in Australia: Western Australia, the Northern Territory and Queensland. Attitudes differed in each area and were largely influenced by the history of interaction between people and crocodiles.

The Northern Territory had the most crocodiles and a significant proportion of local people coming into contact with crocodiles. It had by far the most advanced research programmes. The Northern Territory Government also instituted an education drive which significantly altered the public attitude towards crocodiles. Crocodile industries in farms, tourism and approved skin exports also helped the cause of the crocodile in the public view through income and employment.

In Western Australia—except for the town of Wyndham, a place we will look at later with particular interest—there was little contact between crocodiles and people up to 1988.

Figures given by Dr Andrew Burbidge of the Western Australian Department of Conservation and Land Management after the death of Ginger Meadows in 1987, and quoted in *The West Australian* newspaper, were based on regional surveys by Professor

Harry Messel's Sydney University group. The figures, from surveys in 1977–78 and 1986 in the Prince Regent, Roe and Hunter Rivers of the Kimberley region, showed a 30 per cent rise in the number of non-hatchling crocodiles in that period. More significantly, the number of crocodiles measuring more than 1.8 metres had risen from 20 per cent of those counted to 40 per cent.

There were more crocodiles in Western Australia, in short, and especially more big crocodiles.

With the increase in tourism in remote areas, it seemed that contacts between humans and crocodiles were bound to increase. But crocodile density was unlikely to ever approach that of the Northern Territory. Geographically there is a lack of good wetland habitat on the WA side of the border. The fiord-like rivers of the Kimberleys—lined by spectacular red cliffs—do not offer the same breeding conditions as the Territory's flat country floodplain systems of swamps and billabongs.

Queensland differs from both the other areas. It has the longest 'crocodile coast' in Australia, extending from the Gulf of Carpentaria up and around Cape York and down south past Rockhampton, and even (in the past) Bundaberg. It is a tropical crocodile frontage roughly equivalent to the distance from Perth to Sydney.

Yet it does not contain as many crocodiles as might be expected in terms of sheer distance—though Queensland has recorded a large proportion of the fatal attacks. Messel's estimate is a non-hatchling population of 3000 (against 2500 in a much shorter distance in Western Australia). The reason for the lower density, again, is both lack of suitable breeding habitat and (in some areas) human interference. The 'best' areas appear to be on both sides of the wilderness zones of Cape York. Numbers are greatly reduced in southern areas such as Cairns, which have long been cultivated and where crocodiles—though not apparently endangered—are not common today because in the past they were unwelcome neighbours. The most conspicuous recent example of this was the Daintree River shoot-out. We have already recorded that sad history. But it did turn crocodiles into a political rather than a research issue. Rationality went out the window in the emotive public reaction to Beryl Wruck's untimely death.

Queensland politics, in the late 1980s, appeared to be more attuned to public opinion than to the recommendations of research scientists. Nonetheless there were also active and positive research programmes. They supplemented those of the Northern Territory and Sydney University, but unfortunately did not get the same kind of publicity exposure as negative reactions like the Daintree.

From a position of knowing very little about crocodiles in the early 1970s, the scientists knew a great deal by 1988. Through their published information, which was passed on to the public through television programmes on the ABC and commercial stations and through national magazines such as *Australian Geographic, Simply Living* and *GEO*, Australians generally became much better educated on the subject. The perception of crocodiles changed gradually from one of dangerous and disliked vermin, to one—if not of actual liking—of at least some kind of grudging respect.

One of the major scientific events was the Technical Conference on Crocodile Conservation and Management which was held in Darwin, from 13–18 January 1985. Experts came from all over the world. Scientists and researchers involved in crocodile management in Africa, India, the United States and South America attended, read papers and participated in discussions.

The conference was initiated by the Conservation Commission of the Northern Territory. It resulted in a significant compilation of scientific information on crocodilians.

The papers at the conference, discussion points and relevant information were published in 1987 in book form, *Wildlife Management: Crocodiles and Alligators*, mentioned in earlier chapters as an important source of information. It was edited by Grahame Webb, Charlie Manolis and Peter Whitehead and is the outstanding work of its kind in Australia.

And what *have* the scientists discovered in the past 20 or so years in their investigations and interferences with crocodiles in general?

A considerable amount of the information is technical and

would pass the ordinary reader by without the raising of any eyebrows. But there are other glimpses of the life of a reclusive and previously little-understood animal which are quite fascinating.

Crocodiles are ardent lovers, for example.

Like those other reptilian romantic athletes (surprise), the turtles, they obviously enjoy the first stages of reproduction to the full.

Their courtship is elaborate and even imaginative. Females indicate submission by snout-lifting and muted sounds. They are often excited by battles fought by dominant males. It is more usual for the male to advertise his presence by swimming in an inflated position, tail often arched high. He augments this by head-slapping, an explosive and spectacular clap of jaws at water level.

But female crocodiles are by no means passive or docile. They are not shy in initiating sex play when it suits them and often boldly approach the male.

Foreplay includes snout contact, head-rubbing, body rubbing and riding and a variety of sounds ranging from gurgles and grunts to low growls.

Male crocodiles can also give off rapid vibrations which cause hundreds of tiny bubbles to agitate the water around their flanks.

Female crocodiles appear to find this bubbling (like the fizz in the 'Schweppervescence' television advertisements) difficult to resist. It sets them all a-tingle.

Unlike the American alligator which bellows come mating time, *Crocodylus porosus* is not a noisy animal. He may growl while attacking or mating. But people who think they have heard Australian crocodiles bellowing in the depths of the mangroves have probably been listening to the great billed heron. This is a bird which puts out a surprising volume of sound from a slender body and has fooled a lot of people, including your author.

With low growls, then, the Australian saltwater crocodile proceeds to lovemaking. He has a formidable penis, though this is normally kept withdrawn inside a body vent. It is difficult to tell males and females of similar size apart in an unexcited state.

Scientists can do it by feeling with their fingers in the cloaca.

But crocodiles resent this kind of interference as much as humans and it is not a recommended procedure with a four- or five-metre crocodile in the wild.

The best way to tell sex and keep your arm is to wait and see who lays the eggs. But in copulation, the male—usually much larger—takes the dominant role and can be readily identified.

The fortunate male mounts the female on her back while she lifts her snout in submission and he curves his body around, intertwining tails, to enter her from below. Woe betide any other crocodile or creature interrupting at that tender moment.

Copulation can take 10 to 15 minutes and is often repeated. Couples in captivity may keep at it for days with crocodilian smiles.

A dominant male may couple with a number of females within his territories. But some females—obvious hussies—who cross territorial borders for an additional share are serviced by several dominant males.

The result of all this fun is that three to six weeks later the lady lays her eggs.

Most of the crocodilians, including alligators, dig holes or scratch up mounds for incubation. In Australia *Crocodylus porosus* makes a large mound of vegetation, the smaller freshwater *Crocodylus johnstoni* digs holes in sandbars.

The saltwater crocodile is a good mother. Field studies by the Crocodile Research Station of the Northern Territory Conservation Commission have shown that about 80 per cent of females lay eggs, the average clutch is 52 eggs and overall about 75 per cent of eggs do not survive to hatching.

Why such a large mortality?

Mother *porosus* likes to use long grass to build and conceal her nest, near permanent water. Such areas are prone to flooding and if she lays too late in the season the drenching rains of the Wet raise water levels too high. Wet eggs don't hatch. Crocodile embryos (like chickens) breathe through small pores in the egg shell. Oxygen comes in and carbon dioxide goes out. If eggs are covered with water the embryos drown. In some areas, Webb found, flooding destroys 90 per cent of nests each year.

Once the eggs are laid, the female crocodile relies on the increasingly warm summer sun to maintain the compost effect of the rotting vegetation and keep the eggs warm. She mounts guard in a wallow by the nest.

Dangers to crocodile eggs, besides rising water, have always included monitor lizards, dingoes and Aborigines. Introduced pigs are a modern problem, and water buffalo and cattle are a major, though indirect, cause of mortality. Their trails through foliage form run-off rivulets which drain swamps. Many crocodile nests are on floating mats of vegetation.

When buffalo trample the water's edge they break the attachment of the raft to the bank. It may float away to be lost on floodwaters.

Even after all these losses, when little crocodiles hatch they still only have a long-odds chance of survival.

Obviously the natural mortality of eggs and hatchlings could be greatly reduced by artificial means. A good deal of the Northern Territory research has been directed into practical methods of achieving this. For instance eggs doomed to failure by flooding could be rescued and artificially incubated. In theory the resulting hatchlings could be divided into groups going into crocodile farms and others returned to the wild to increase the natural population.

Since many of the nests are in the Aboriginal Reserve of Arnhem Land, egg collecting could provide a paying and congenial industry for Aborigines. It could also benefit outlying cattle stations at a quiet time of year.

So there are side-benefits as well.

If this all seemed too easy an answer to problems, there are indeed snags. Eggs brought in often failed to hatch and eggs became the subject of major research, with Grahame Webb's consultancy group advising the Northern Territory Conservation Commission.

It costs him blood, literally, because in the course of it he was attacked by a zealous crocodile mother and bitten on the leg. He still carries the scars.

Through the 1980s some thousands of nests were examined, often in inaccessible areas where the only means of reaching them was by helicopter. Researchers had to fend off angry mother crocodiles while they measured, weighed and photo-graphed eggs and took samples for laboratory analysis.

It was found, among other things, that if eggs were rotated during collection the embryos died. They had to be marked and maintained right side up. The temperatures of incubation deter-mined sex and it was possible to produce varying ratios of males and females and other results from different temperature levels.

For instance, low incubation temperatures produced large 'good-looking' hatchlings. But they did not often survive.

Despite the difficulties it was found that it was possible to get a high success rate in hatching and that once out of the egg, little captive crocodiles were 80 per cent likely to grow to commercial skin size. About a 79 per cent better chance than in the wild.

However, as Professor Messel showed in his research, the other major area of mortality was in juveniles of less than two metres forced out of the river systems by larger crocodiles. This represents about a 70 per cent loss and one of the recommenda-tions has been that some of these unfortunate youngsters be cap-tured for farms and raised past their vulnerable stage for the wild, rather than disrupting nesting and upsetting mothers.

There are many other scientific and lay aspects of interest in studies of crocodiles. There is the four-chambered heart for in-stance, not found in other reptiles, which permits the furious burst of energy when the crocodile attacks.

The question of how fish, seabirds and other marine animals cope with the elimination of salt has always been intriguing. Most seabirds, like albatrosses, petrels and common gulls, have salt glands in their beaks. Turtles use eye ducts and hence the 'tears' as the turtle crawls ashore. Crocodiles also excrete high salt con-centrations but they do it through glands on their tongue. Queensland research scientist Laurence E. Taplin (*GEO* maga-zine) writes that the freshwater crocodile, *Crocodylus johnstoni*, also has salt glands, indicating that in some distant past the spe-cies may have spent time in saltwater.

On the other hand American alligators and South American caimans have no salt glands and therefore—presumably—have always lived in freshwater systems as far back as their history goes.

Other important glands are scent glands. These are located in the cloaca of both males and females, giving off a musky aroma to attract the opposite sex, and under the jaw (like a lady putting scent behind her ears?). Their function is as a supplement in attracting partners in the mating season.

Humans do it too.

Crocodiles often carry stones or other foreign objects in their stomachs. The reason for it is still unclear. It has been argued variously that they are to aid digestion or for ballast purposes. Yet captive crocodiles with no access to stones seem to digest their food perfectly well and they also have no trouble submerging. In fact it seems most likely that crocodilians used their breath either to inflate and float high for aggressive territorial displays or to deflate and sink low when they wish to stalk and show only eyes and nostrils.

The stones may be accidentally swallowed, or they may be the result of whimsey. But they are regarded seriously by primitive tribesmen who see the stones as objects of magic power. Some tribes in the Northern Territory prize them as religious objects.

The Chinese have provided a traditional market for poachers' wares, which contributed to the threat of extinction of rhinos and tigers. This is through the illicit trade of powdered horns and whiskers as supposed aphrodisiacs. In Africa black rhino numbers fell from millions last century to 65,000 by 1970. As a result of poaching they are now down to a mere 3800 animals. Crocodile penises and gall bladders are in demand for the same purpose. It is hoped that Australian crocodile farms, with others worldwide, will provide the product legitimately and put poachers out of business.

On a happier note, few people realise that crocodiles actually play games. Bob Hall, caretaker of a mothballed mining camp at Ja Ja in Kakadu, found this out in an inconvenient way.

During the Wet, when local dirt roads were closed, he needed to keep open a connection by boat to the main sealed road to Darwin at South Alligator crossing. In fact Val Plumwood was evacuated by this route when she was injured in February 1985.

A methodical man, Bob marked the deep channels with anchored oval fishing floats. When floats kept moving about the place irrationally without the impetus of current and the channel was 'lost', he was momentarily nonplussed. But he soon found the answer in crocodile teeth marks on the floats. Some of the floats were actually crushed flat. The jaw force required to flatten the hard polystyrene was enormous. But it was no trouble to the local crocodiles.

It seemed obvious that they were taking the floats and dragging them around as playthings and the experience has been repeated elsewhere with crushed tins, buckets and other random objects crocodiles have taken, apparently to amuse themselves. While we can accept the idea of a dog running after a thrown stick or a kitten playing with a ball of string, the notion of a crocodile playing with toys is something of a foreign concept.

This is departing somewhat from the scientific aspects of crocodilian life. But it shows how much we still have to learn about them.

Another area into which research will undoubtedly one day probe more deeply is the ability of crocodiles to navigate and to locate prey underwater in conditions of nil visibility.

Many of the northern rivers are so heavy with soil washed down by the rain in the Wet that they are little more than liquid mud. Yet crocodiles move around in them freely, going about their business, avoiding snags, pursuing prey as an everyday occurrence. Perhaps we should say an 'every night' event, for they are basically nocturnal feeders, which makes it even more remarkable. How do they locate and catch a fish in the blacker-than-black waters of a mangrove creek at midnight on a moonless night?

We know that they see well both under and above the surface in daylight and clear water. But when the water is turbid other senses must come into play.

Dolphins do remarkably well in these circumstances using echo location. An inbuilt sonar guides them unerringly even when blindfolded in experimental tests. Scientists know that they do it and that there is a connection with the audible sounds they make —whistles, buzzes and clicks. But they have not yet fathomed exactly how this system works.

So far no one has tried blindfolding crocodiles. But sooner or later some scientist will investigate crocodile navigation and it will be interesting to learn how they actually do find their way about in the dark.

Other crocodile senses, like their hearing, are also acute. They are particularly sensitive to vibration, such as splashing in the water and footfalls on the bank, and their ears, like their nostrils and gullets, have neat flaps to keep the water out.

Like an efficient submarine, the crocodile seals all hatches when submerging.

People who go to places like the East Alligator River where crocodiles proliferate are often disappointed. They look out across the shining stretch of water and fail to see a single crocodile. "Where are they?" they ask.

The crocodiles are there all right. But their natural tendency is to submerge at any intrusion. To become an unseen presence. With patience, sitting quietly under a tree without noise or movement, a pair of 'walnuts' will appear here or there and eventually a number of crocodiles may surface and resume their ordinary activities. A pair of good binoculars are a great help in observing them, for they show remarkably little of themselves in natural circumstances.

Crocodiles in the wild tend to be shy, except in areas like the Adelaide River where they are fed for the benefit of tourists. Watching the speed and agility of crocodiles leaping to take meat two metres out of the water is an awesome sight.

Probably the best place to see and study large crocodiles in safety is at crocodile farms.

At present there are seven crocodile farms in Australia. One is at Broome in Western Australia, three are in the Northern Territory and three in Queensland.

The oldest established farm, set up basically for the benefit of the Aboriginal community by the Commonwealth Government, is at Edward River, near the tip of Cape York in Queensland. It has about 5000 animals and its function is an export trade in skins under strict controls and the supply of eggs and hatchlings to other crocodile farms.

The biggest farm, 40 hectares with 6500 animals in 1987 (both *Crocodylus porosus* and *Crocodylus johnstoni*), is the Darwin

Crocodile Farm. This combines excellent tourist displays with breeding for skins.

The commercial returns on breeding market crocodiles are good. The skin from a two-metre, three-year-old *Crocodylus porosus* was worth $300 in 1988—$19 a belly-inch of leather, in the vernacular of the trade.

While some people question the ethics of breeding animals for killing—ignoring their own breakfast chop or dinnertime takeaway chicken—it can be argued that a regular, controlled skin trade is the best answer to the evils of poaching. Illegal hunting still threatens whole crocodilian populations in South America and Africa. However by commercial logic, skin buyers prefer a stable and controlled source. Also the skin quality of farm-bred animals is very much better. With regularised trading from reliable sources the market for poached skins might dry up altogether.

There is also a considerable potential for crocodile meat. Crocodile flesh has a taste of its own, somewhere between veal and chicken. It cuts up well into steaks or hamburger meat and there is a big tourist demand throughout northern Australia. In 1988 the meat was worth $20 a kilogram in the Territory and more than $30 a kilogram in the south. A three-year-old crocodile provides eight to nine kilograms of meat, putting on an extra $180 of value to the $300 skin.

In addition to all this, there is still the traditional Chinese requirement and high prices for crocodile penises and gall bladders. Adding up skin, flesh and aphrodisiacs, a three-year-old farm crocodile becomes a valuable beast worth more than $500. Because the best markets for these products are in Japan, Europe and Asia the exchange rate situation in 1988 made export particularly valuable.

Apart from the people employed in the farms, feeding and caring for growing crocodiles, specialists are needed for skinning and preparing flesh for market. Crocodile Farms (NT), the company which runs the Darwin Crocodile Farm, began its commercial operations by employing 15 people in its abattoir section.

The tourist aspect is of prime importance. Tourism is the Territory's major dollar earner. Crocodiles are high on the list of sights which visitors—particularly from overseas—want to see.

At the farms, big saltwater crocodiles—impossible to approach in the wild—can be seen at close quarters and every feeding time produces fascinating glimpses of crocodilian speed and power.

Most of the big crocodiles in the farms are 'problem animals' which have been removed from specific locations because they had become a nuisance or a danger. A more humane solution than the .303 bullet of years ago.

By 1988 the image of crocodiles in Australia had changed markedly through scientific study and public education. Their numbers appeared to be increasing steadily and satisfactorily under protective legislation in their northern habitats.

But what of the future? As increasing numbers of people, tourists and residents in the north, and increasing numbers of crocodiles which have never had to fear a human being, come together, what sort of situation is likely to evolve?

WHAT OF THE FUTURE?

▲▲▲▲▲▲▲▲▲▲▲▲

*T*he little town of Wyndham on Cambridge Gulf, in the north-eastern corner of Western Australia, should be of particular interest to anyone engaged in crocodile research.

Wyndham, through the years, has had more large wild crocodiles in close proximity to people than any other town in Australia. Perhaps in the world.

Some of the town's backyards are only 30 metres from crocodile-basking territory of black mud and mangroves, where the coffee-coloured waters of the gulf lap the shoreline and the saurians come to bask.

Cambridge Gulf, fed by the King, Durack and Ord Rivers, is in any case prime natural crocodile habitat. But it was the meatworks, which saw the slaughter of more than two million cattle between 1919 to 1986, which was of particular significance. They attracted crocodiles to the town through the blood trail which ran into the gulf from a drain by the town wharf.

The blood and fatty residues attracted fish and dozens of kite hawks to the red murk which flowed out from the drain.

At the mouth of the pipe crocodiles lay sometimes row on row in the killing season. They ate the fish and the birds and appreciated the flavour of the drain.

As many as 20 crocodiles at a time could be counted there, some of them huge beasts. During the years when there was a good price for crocodile skins and they were unprotected, many were shot. In fact it was claimed that 3000 skins were taken out of Cambridge Gulf, a figure which seems unlikely.

One of the early shooters was Tex Boneham who found the gold signet ring of John Thompson inside a crocodile. He told me that the figure was far too high. "There were never that many crocodiles here."

But unlike other areas, the crocodiles—attracted by the meatworks blood—were never shot out at Wyndham. After protection in 1969 they were soon back in force, basking at the drain, swimming by the wharf or sunning themselves on the mud banks within stone's throw of the houses.

The important point is that despite this heavy population of saltwater crocodiles, no Wyndham local resident has ever been attacked or eaten.

The two official fatalities, the police corporal in the 1890s and the truck driver Paul Flanagan in 1980, were both visitors to the town. John Thompson was a ship's engineer.

Wyndham people themselves have been far too aware of crocodiles to be caught. The crocodiles were visible and obvious and through the years everyone had them in mind when they went near the water.

The crocodiles were thickest when the blood drain was working during the winter killing months at the meatworks. But there was still a regular population during the rest of the year. Just off the town wharf lies the submerged wreck of the state ship *Koolama*, sunk by Japanese bombs in 1942. Wrecks attract shoals of fish. Fish attract crocodiles.

"The crocodiles used to seem to know when the season was about to start," a resident told me. "The meatworkers would get telegrams telling them the date when operations would begin. We used to joke that the crocs had got their telegrams too. They'd be there a couple of days beforehand, ready and waiting."

When I was there in 1987, a sadness had fallen over Wyndham. The meatworks had closed the previous year and the loss of the 50 families of the 300 workers employed there had left a big hole in local trade and social activities.

But the crocodiles were still at the drain. Not so many as before, but a few were still living on memories it seemed.

I asked Barry Hetherington, the Marine and Harbours skipper, why there had been so few crocodile attacks at Wyndham.

"You know they're there, mate," he said: "We're all very much aware of them. When I have to go out at night in the boat and launch the dinghy at the ramp, I always take a torch and have a bloody good look before I wet the dinghy. We take no chances."

What about children? In the peak years there were 308 at the local school.

"All the kids know too. They don't play in the mangroves or on the banks. It's drummed into them from the start. No one would consider swimming in the gulf. It's a very crocodile-conscious town."

Perhaps there is a message there for other Australian towns with nearby crocodile populations.

Different areas have their own answers. The Northern Territory has areas like Kakadu where the rule is that people have to watch out for crocodiles which have the 'rights' of protected wildlife in a National Park. But in the capital of Darwin, crocodiles appearing in the harbour are trapped and relocated to enable swimming and yachting to be carried out safely.

In Western Australia the Prince Regent River and St George Basin are part of a huge wildlife reserve where crocodiles are sacrosanct. But a maverick three-metre crocodile, hundreds of kilometres south of normal *porosus* territory, living in mangroves at Port Hedland, was scheduled for relocation.

That is, he would have been relocated if anyone could have caught him. His tracks were seen and he left teethmarks in baits. But the crocodilian Scarlet Pimpernel managed to elude all attempts by wildlife officers to catch him throughout 1987.

The question of which areas to declare as 'crocodile-free zones' and which should be classed as wildlife parks, was as much a matter for political as for conservationist consideration. People have votes and many people, particularly in Queensland, did not want crocodiles on their doorstep.

In Wyndham they were seen as a potential tourist attraction which might help save a dying town. People had been living with crocodiles there for the best part of a century and saw no alarm in continuing to co-exist.

In the Northern Territory many of the locals were particularly proud of their crocodiles. They also appreciated the tourist dollars.

Up to the present time it is the Territorians who have had to make the greatest adjustment to living with crocodiles.

In the 1960s and early '70s when crocodiles had been so thinned by shooting—and were so timid of men—Territorians swam and fished in rivers and waterholes with impunity.

Today it is a different story. "People in the Northern Territory have accepted crocodiles and adjusted their lifestyle," Grahame Webb says. "I think they've adapted wonderfully well to what other people might have seen as an inconvenience. I doubt that many people in Melbourne or Sydney would have sacrificed leisure activities in the same spirit."

What people in Wyndham and the Northern Territory can do, others elsewhere in Australia could also manage if they were prepared to accept living alongside crocodiles.

Among the conservationists there are conflicting ideals.

Some see the crocodile farms as an anathema. They are against captive animals in principle. In their eyes zoos, dolphinariums and crocodile farms should all be scrapped. Certainly they are against growing crocodiles 'like battery hens in cages' for skin exports.

Pragmatists like Grahame Webb argue that unless crocodiles have a dollar value their future may still be dubious.

"People have to have a reason for limiting their activities and being inconvenienced," he told me in the transportable on chocks which forms his Darwin office. Crocodile skulls, photographs, harpoon lines and research data were piled in organised confusion around him.

"Crocodiles have to be made valuable to the community," he said. "The effort can't just be for the benefit of the 5 per cent of southern visitors who appreciate their value as wildlife.

"In the Northern Territory and other crocodile places, people are going to be involved, like it or not. If they don't like it, as happened at the Daintree, then no crocodile programme can succeed.

"The secret of acceptance is partly education. But the real incentive for living with crocodiles will be their commercial value. If crocodiles provide jobs, earn tourist dollars and become 'useful' animals then they'll have a place in our society.

"We're already well on the way. The recovery of population here in the Territory has surprised many people. The research programmes have shown that crocodile industries are a practical proposition. Tourism is booming and everyone who comes wants to see a large live crocodile. That's good, because the Northern Territory is now the only place in the world where the saltwater crocodile is relatively plentiful.

"That fact and the movie *Crocodile Dundee* have had a huge effect in attracting visitors to the Territory from overseas. It encourages me to believe that *Crocodylus porosus* has a sound future here."

After years of working with crocodiles his interview had a brisk, practical note. The careful recounting of documented facts by a scientist and pragmatist. But he could not help letting a glimpse of his own involvement show at the conclusion.

"After all," he said, "the saltwater crocodile is the largest carnivore out of the ocean. The species is more than 160 million years old. They *are* a remarkable animal."

They are indeed.

ACKNOWLEDGMENTS

▲▲▲▲▲▲▲▲▲▲▲

Most writers need some assistance with a book through that long and arduous journey from the opening sentence of Chapter One to putting pen down some 90,000 words and many months later at THE END.

A book on crocodiles has needed help on a grand scale. While it would have been possible to write a book (of sorts) from magazine and news files and other second-hand sources, there is no substitute for eyewitness views or standing on the actual spot where particular events occurred.

Often, in the first person, a completely different view emerges. The only way to comprehend the complex splendour of crocodiles themselves is at first-hand and as close to them as you dare to get without too much camera-shake (something the designer has complained about). For these reasons the book involved months of travel in the Kimberleys of Western Australia, the Northern Territory and Queensland.

For helping me come close to some understanding of these magnificent creatures I am indebted in varying measures to kind people all around the continent. Some are mentioned in the text, some are not. I may have accidentally omitted a name or two even from this list but they were all important and I am grateful.

In the order in which I met them, my thanks to:

Paul Hogan, who needs no introduction to anyone and who wrote the foreword. To Jane Burchett and Val Plumwood for unstinting personal accounts of harrowing experiences. To Malcolm Douglas, adventurer, fellow enthusiast for wild and remote places and proprietor of the Broome Crocodile Park, and Martin Johnston, his manager. Peter Sartori, skipper of the *Kimberley Explorer*, Barry Hetherington, of the Marine and Harbours Department, Wyndham. Hugo Austla and Bev Hamilton of The Three-Mile at Wyndham. Dr Grahame Webb, Northern Territory Conservation Commission, for a mass of generously proffered scientific information and for reading and correcting the scientific chapters. Colin Stringer, author of *The Saga of Sweetheart*, The Darwin Crocodile Farm and Nick Robinson. Clive Cook, superintendent of rangers, Kakadu. A Darwin taxi driver whose name I have forgotten but who gave me a fascinating account of the ordinary Territorian's view on crocodiles. Dr Colin Jack Hinton, most hospitable and helpful director of the Darwin Museum, and his assistant, Wendy. In Queensland my old friend Ben Cropp, a diving companion of many years and a film-maker famous for his documentaries on crocodiles, sharks and other denizens. John Monk, who accompanied me to the Daintree, and his wife Dianne. John Robb and Michael Turner, who provided the Daintree first-person information, though it dealt with a death they would understandably rather have put out of their minds. Managing editor Kevin Kavanagh of the *Cairns Post* for access to his newspaper files. Bill Green, of Sydney University's crocodile research section. Professor Harry Messel, research pioneer. Alf Casey at Proserpine, and George Craig at Green Island. To Broome Coroner Dr John Howard R.M. and Perth Coroner Mr David McCann for access to official records, and clerk Glen Spivey. Also to Vic and Sandy Cox of Cockatoo Island, Peter Tyler and Constable Mick Scanlon of Koolan Island, Fisheries Inspector Peter Johnson of Broome, Craig Muir of Alligator Airways and Greg Parker of the Ballarat Wildlife and Reptile Park.

On a personal level thanks to my old mate John Cornell of *Crocodile Dundee* fame for the right words of encouragement at

2   the right time. Margot Lang for Western Australia research. Professor Alan Edwards, Duncan McLaurin, Bruce Lawson, Elizabeth McDonald for checks and opinions. Glenda Hemery for keeping life interesting.

To Ansett and Joanne Cross and *Australian Geographic*, *GEO*, *Simply Living* and *New Idea*.

And to a lot of other people around Australia who, with kindness and courtesy, unknowingly helped this book along.

Sometimes the last should be first. Without the initial cheerful confidence and continuing faith (during some dark periods, especially one rainy day in Sydney in November 1987) offered by Denis Cornell and his Swan Publishing partner Austin Robertson, *Crocodile Attack* would never have come to the surface. The completeness and quality of the work is as much a tribute to them as anyone else.

Finally, for hundreds of pages of clean copy which emerged from scribbled and near-illegible longhand pages penned in boats, aeroplanes and other unlikely places—pages I sometimes stumble over myself, but which she could always decipher—my thanks to my patient typist Margaret Wallace.

And to crocodiles. These magnificent, misunderstood partners of our planet.